Sword and Scalpel

A Surgeon's Story
of
Faith and Courage

Second Edition

by

Lorry Lutz

Sword and Scalpel:
A Surgeon's Story of Faith and Courage
Copyright 1997 by Promise Publishing Co.
Published by Promise Publishing Co.
Orange CA 92865

Library of Congress
Cataloging-in-Publication Data

Lutz, Lorry

Sword and Scalpel:
A Surgeon's Story of Faith and Courage

ISBN 0-939497-21-2

Table of Contents

Foreword

As president of Samaritan's Purse and World Medical Mission, I have had the opportunity and privilege of working with Africa Evangelical Fellowship (AEF) through the years. I believe AEF is one of the great missionary societies in Africa today because God has His hand on Bob Foster. Bob has been a spark plug for many years,

If you don't know Bob Foster, this book, *Sword and Scalpel*, will introduce you to him. After reading it, I believe you will see why I think Bob Foster is not only a great surgeon but a great preacher as well. You will also see why I believe Bob is the number one missionary statesman in the evangelical world tday and the man God has used in a mighty way to open up new frontiers for the Gospel in some of the roughest areas of Africa.

On occasion when I've been in Africa, I've traveled with Bob Foster. Taking a trip with him is fun because no matter how rough a situation gets, no matter how gloomy it looks, Bob is always laughing and smiling. Bob Foster has learned what the Apostle Paul was trying to teach when he said we should "rejoice in all things." Bob doesn't run away when things get tough. He keeps pushing ahead, trusting God, and believing God will work the impossible.

- Throughout the war years in Angola, Bob lived in the middle of the fighting. It was practically impossible for foreigners to survive in that part of the world at that time, but Bob and AEF were there.

- For years, the door to missions had been closed in Mozambique, but Bob went there and by faith met with Marxist government officials and was granted permission to re-establish evangelical missions in that country.

- In Madagascar, God again used Bob to help open the door for missions in this Marxist country.

One of the qualities of a great leader is having good people surrounding him. A great leader will have great men and women around him. The people Bob has recruited, missionaries throughout Africa, are probably the most highly motivated force in Africa today. Like Bob, they share an overwhelming commitment to the cross of Jesus Christ.

Bob Foster has inspired and challenged me, not only in the ministry with which I'm involved but also in my personal spiritual journey. When I get to the end of life's road, I pray that God will have used me even a fraction of the way He has used Bob Foster.

---Franklin Graham

Introduction

During the past few years, as I have ministered in Missions Conferences and churches, friends have repeatedly said to me, "Bob, when are you going to get something into print?"

Life has always been too full with "doing" to find time for writing. However, two or three things happened that spurred me to get something recorded. Four years ago, I discovered that I suffered from a lymphoma and that I'd better number my days and get on with the task if it was to be accomplished. At that point, I met Lorry Lutz, a former AEF missionary and writer of note, who said she would be glad of the challenge of writing the Foster story, though she didn't see how she could do it because of her many commitments. Unexpectedly, her situation dramatically changed so that she was free for this assignment. In addition, a number of supporters and personal friends in Canada and the United States provided the capital to launch the project. So, the right time had come.

During most of the last two years, Lorry has been researching the files, travelling extensively to interview co-workers and friends, and writing.

It is our prayer that the record of God's working in our lives will truly glorify our Savior, the Lord Jesus Christ, and encourage many to take God at His word and act upon it for **"NO WORD OF GOD LACKS POWER"**.

To my wife,
Belva,
without whose loving support
and encouragement
nothing
would have been written.

Prologue

Is There Healing for These Wounds?

The lioness padded stealthily through the grass, her giant paws imprinting themselves on the sandy African soil. Later, her trackers would be able to identify her every move.

Scampering behind, her two cubs rolled and tumbled as they tripped over their ungainly feet or lunged for their mother's swinging tail. The lioness had been sleeping through the heat of the day as the searing Angolan sun baked the dry earth. She seemed oblivious to her cubs sprawled across her forelegs, their feet twitching against her mouth as they dreamed of chasing zebra across the open plains. But even the subtlest new sound in the grass brought her majestic head off her paws and a rolling growl rumbled in her throat.

Now she was leading her cubs to a watering hole. Instinctively, she knew the way even though she did not usually hunt in this area. It was too close to the villages where dangerous humans lived. Their powerful weapons had destroyed several of her pride.

At the edge of an open field she stopped momentarily, allowing the cubs to catch up to her. Suddenly, a shift in the breeze brought a familiar smell; her ears shot up and the fur along her back stood up. Then she saw the woman hoeing in her garden. She could hear her singing to herself as she came towards the shaded spot where the lioness stood.

Without a sound, the lioness turned swiftly ready to lead her cubs out of danger. But from a bush not twenty feet away, she heard a wailing which pierced the air and brought the woman running towards them. The cubs heard the baby's cry at the same moment and began scampering back to their mother for protection. Angered, the lion stopped, poised to attack. With a bone-chilling roar, the lioness bounded out to intercept the woman who posed a threat to her cubs. Terrified, the woman threw herself over her child just as the lioness attacked, pulling her poisonous claws through the soft brown flesh and the red sinewy muscles until they exposed the glistening white bones.

Drenched in her own blood, the woman screamed for help. In her terror she wrapped herself more closely around the crying child beneath her, shielding it from the tearing claws of the lioness. Frightened by the strange screams and cries they'd never heard before, the cubs scampered back to the protective covering of the tall grass. The lioness heard their fearful whimpering and with one final shake of the limp body beneath her, she bounded to their side confident this human could no longer do them harm.

Flies buzzed around the bloodied body as the sun grew lower in the sky. The baby fell asleep, exhausted from crying for the food its mother never provided but warm under the protective covering of her body. By sunset vultures were circling the spot, uncertain of their target.

In the village nearby, the anxious father began visiting neighbors, looking for his wife and child. No, they shook their heads, they'd not seen her since she'd gone back to the fields to finish hoeing her maize after the sun was high in the sky.

Calling his older son, the father ran to the family plot about a mile from the village. In the twilight, he could only make out shadows but there was no one hoeing in the maize; no sound of a mother or baby.

Then he saw the vultures. His heart leapt to his throat as he raced to the scrubtrees where the birds were slowly circling. A cry broke from his lips. The bloodied mass on the ground was hardly recognizable. Surely she was dead. But where was the baby? Lioness tracks led off into the bush. Had she carried the child away?

A muffled whimper reached his ear. Falling on the ground, he gently moved his wife's body to uncover the child. As he did so a moan escaped her lips. She was alive!

"Son, run to the village for help. Tell them your mother has been attacked by a lion."

But what could anyone do, he thought. The lioness' claws had torn the flesh from one whole side of her body. Her arm lay limp and disjointed, pulled from its socket, the muscles hanging in shreds. The congealed blood oozed thick and red at the slightest touch. He'd never seen anyone survive such an attack. It seemed the whole village had come to help - or look - or give advice. Some of the men who had weapons agreed to follow the tracks of the attacker. The women had brought blankets to make a stretcher so the injured one could be carried back to the village and the baby's auntie was already suckling the famished little one at her breast.

Someone suggested calling the witchdoctor to treat the wounds but the people shook their heads. They had never seen wounds like this healed by anyone. Then a young man who had recently come back to the village made a suggestion.

"There is a doctor at Cavango now."

The people didn't believe him. There hadn't been a doctor at the leprosy village for many years. A few African nurses cared for the patients with leprosy who still lived there but they could not treat these hideous wounds.

But the young man held his ground. "It's true! They call this man Kahaya after a powerful witchdoctor in Zambia. Kahaya has come to build a hospital and stay at Cavango. Take her to him - he and his God can heal her."

It was the end of another long day at the Cavango hospital, six hundred miles inland from Angola's capital of Luanda. Hospital was a misnomer because the primitive buildings which had served as a clinic for previous mission doctors, were a far cry from a modern hospital.

But Dr. Bob Foster, his son Stephen and two daughters, Sharon and Sheila, had spent the day utilizing their considerable energy, training and experience to help hundreds of African patients who came for treatment. Though Bob had been there only six months, news had spread far and wide of his skills. It was the only hospital for a hundred miles in any direction.

In spite of the long day of backbreaking work, the constant tests of ingenuity in this isolated outpost, the Fosters had a knack of making each evening a social experience. With Steve, Sharon and Sheila's arrival from the United States for their summer holidays (winter in Angola), all seven of the Foster children were home. No matter how late surgery and emergencies took, Bob's wife, Belva, kept a hot dinner waiting and the family sat around talking long after the meal was finished. At times like these, Bob's booming laugh could be heard half way across the station as he recounted an amusing incident at the hospital.

Even at the end of an exhausting, twelve-hour stint, Bob's eyes sparkled behind his dark rimmed glasses. His high forehead was accentuated by the deeply receding hairline of his once-dark hair, his high cheekbones framed by heavy, graying sideburns. The broad mouth which broke so frequently into smiles could also be clenched into stubborn determination, as his co-workers knew so well.

These days there was lots of talk of the new hospital building. Since Bob had already built two hospitals in Zambia, this was a new challenge to improve on past mistakes. Coming so recently from her own nurse's training, Sharon had ideas and new procedures to share. As a third year medical student, Steve scrubbed up each day to work with his dad in the simple operating room.

So this evening the family again lingered around the table, Stuart and Stirling talking about their studies that day; listening to seventeen-year-old Stacey tell of his latest hunting foray and laughing at six-year-old Shelley's comments.

Suddenly, they heard a commotion at the back door - one of the hospital orderlies came for Dr. Bob. A woman had been carried in from a distant village near death from a lion attack. Her relatives said they'd found her just before sundown; they didn't know how long she'd been lying there but she'd lost a lot of blood.

Without a moment's hesitation, Bob jumped up from the table, instructing the orderly to prepare the patient as he donned his hospital jacket he'd shed just an hour earlier. It was as though he pulled on authority and self-confidence at the same time. It was clear to anyone watching him sprint out into the night, that here was a man whose energies and intellect were ready to synchronize into high gear upon demand. There was no task he was unwilling to tackle, confident that God would give him what he needed to make things work; a man so sure of God's resources that he was completely sure of himself.

As Bob headed out the door, Sharon and Sheila were on their feet to follow him a half mile to the hospital. Since their early teens, they'd often assisted their dad in surgery, learning step by step the names of the instruments and how to handle them. Now both Sharon and Sheila were studying nursing at Rutgers University so they both had a keen interest in working with him. In the primitive operating room, Bob took one look at the woman's torn body.

"What a mess!" The African staff was already removing the shredded clothing and draping the woman with sterile cloths. Her contorted arm dangled grotesquely; the muscles holding the shoulder in place had been ripped away. With a gesture Dr. Bob silenced the team that had gathered. Bowing his head, he asked God for guidance and strength for the work ahead.

As the small generator outside puttered comfortingly, the team in the operating room began the long slow process of repairing the shocking damage.

"Lions' and leopards' claws cause some of the most filthy wounds I know," Bob commented as he worked. "The infection is terribly difficult to get rid of."

For hours into the night, he cut away torn flesh and sewed damaged tissue together. Sharon continually irrigated the deep wounds with saline solution. They could not be closed up because of the danger of infection so Bob put in drains. In the days ahead, iodoform gauze would have to be pushed down into the deep wounds to fight any infection.

The woman would have some ugly scars but even more serious, Bob wasn't sure whether or not she could survive the infection in spite of massive doses of antibiotics. Whether or not she would ever use the arm, so nearly torn off, was problematical.

But as the four Fosters walked back to the house in the early hours of the morning before the African dawn brought its shades of pink and gold to the bush, Bob must have marvelled at God's appointments. Six months ago, the woman would have died an agonizing death from infection and gangrene. She could never have survived the twenty-mile trek out to the nearest mission hospital. How many in years gone by had died like animals in the fields, with no one able to care for them?

So often in moments like these, he thought of his parents who had come to the interior of Africa more than fifty years earlier to work on a station three hundred miles from any medical help. The tragedy in his parents' lives might have been avoided if there had been a place like Cavango - and a man like "Kahaya".

Chapter 1

A Costly Sacrifice

Charles Foster saw the fright in Kanono's eyes. The African lay on his dining room table watching Dr. Fisher place the shiny instruments on a cloth on the sideboard. Miss Shoosmith, the young missionary Charles had recently brought through the bush for her first assignment in Africa, listened carefully as the doctor explained what he wanted her to do. She'd had some training at a missionary school in London and she was the closest thing to a nurse within three hundred miles.

A doctor seldom passed through Musonweji, but a year ago when June Foster had gone to the Kalene hospital on the Congo border for the birth of their daughter, Mabel, she'd urged the doctor to visit Musonweji. Many Africans were dying without medical help and the two single missionaries who treated people who came to the station felt inadequate and frustrated.

At last, Dr. Fisher had come just for a few days and Edith Shoosmith and her co-worker, Peggy Cowell, gathered a number of seriously-ill patients for him to treat. The worst was Kanono's ulcerated leg, which was showing signs of gangrene.

"This leg will have to be amputated if we're going to save the man's life," Dr. Fisher warned after examining Kanono.

There was only a mud and thatch clinic on the station, and it was too small and far too dark for such a delicate procedure. After consulting with his wife, June, Charles agreed that the best place on the station was on the dining room table in their house.

Now as Miss Shoosmith placed the chloroform-saturated cloth on Kanono's face, Dr. Fisher began washing the leg above the ulcer. Peggy stood across the table from him, ready to hand him the instruments while Charles apprehensively waited on the sidelines to see if he was needed. For a moment, the room was silent except for the deep breathing of the patient, already succumbing to the anesthetic.

Suddenly, Edith fell backwards to the floor, dropping the cloth. The escaping fumes, the heat and the tension were too much for her. While Charles rushed to help her out of the room, Peggy retrieved the cloth and continued to administer the anesthetic. Dr. Fisher carried on with his grisly task. Kanono's life was spared though he hovered for weeks between life and death. He lay in the grass hut that had been built especially for him behind the Foster home. Time after time, Edith found him lying in a pool of blood which had collected in the hide placed around the stump.

"You've got to stop trying to walk around, or it will never heal," Charles advised sternly. But the African boy watching over Kanono assured them he hadn't been off his mat. Finally, Edith probed the incision with a forceps and found a piece of catgut that would not be absorbed. Dr. Fisher had to make do with the inferior medical supplies available in the interior of Africa, especially during World War I.

To serve God here in the heart of Africa was June and Charles Foster's deepest longing. When they left Chicago four years earlier in 1917 to become missionaries with the South Africa General Mission in Northern Rhodesia, they knew they were going to an isolated and primitive area, but the exact place would not be determined until they arrived at the headquarters in Capetown. Just getting to Africa was risky, for the Germans were attacking ships in the Atlantic. Delayed by passport difficulties, the Fosters missed their scheduled passage on the "City of Athens". A month later, their disappointment turned to thanksgiving when they read the headlines that the ship had been blown up outside of Capetown early in 1917.

When one of Charles' aunts heard of their close escape, she remonstrated him, "Don't you think it's foolish to go?"

Charles responded, "Don't you think it's foolish for these thousands of young men to be shipped to France, facing almost certain death? If those young men can die for their country, then we can die for Christ, if it's necessary."

Besides the dangers, there were also financial insecurities for missionaries going out with the SAGM, as the mission was called in those days. Many years later, Charles Foster would tell young missionaries, "The mission took absolutely no responsibility in a sense, for our support. We were not going forth looking to the mission for support. We were to depend on God. If there was a shortage of funds, it was a call to prayer. It was not the mission's responsibility, it was God's. They would do what they could, but if funds failed they were not responsible. We should have our faith and our eyes fixed on God."

If there was enough money in the general fund, Charles would receive $45 a month for his support and June would receive $40.

"You see, women weren't worth quite so much then," Foster quipped in later years.

With the $50 equipment money they were allowed, Charles and June purchased a folding table and chairs and other camping gear - even a folding bathtub for their long treks into the bush. After they arrived in Capetown, they learned that their huge steamer trunks filled with clothing and household goods, were useless. They had to re-pack everything into ninety-pound packages for the carriers who would accompany them into the bush.

In Capetown, the mission leaders hesitated to send them north at this time of year. It was November and the beginning of the rainy season, which meant they could be stranded on their three-week trek to the station from the railhead. Nevertheless, the Fosters and three other missionaries decided to take the risk and boarded the train for Broken Hill at the end of the line in Northern Rhodesia.

The journey across the South African Karoo and through Southern Rhodesia was like a dream come true. The countryside changed from the rugged mountains and verdant greens of the Cape to scrub bush and finally to barren desert. This was not the jungle they expected, but the heat building up in the coach as they headed north into the tropics was reminiscent of all they'd ever heard of the "dark continent".

The Vernons, a newly married couple, had joined them in Capetown. Miss McGill, an SAGM missionary heading for Angola, also travelled north with them. After the train crossed into the Bechuanaland Protectorate, it skirted north of the Limpopo River and into Southern Rhodesia. In 1917, the independence of the territory was still in question and Smut's government in South Africa hoped to annex this vast region rich in copper and other minerals.

But the young Americans thought little of the political tug-of-war going on. Crossing the rolling hills of Southern Rhodesia, they eagerly pointed out game running alongside their train. Charles' fingers itched to get out his rifle; but he would have plenty of time to hunt since he would have to provide the only meat on their table for many years to come.

When they crossed the Zambezi at Victoria Falls, the engineer stopped the train on the bridge so the passengers could take in the awe inspiring sight that had so overwhelmed the famous missionary explorer, David Livingstone, the first time he saw it. By now the young missionaries could hardly contain their excitement. Soon they would reach Broken Hill, the end of the rail line in Northern Rhodesia, and begin their final trek through the bush to Musonweji mission.

Broken Hill, on the edge of the Copper Belt, was just coming out of the depression caused by the closing of the mine in 1906. With the war in Europe, a lead and zinc mine was being re-opened as well, and the town now boasted a bank, a post office, a couple of general stores and a small mine hospital. Boone's Hotel, where the Fosters stayed while buying provisions for the journey, was a whitewashed cement block building with a dirt floor and a low galvanized flat roof. With the European War spilling over into British and German territories, Broken Hill became a staging point for troops passing through to the north. But to the travel weary young missionaries, it was the gateway to their future place of service.

A missionary couple, the Drummonds, had come to lead them back to Musonweji, three hundred miles west. They'd also brought a hundred carriers to take their goods and all basic necessities into the interior for them. At twenty-four, Chicago-born June Foster had little preparation for bush life or its modes of transportation. Each missionary had brought along a bicycle, but June had never ridden one. Before leaving Broken Hill, Charles gave her a few basic lessons. It took several days before June felt comfortable riding on the trail, her long skirts tucked modestly underneath her to avoid getting caught in the spokes.

Initially, June rode in a makila (hammock) carried on poles by six Africans, but after the first day she gamely succeeded to stay on her bike, and rode the rest of the three weeks on the bumpy and sometimes muddy footpaths leading from village to village.

Before leaving Broken Hill the missionaries stopped for prayer. Charles would later recall, "We'd left Broken Hill near the end of November, but in that three weeks' journey, we were never rained upon once. Rain at night, yes; but not in the morning when it would have held us up from starting out. We could see rain falling over there, but never where we were. The Lord definitely answered our prayer."

The Fosters were to work among the Bakaonde, a tribe of about 40,000 people living in widely scattered villages over a 20,000 square mile area in the central part of Northern Rhodesia. Just seven years earlier, the first missionary, Mr. Bailey, arrived to work among the Bakaonde and the first baptized believer, John Pupe, was now in charge of the young missionaries' carriers. He could speak a little English and along the way, they began to pick up Kikaonde words and phrases, so that by the time they reached Musonweji, they could give simple commands and ask basic questions.

The Kikaonde language had never been put in writing, and Mr. Foster soon realized that he had an ear for language and a desire to translate the Scripture into Kikaonde. Until they heard the Word of God, the people would continue to live in fear of evil spirits and the displeasure of their ancestors. From those early days on trek, Charles Foster never deviated from his lifelong purpose to teach the Bakaonde the Word of God. In later years, he articulated the need that gripped him as he travelled from village to village.

"We need to give them a clear view of God's great love and what He's done for us, how He sent His son, and gave Himself for us through His blood. Through His death, we have redemption and salvation. We have to get those truths across to the Africans."

But on this first trip into Kaondeland, Charles and June threw themselves into the joy of getting to know as much as they could about the people with whom they planned to spend their lives. In halting Kikaonde, they greeted the friendly, half-naked people who came out of their villages to meet them. They inspected the thatch and mud huts where the people lived on dirt floors while chickens and scrawny dogs ran in and out freely. They noted the neat gardens cut out of the bush, growing richly in the wet black soil near the rivers and swamps. As they sat around the blazing campfires at night, they listened to the other missionaries tell of the customs and beliefs of the Bakaonde.

"If we ask them where they came from, they reply 'Shakapanga made us.' *Sha* is the word for Father and *kapanga* means to create."

They learned that the peoples' sacrifices were not to the GOOD Shakapanga who doesn't require any appeasement, but to the evil spirits that cause them trouble. So much of the Bakaonde's customs were shaped by their belief in witchcraft. If a man's wife died, it was because an evil spirit from him had killed her. He had to pay everything he possessed to the wife's relatives to recompense them. If his child became ill, it was the witch doctor who would investigate who or what had placed a curse on him. The Fosters listened, fascinated, for they'd had little preparation for the ministry that was before them.

One day, just before they were to reach Musonweji, a group of villagers came to the camp with exciting news. They had spotted a huge herd of animals several miles away. Would the Bwanas come with their rifles and kill some? Mr. Foster and Mr. Drummond pulled out their weapons and ammunition and raced after the African trackers through the bush. Suddenly, they came upon a huge herd of wildebeest grazing peacefully. Sixty years later, Charles could still recall the excitement of that hunt.

"We saw a big herd - about a hundred of them. I shot, but nothing happened. They just stood facing me, pawing the ground. We didn't know if they would charge us."

Charles shot five precious cartridges without hitting anything. Determined not to arrive at the mission the next day empty-handed, he sent an African back two miles to the camp to get more ammunition. Again, he took careful aim.

"I loaded my magazine again. Down went the wildebeest. I took two more shots. Down went another. We had lots of meat to take into the mission!"

And what a welcome by the Wilsons and the Africans as the weary party rode their bikes into Musonweji the next day, followed by a single file of carriers, each with his load on his head.

It was only a week before Christmas, but the new arrivals had no time to get homesick. Mrs. Wilson put on a Christmas dinner beyond their imagination "right here in central Africa". But June and Charles would find out they didn't always eat that way. Before the year was out, they were bone tired of pumpkin and maggoty flour, and they knew what it was to skimp and stretch the basics because the nearest well-stocked store was in Bulawayo, a thousand miles away and orders had to be placed months in advance.

One time, they discovered their basic supplies were running low, and they sent an order to Bulawayo to be shipped by rail to Broken Hill where the carriers would pick it up. When the time came for the things to arrive in Broken Hill, Mr. Foster asked Ezekiel, one of the promising young Africans who had become a Christian, to organize a party of carriers to get the order.

Ezekiel came back from the village with disturbing news. No one was willing to make the journey. The rains had been especially heavy that year and all the streams and rivers were overflowing their banks. Fording those flooded waters carrying a heavy load on their heads could be disastrous. No amount of persuading could change their minds. The Fosters watched their dwindling supply of flour, sugar, coffee, and other basics gradually disappear. They couldn't wait until everything was gone, for it would take three weeks for the carriers to pick up their order, which by now was sitting at the railway station.

For two weeks they prayed, asking the Lord for just twenty carriers - a seemingly small number when they recalled the line of a hundred that had brought them to the station two years earlier. Then one morning, they heard singing outside their window and looking out, they saw a line of carriers coming into the station, led by a triumphant Ezekiel. They hardly needed to count; they knew there would be just twenty.

In 1920, June had to make the long trip to Kalene hospital near the Congo/Angola border to deliver her second child. Their first child, Harold, had been born in 1918 at Musonweji, just exactly one year to the day after they arrived in Africa. It was a complicated delivery without any medical help. As a result, they felt it necessary to make the long trip to Kalene more than three hundred miles through the bush.

Trusted African men carried her in a hammock for almost a month. Yohano, who later became a pastor at Mukinge remembers the journey: "Because we had to carry her on our shoulders, we took a long time. We only went about 15 miles a day."

While at the hospital in 1920, June made friends with the mother of Stephen Olford who was also there to deliver her second child. The Olfords were missionaries in Angola, but this little Brethren hospital became the meeting point for missionaries from different denominations for hundreds of miles in all directions.

At the field conference that year, the missionaries pled with the mission to send a doctor to Northern Rhodesia. Too many Africans and missionaries were dying because of lack of medical care. The mission leaders agreed to pray with them about it, but made no promises.

If mission life was not what June Foster expected, or if it disappointed her, no one ever heard her complain. She managed her mud and thatch house with efficiency and energy. She soon learned enough Kikaonde to keep the houseboys in line as they chopped wood, fetched water, and built fires. She couldn't worry too much about keeping Harold and Mabel clean as they crawled and played on the dirt floor. But there was the constant awareness of danger from snakes coming into the house and it was important that an African boy watch over them.

She learned to nurse the African soil into producing the best vegetables of any missionary in the area. "She can even grow celery," was the awesome observation of one young missionary. "She would bring us a few stalks once in a while and we would savor it as a delicacy, and then cook the leaves in a soup."

But in the early years, June dealt with far more basic needs than celery. She made her own yeast, her own bread, learned to cook the strange new African vegetables and the tough little chickens Africans sold to her at the door for six pence. When Charles brought a duiker or wildebeest home from a hunt, June learned to cut up the meat and salt it to preserve it for the months ahead.

Hippo hunts brought the biggest excitement of the year. Jesse, who later became a teacher at the mission school, still remembers those hunts. In his expressive African English, he told of one rewarding hunt: "We found hippos - but hippos; birds - but birds; animals - but animals. On the second day, Mr. Foster killed a hippo in the early morning before the sun rose. He called me, 'Jesse, come here. Take your bicycle and go to the village. Tell the people to bring their canoes to help us take the hippo from the water.' What a celebration as the people helped pull the two-ton beast to shore."

Jesse remembers, "We were there for three days. We carried the hippo. We roasted meat in the fire, and rendered the fat." The victorious party returned to Musonweji with thirteen four-gallon cans of rendered fat - enough to last them for a year. Every carrier was loaded down with as large a piece of hippo meat as he could carry.

Now it was June's turn to carve up the pieces and dry them slowly over an open fire so it would keep for months to come. In later years, the Fosters would take their annual holiday to go hippo hunting. But one can just imagine the enormity of the task this city-bred girl faced, trying to preserve the meat before the African heat rendered it too rancid to eat. What they couldn't eat, she bartered for other commodities from local Africans.

But though hunting was his relaxation, in those early years at Musonweji, Charles was anxious to conquer the language. He started putting Kikaonde into writing and soon began translating passages of the New Testament. None of the Africans had ever been to school, so he opened a small school for the boys on the station. They worked in the mornings and studied in the afternoons. They learned basic reading, writing and arithmetic, and their textbook was always a newly-translated portion of Scripture.

Pastor Yoano Shikelenge, Pastor Yoba Shamambo, Pastor Ezekiel Musompa and Teacher Jesse Sandasanda were some of the "boys" who worked in the Foster's home and became Christians under Mr. Foster's teaching. Though he had little cross-cultural training, almost intuitively Mr. Foster knew the African should be taught to preach as soon as possible. Within two years, he himself could preach fairly well in Kikaonde. But when he went out to the villages, he would preach a message and then have one of the Africans repeat it to make sure the people would understand.

Ezekiel frequently travelled with him. On one lengthy trek to Kabuita, a village on the Muvungwe River, Mr. Foster and Ezekiel stayed for two weeks. Charles decided to give them a whole series of messages, beginning with creation, the fall of man, the promise of the Redeemer, and the birth, life and death of Christ. They met three times a day for ten days. Though the people didn't make definite confessions of faith, they seemed very interested and invited Bwana Foster back.

Later Ezekiel told Mr. Foster, "Bwana, I made profession of faith years ago and was baptized, but I really didn't know what it meant to believe on the Lord Jesus, not until I went out to those villages and heard you preach day after day. Then I really understood."

Experiences like this reinforced Charles' conviction that the African had to have the Bible in his own language so he could study it and receive regular teaching. There was nothing he loved better than to bury himself with his Greek and Hebrew dictionaries, commentaries, and his Kikaonde grammar notes. He and John Pupe, the first Kaonde convert, worked endless hours to translate the Gospel of Mark. The Fosters were making plans for their first furlough in 1922, and he hoped somehow the Gospel would be completed before they left.

One night late in March, their third son, Edgar, three-months old, seemed flushed when June put him to bed. Before morning his little body raged with fever and he threw himself around in her arms as though suffering great pain. Edgar was too young to be teething, and surely that would not cause such a high fever. June's first thought was malaria; everyone on the station had come down with it more than once. She gave the screaming infant a tiny dose of quinine, which usually controlled the attack. But by morning

Edgar's fever had not gone down; in fact his shallow breathing and weakened whimpers frightened June. Charles gave the boys their orders for the morning's work and returned to the house to keep his vigil beside the little one's cot.

June sent a message to the grass clinic Miss Shoosmith held every morning, to have her come as soon as she could. The two women bathed the burning little body and tried to get fluid down his throat. He wouldn't nurse, nor would he take the water they offered. Edith was concerned about dehydration, and stayed at the Fosters most of the day, trying to keep the raging fever down with baths, and forcing drops of water into the parched little lips. After a few days without any relief, Miss Shoosmith urged the Fosters to send a runner to Dr. Fisher, three hundred miles away, to ask him to come as quickly as he could.

It was a desperate effort, because they all knew it would be at least three weeks before the doctor could get to them. But how could they let the little one suffer like this without any help? He would never survive such a journey - better that he stay at Musonweji under the careful ministrations of his parents and Miss Shoosmith.

All the Africans on the station were aware of the tense drama going on at the Foster home. News spread out to the villages where Charles had trekked, that the Bwana's baby was very ill. It took little urging to convince the messenger of the seriousness of his mission as he sped off on the mission bicycle with the letter to Dr. Fisher.

June anxiously watched Harold and Mabel, praying they would be protected from the fever. But before the messenger returned, two-year-old Mabel, the darling of her Daddy's heart, came down with the same chills and high fever, holding her head and crying, "Hurt, hurt."

Charles walked the floor with her at night, agonizing in prayer for her life. By now, they realized this disease was far more than a simple case of malaria and only a miracle could cure the children. Edgar's fever had abated but he lay limp and immobile in his cot. His silence troubled June almost more than the painful screaming of the first few days. After six days of fever and pain, Mabel died. Charles wept uncontrollably. It was June who put her strong arms around him to comfort him and gently wipe his tears, reminding him that his little darling was "safe in the arms of Jesus". When the runner returned, he brought a letter from Doctor Fisher saying he could not leave his critically ill patients to come such a distance.

"From your description," he wrote, "it sounds like cerebral meningitis. Either Edgar will have recovered by the time this reaches you, or it will be too late. There's little I can do, in any case, for this dreadful disease."

Though Edgar's symptoms had disappeared, there was obviously something seriously wrong. He no longer responded to their smiles or conversation; he made no attempt to sit up or roll over in his cot. It seemed as though the light had gone out of his once sparkling brown eyes.

The Fosters were scheduled to go home on furlough later in 1922, but they decided to go in May to seek medical help for Edgar. They seldom spoke about Edgar's illness in years to come; no one ever heard them complain or question God's judgment. But years later, Charles wrote an article about Edgar explaining his condition:

"On our first furlough home, we sought expert advice. Tests at two Chicago hospitals provided similar reports: Edgar's brain had been destroyed. The doctors could give us no hope that he would ever be other than a baby without muscular, nervous, mental or emotional development."

It's no wonder that when June discovered she was pregnant again, she and Charles prayed that God would give them a son who would be a doctor - a doctor to serve in Africa. And when in September, 1924, their fourth child was born, this time in a mud brick house at Musonweji mission with only Miss Shoosmith in attendance, they named him Robert Livingstone Foster.

Chapter 2

The Most Difficult Choice in Life

"If you have raced with men on foot and they have wearied you, how will you compete with horses? And if in a safe land you fall down, how will you do in the jungle of the Jordan?" Jer. 12:5.

"My parents knew what total commitment meant and they were prepared to serve in any difficult place. They went to Africa in 1917, to the northwestern province of Northern Rhodesia, now Zambia, where there was not one Christian. It was absolutely unreached. They had to start from scratch to learn the language. There was no grammar, no lesson helps, nothing written. Over the years, my dad reduced the language to writing, recorded its grammar, decoded its tonal structure and translated the Bible and a number of other books and Bible study materials. The University in Johannesburg

was prepared to honor him with a doctorate but he wasn't interested. That wasn't his motivation.

"My parents continued their church-planting ministry for fifty-eight years in the Zambian bush. I never once heard them complain or find fault with God for all of their problems; there was never any sense that God had been unjust to them. I'm sure it wasn't with too much joy at first, but they could look back and really thank and praise God for the way He undertook.

"Their faithfulness was rewarded in part when two of their three sons finally joined them in the Lord's work although they never exerted any coercive pressure other than prayer and example. But their greater rewards are the Kaonde Bible and the growing Zambian church."

--- Dr. Robert Foster

****

The African runner standing outside the Fosters' door carried a crumpled letter in his hand. Charles Foster recognized him as working for Mr. Sutter who lived at the salt pan, three days journey from Musonweji. The missionaries purchased their salt from him.

According to the note, Sutter was very ill and asked that one of the missionaries come to see him. Charles discussed the matter with Herbert Pirouet, who had come to Musonweji late in 1919 after the Wilsons left, and they decided that Pirouet should make the journey to see what could be done for the trader. While there, Pirouet spoke to the Africans working at the salt pan, explaining the simple message of the Gospel.

As so frequently happened, there was little response, just a skeptical curiosity. By this time, the missionaries realized that the Bakaonde were not waiting with open arms for the Gospel message. They listened and asked questions, indicated they "accepted" (that is; they had heard) the message and even invited them to come back again. But it seemed they wanted to evaluate what they'd heard through their own world view. Even with this reluctant attitude, about one hundred Bakaonde a year accepted Christ in those early days. However, on this trip to the salt pans in 1920 Herbert Pirouet saw no response from the white trader (who did, however, respond to his medication) or from the African crew. But unknown to him, the message made a deep impression upon the boss-boy, Sokonyi. He could not get the story out of his mind. Three years later, when Sokonyi heard that the Gospel of Mark had been printed in the Kaonde language, he saved up enough money to purchase a copy, even though he couldn't read a word. Each time a visitor came through the village, he would ask, "Can you read?" If they said, "Yes," he would pull out his Gospel saying, "Sit down, I want you to teach me how to read this book."

Starting with the first chapter, Sokonyi laboriously worked his way through the Gospel, learning to read as he learned about the life of Christ. Finally one day, while the Fosters were on furlough, Sokonyi came to the mission. There were so many things he didn't understand, even after painstakingly reading through the Gospel. He had been telling others about the stories he'd been reading, but he knew there was a deeper meaning for him. As one of the missionaries spelled out the salvation message, his heart, so ripe and ready for truth, responded and he gave himself to the Savior. Sokonyi stayed at the mission a few days, drinking in every bit of teaching he could, and learning the hymns that were sung each morning during station prayers. Then with his tattered Gospel of Mark in his pocket, he walked back to the salt pans to become the "salt" Jesus told him to be.

Word drifted back that Sokonyi was preaching in his village and almost everyone had turned to Christ. With the Wilsons and Vernons gone and the Pirouets now living at Chisalala station almost two hundred miles away, it was almost impossible for the two SAGM missionary men in the region to follow up every contact they made. It would be years before Charles Foster met the man who had taught himself to read so he could read the Gospel of Mark which Charles had translated into Kikaonde.

The paucity of missionaries in the region simply followed accepted mission principles which had been outlined at the Edinburgh Conference in 1910. Mission leaders determined that one couple should be able to serve 20,000 people. The Bakaonde numbered only about 40,000 so, theoretically, the field was adequately staffed with two couples. When the missionaries wrote for reinforcements, they were told, "You can't expect to have a bigger staff. You're already overstaffed."

But the people were scattered over an area of 20,000 square miles, and with the missionaries hundreds of miles apart, the mission decided that they could work more effectively out of one place. Charles and Herbert surveyed a region where they could start a more central mission station. They trekked through swampy *"dambos"* (shallow depressions where water collected in the rainy season), and six to seven foot high elephant grass looking for the ideal location. As they climbed Mukinge Hill in the Kasempa district overlooking the Lufupa Valley below, they felt certain this was the place. Located more than 4,000 feet above sea level, it would provide a more temperate climate than the lowlands; springs in the valley provided abundant water; the nearby *"boma"* (local seat of government) would expedite business.

Still, there were several obstacles to overcome. Would Chief Kasempa agree to having a mission in his district? And would the British authorities grant them a substantial piece of land? Indeed, Chief Kasempa urged the mission to move near his village. He knew the benefits brought by missions' education, jobs, medical care. In time, he would come to know the most important benefit of all, when he himself accepted Christ as his Lord. The colonial authorities not only approved, but allocated 1,000 acres at a yearly rental of one pound.

In 1926, when Robert was two years old, the great move from Musonweji to Mukinge took place. At first, four men and six of the African boys, like Jesse Sandasanda who had been working and studying at the station, went over to Mukinge to build a three-room grass hut for the Fosters to live in initially. It was here that the Fosters' fourth son, Herbert, was born, shortly after the family moved. Every usable piece of furniture and equipment at Musonweji was salvaged and taken by carrier more than sixty miles to the new station. They even took out the casement windows and door frames of the mission house to use at Mukinge Hill.

Jesse remembers carrying the two Foster boys in a hammock. Edgar was carried "in a very big box with a bed inside," he recalls.

By November 1926, the move was complete and the large sunbaked brick house on top of Mukinge Hill, to be known as the Foster home for years to come, was complete. Its steeply pitched, thatched roof held by a frame of poles reached almost forty feet high, giving the interior a dark, cavernous look. A wide verandah ran along the full length of the house. Before the end of the year, the Pirouets had also moved from their station at Chisalala to Mukinge. Two single missionaries completed the staff. With six people on one station, they were able to start a small boarding school, and opened a clinic in a two-room dispensary down the hill from the Fosters.

After the Fosters returned from their furlough, Charles planned a trek to visit some of the villages, including Kuwani where Sokonyi lived. Usually he slept in a tent, pitched by his carriers on a level spot near a village. The Africans would chop wood and build a roaring campfire. The villagers would begin drifting near the camp, curious to see the strange contraptions this white man sat on; marvelling at the light in a bottle; laughing at the weapons he used to put food in his mouth.

Once dinner was over, Charles invited them closer. He and the African carriers would begin to sing and soon he was teaching the villagers a song about Jesus. Far into the night, they crowded around the campfire, listening to the words the white man or his African companion taught them. When Charles neared Sokonyi's village, he sent word ahead that he was coming. What a welcome he received. A special shack had been prepared for him to stay in. Sokonyi took him around the village and proudly showed him the mud-plastered and whitewashed house the villagers had built especially for worship. "Bwana," he explained, "this is where we come every morning before people go to work. We sing a hymn, or read something from the gospel, and then we have prayer. In the afternoon, before sundown we do something similar."

And in the surrounding villages, Sokonyi's message was bearing fruit. Other villages were putting up worship houses on their own. The gospel was beginning to take hold among the Bakaonde. Without encouragements like Sokonyi, Charles and June could not have withstood the terrible heartache that engulfed their lives. Sorrowfully, they watched Edgar's body grow, with never a flicker of recognition in his glassy eyes, never a voluntary motion in his limp body. Epileptic convulsions often seized him and his hands sometimes thrashed about so violently that the African boy feeding him would have to tie them down.

June's gentle amber eyes filled with compassion and the Africans remember her holding the young boy's body on her lap, crooning and rocking him to soothe the violent contortions that so mercilessly seized him. But her gentleness turned to anger when she caught one of the African boys eating Edgar's food when he was supposed to be feeding him.

Somehow Charles could not cope with the daily care of a body that could not control any of its functions and seemingly had no purpose. Though he longed deeply for the son Edgar could have been, his sensitive nature recoiled from the reality of what he was. What must the African community around them have thought as they saw the growing boy lying mindless and helpless on the Foster verandah? Sometimes when Charles and June trekked out to the villages, they would carry him with them in the "big box" so that June could supervise those who cared for him while she taught the women. Word spread throughout Kaondeland of the Foster's sick child.

There's no question that the Africans would have looked upon this as the work of a witch doctor. The baby would most likely have been left in the bush to die, or dropped into a rushing river to the crocodiles. African families have been known to leave their village when a deformed or retarded child is born, believing that a curse has been put upon their home. Yet, even today, the memories the Africans share is of a loving mother who cared tirelessly and without complaint for her child.

By 1928, Charles and June had some major decisions to make. They had not been back to North America for six years; furlough was past due and the mission was urging them to come home. What should they do with Edgar? It would be almost impossible to travel from city to city and home to home, with a totally helpless six-year-old. Edith Shoosmith bravely volunteered to care for him while the rest of the family went home. She loved the Fosters as her own family and had assisted at Robert's and Herbert's deliveries. With her training as a practical nurse and the help of faithful Africans who knew Edgar's routine, she felt confident she could manage.

But Charles and June had another more difficult decision to make. Ever since the loss of the two children, they realized illness and death could strike at any time deep in the bush, far from medical care. As they looked at their three, strong healthy sons, they longed to do what was best for them; whatever would give them the greatest opportunities to be the men of God He wanted them to be. Not only were there serious health hazards in central Africa, but there were no schools. June had been teaching Harold at home but she soon realized that with the heavy demands Edgar made, she could not give him adequate training and soon Robert would be old enough to start school.

How they must have agonized over the options. Could Charles spend less time on translation and village work? Should he cut back on the time he was spending training young men in the Word of God? Could they get along without the meat that took so much time to hunt? Would it be possible for one of the other missionaries, already so overworked, to teach their children?

Every question brought them to the same inconceivable answer. To every heart-wrenching cry to God, He seemed to clearly respond that they could not bring their children back to Africa with them when they returned. Every experience of those furlough months must have impressed itself indelibly on their hearts; the long boat trip watching the children on deck, and tucking them into their bunks as the ship tossed and rolled; introducing four-year-old Robert and two-year-old Herbert to the family and friends in Chicago; watching the boys' eager faces as they spent Christmas together.

June's family lived in Chicago. She and Charles had met at the Roseland Baptist Church where she had been the organist and he a student preacher. They had both attended the Moody Bible Institute. The Roseland friends had prayed earnestly with them when they'd brought Edgar home in 1922, assuring them that healing would come as they exercised prayer and faith. For a long time, Charles and June had inner struggles over why God had chosen not to heal in spite of their faith and throughout the months of furlough, they pursued the nightmarish task of arranging to leave Harold and Robert behind.

They had learned of a home for missionary children run by the Sudan Interior Mission in Collingwood, near Toronto, Canada. Everyone who knew Gowans' Home spoke highly of the warm, homelike atmosphere, the comfortable surroundings, and the deeply spiritual teaching the children received.

So it was in July, 1929 that the Fosters gathered in the living room of Gowans' Home. The lovely old mansion had large rooms with high ceilings, and gleaming wood paneling. But bright, sunshiny rooms and colorful decor could not soften the pain Charles and June felt as they knelt down and drew Harold and Robert into their arms to pray for them. Once more they explained as simply as they could, that they loved them very much, that they didn't want to leave them, but this is what God wanted them to do. None of them realized it would be almost eight years before they would see each other again.

In the years ahead, no one ever heard the Fosters complain that God had expected too much ...not during the depression, when they sometimes received only $57 allowance after the children's monthly fees at Gowans' Home were taken out ...not when they left Herbert and their daughter Rhoda, who was born in 1929, at Gowans' Home and returned to Africa alone ...not when they left Edgar in a home for retarded children in South Africa in 1938 where he would die four years later.

There was joy, too, as the Fosters saw the church in Kaondeland grow to more than 20,000 believers. And the day came when they returned to Africa in 1977, two years after their retirement, to present the first copy of the completed Kaonde Bible to the people with whom they had spent fifty-eight years. Perhaps the greatest personal joy was to see the curly-headed four-year-old they'd left standing on the stairs of Gowans' Home that summer of 1929, return to Africa as the first missionary doctor in Kaondeland.

Chapter 3

When Father and Mother Forsake Me

"'When my father and mother forsake me, then the Lord will take me up.' I can remember memorizing that verse. I knew in a sense, they hadn't forsaken me. They loved me; but in a physical sense, they had [forsaken me]. And I said, 'Lord, You've got to make it up to me.' The Lord gave me peace and contentment that most kids never have. Others were upset, fussed and fumed and didn't adjust but, my having been left so early, and memorizing Scripture, and just asking God to make these things real to me, gave me stability. If I'd had my parents to depend upon, I would never have learned to depend upon the Lord in the same way. This is one reason I can't be angry at my parents. I've realized that my folks made a sacrifice. I've always appreciated the fact that my folks put the Lord first, and that has been a tremendous example to me - to put the Lord first and to know that the Lord honors those who

put him first. I know I have a responsibility to my
family, but family responsibility is not first, not for
me."

--- Dr. Robert Foster

****

When Charles and June sailed back to Africa with two-year-old Herbert, their sons (ten-year-old Harold and Robert who was not quite five) became part of a family of twenty-six missionary kids in the Gowans' Home. Harold missed his parents dreadfully and probably cried himself to sleep many a night. He never could quite get over the sense of desertion he experienced.

But Bob, outgoing and independent even at this young age, soon adjusted to his new family. He cannot remember painful loneliness or a sense of deprivation in those early years. But some of his colleagues feel that the deprivation of his parents affected his personality. "Bob would have had a more mellowed personality if he'd had his parents," said one. "It didn't sour him, but he had to fight for himself. His character was forged to 'go it alone'; he was left without the 'rounded corners' companionship with his mother and father would have provided." Bob has his own theory about the difference in reactions between Harold and himself.

"I personally think if you're going to leave your kids, you must do it before they are old enough to really understand; that means four or five years old. Or you have to wait until they are old enough to really understand; that means sixteen or seventeen. If you leave them when they are ten or twelve, it's much more difficult."

Gowans' Home was operated by the Sudan Interior Mission although it was open to missionary children from a number of other organizations, including the South Africa General Mission. The home was named after Walter Gowans, a young missionary pioneer and one of the co-founders of the Sudan Interior Mission. He succumbed to malaria in his first year while trekking into the interior regions of the Sudan where only marauding slavetraders travelled.

The year after Bob was left at Gowans Home, the following ad appeared in "The Evangelical Christian."

Wish My Mummy Were Here

"The heart-echo of a lonely, homesick little lad of five; some missionary's baby.

"Away out in some foreign field, a lonely, yearning mother can sense that cry but cannot respond; salty surges roll between, the dearest things in life have been forfeited to serve Him.

"Because of the lack of educational facilities, the prevalence of moral degeneracy and physical disease, little ones have to be left behind while parents 'Seek first the Kingdom.' Think of the cost of sacrificial service.

"In the Gowans' Home for Missionaries' Children at Collingwood they are being cared for, educated and trained to serve the God of their fathers. Perhaps someday they, too, will hear the call of the far distances and follow after. As the season of remembrance draws near will you remember by your prayers and gifts this very needy branch of the Lord's work, and feed His lambs? "

--- R. V. Bingham, President, Toronto

The staff at Gowans' Home tried to provide a real family atmosphere rather than an institutionalized regimen. Indeed, visitors to the Gowans Home in those early years came away with the deep impression of happy, rosy-cheeked children enjoying their own ice rink in the winter, and long cozy evenings around the piano. Of course, the children had to be up at 6:30 every morning, and appear at meals on time. But the stately 32-room Victorian house with its wide verandahs, dormers, gleaming oak paneling and carved banister, provided a gracious atmosphere. Situated on four acres of land in the center of the town of Collingwood, Ontario, the children had a far more comfortable home than most of them had known in the far away places where their parents served.

A former businessman, Mr. Stock and his wife took the responsibility for the running of the home. But it was Miss Linda Kaercher, a nurse, who acted as surrogate mother, especially to the boys. A perfectionist, Miss Kaercher could not abide laziness or untidiness and expected each child to do his or her own chores without complaining.

She carried herself ramrod straight so that she seemed taller than she really was. She went about her duties with an unsmiling and stern demeanor which demanded obedience. When Miss Kaercher spoke in her resonant voice, the children listened. Yet her appearance and demeanor belied her deep love for the children. She cared for them as though they were indeed her own. During the depression years, it was difficult to provide food and clothing for the children on the meager allowances their missionary parents could provide. Miss Kaercher cut every corner possible and spent many hours canning fruits and vegetables.

Once she wrote Rev. Bingham, "Expenses are heavy this time of the year when we need to prepare for winter. I can buy apples, early winter, at $1.77 a barrel, then Mr. Sherrick (a neighbor) will take the boys to pick up apples for present use. These will cost very little. I feel we should have plenty for the children. They are the cheapest fruit we can buy. Oranges are prohibitive except for sickness."

In another letter she advises Rev. Bingham that she had taken on a daily cleaning woman for $16 a month. Later, during the war years it became impossible to find workers. Though she lived on a missionary stipend herself, Miss Kaercher was often known to pay for music lessons for a child who demonstrated talent but whose parents could not afford to pay for them or for necessary dental care! And she seemed to have a special place in her heart for the curly-headed youngster whose parents left him with her when he was less than five years old.

Bob recalls, "Miss Kaercher was the one who really took care of me. She made it her responsibility to 'mother me' and in many ways, I looked upon her as mother."

There were poignant moments. One six-year-old had been waiting eagerly for her mother's return when the mission wrote the home to inform her that her parents would not be coming for another two years. Philosophically, the little one dictated her next letter to her mother, "It's all right, Mommy, if you can't come. We'll go to camp and we'll have marshmallows."

It was natural that parents sometimes felt supplanted by caregivers. As a furloughing mother gave her son a bath, she noticed two spots on his fingers. When she asked what those were, the boy replied, "Those are for the two I love best - God and Aunt Hattie (who had taken him to her home at Christmas time)."

As far back as Bob could remember, he received a weekly letter from his parents, assuring him of their love and challenging him to excellence. But in a sense, the children shared each other's parents. Anticipation built for the arrival of each missionary on furlough. The children were allowed to stay up to see slides and hear stories from far off Africa, India, and other places all around the world. It was the spiritual atmosphere that stands out in the mind of any Gowans' Home resident of that era; the daily Bible reading and prayer, the Scripture memorization every night after dinner. Miss Kaercher asked the children to recite whole Psalms together or went around the table asking each one to recite a verse he or she had memorized.

"We learned the ABC of verses," Bob recalls, "from 'All we like sheep have gone astray' to 'Except the Lord build the house they labor in vain.'" To this day, Bob can recite Psalms he learned at Gowans' Home - 1, 2, 5, 8, 16, 23, 24, 32, 34, 37, 90, 91. They even learned the whole of Psalm 119, plus whole chapters of John and Romans and the entire book of Ephesians. Is it any wonder that most of the children, including Bob, aspired to be missionaries? Bob admits, "As long as I can remember, I felt that I wanted to be a medical missionary." And many did, indeed, become missionaries, including Ian Hay, present General Director of SIM; two Beacham boys to Dahomey and Nigeria; Betty Collins to Central Africa Republic; John, Agnes and Margaret Hall to Nigeria; Jean McDonald to South Africa; and Bob and Herb Foster to Northern Rhodesia.

When Bob was about ten years old, an evangelist came to Collingwood to hold an evangelistic campaign. One night, Harold went forward to make a decision for Christ. After the meeting, he came to Bob and asked, "Aren't you going to give your heart to the Lord?"

Bob thought about it for a few nights, and later in the campaign he, too, went forward - a child whose mind had been nurtured, prepared and molded to love God, but whom the Spirit had now stirred to respond with his heart.

Bob's contemporaries at Gowans Home remember him as a strong natural leader, taking his responsibilities seriously, and not infrequently lording it over the younger children. But others also remember him carrying little boys around on his shoulders and comforting a little one crying for his parents. His deep sense of independence surfaced in the fall of 1936 when Miss Kaercher decided to send him out to Lakefield to live with the Stocks who had taken the older boys and retired to a farm. Since Harold was already living on the farm, Miss Kaercher felt Bob should be with him when their parents arrived from Africa later that year. Bob begged not to be moved. Gowans was his home; the other MK's were his brothers and sisters. At school, he excelled in his grades and he was a keen hockey player. Every Saturday night, the older children at the Home crowded around the radio to listen to the Maple Leafs play, and now and again Bob vacillated between his desire to be a missionary and a sports announcer.

But the decision was made, and Bob spent the summer at Lakefield working on the farm picking berries, milking cows. As the summer drew to a close, Bob could not imagine attending a new school out in the country while all his "family" back in Collingwood were getting ready to return to school with its familiar friends and teachers.

Then the plan struck him. He'd just go back. Though he hadn't travelled by train alone before, he made discreet inquiries as to how to get back to Collingwood. The Stock's farm was ten miles from Peterborough where he had to catch the train. He made arrangements with one of the people in Lakefield to drive him to the station.

Early in the morning Bob slipped out of the farmhouse, leaving a note on his pillow to say he'd gone back to Collingwood.

When he arrived in town, his friend wasn't even up yet. Bob thought for sure he would get caught. But the driver made it to Peterborough just in time for the train. Because there was no direct line, he had to change trains two more times and he reached Collingwood late in the evening.

To his chagrin, there was Mr. Stock waiting for him. He and Miss Kaercher said very little that night, probably just relieved that the twelve-year-old had arrived without any mishap. But the next morning they made it very plain that Bob HAD to return to Lakefield to attend school with his brother so that the family would be together when his parents arrived. Bob recalls that the only thing that redeemed the situation that fall is that he won five or six track meets which relieved some of the stigma of being "the new boy."

One can hardly imagine the anticipation in the hearts of Bob's parents as they headed for home to meet the sons they hadn't seen in more than eight years. The mission had made it clear they couldn't leave Edgar with a missionary again, and so they had delayed their furlough until they were at last able to place him in a home for the mentally retarded in South Africa. Now they were returning with ten-year-old Herbert and their daughter Rhoda who had been born in 1929 just before they had returned to Africa. Though Bob does not recall their meeting, anticipation must have been building as the Stocks prepared the two brothers for their parents' arrival. Now it was their turn to be the envied children whose parents had come to claim them; to bask in the reflected glory as they told "missionary stories" to the gathered family of missionary children. But Bob does recall the sense of oneness and belonging that engulfed him when he was finally with his parents.

"I didn't know them well, but I felt close to my parents," he remembers. "They'd been in touch with me regularly. They never forgot me or neglected me. When I saw my mother and father and got to talking with them, it was just like I'd been with them, because their letters communicated their love and concern for me."

Thus began what Bob terms one of the more difficult years of his life. The family, except for Harold who had graduated from high school and had a job, moved into Toronto for six months and the three younger children started a new school. Just about the time they'd made friends and were feeling at home, the Fosters moved to Chicago to be near June's family and supporting churches. The American and Canadian school systems differed greatly and Bob found that he was way ahead in some things and behind in others. By the time the year was over and he was back in Collingwood, he'd attended four schools and was feeling very displaced.

Before the Fosters returned to Africa in January 1938, they posed for a family picture - the only one ever to be taken of the whole family. It would be six years before they returned to North America again. By that time, Harold would be working back in Africa and the others were no longer living together at Gowans Home. Even at thirteen, Bob appears studious and mature, already wearing glasses and dressed in a dark suit and tie. Eight-year-old Rhoda, her long pigtail tossed over her shoulder has an impish grin, a smiling image of her introspective-looking mother. Rhoda had not yet faced the pain of farewell nor the empty years of trying to find a place to belong. But she muses sadly now, "I watched my parents leave on the train, waving goodbye until they were out of sight. My life has been full of goodbyes."

Yet the two younger Foster children were fortunate; they had big brother Bob, the darling of Miss Kaercher's eye and one who confidently knew his way around the home and school, to look after them. If sometimes he seemed arrogant and cocky to them, at the same time they relied on his judgment and advice. As the years went by, Rhoda often slipped up to the private attic bedroom where Bob studied, to talk over problems or just to bend his listening ear.

While Herb, who is remembered as an angelic, warmhearted, easy-to-be-around child, seemed to adjust to Gowans Home life readily, Rhoda found it more difficult. Somehow she and Miss Kaercher didn't hit it off. She recalls one day Miss Kaercher brought visitors into the girls' room. Rhoda slipped into the closet and heard Miss Kaercher brag about the Foster family and how wonderful the boys were. "But," she added, "Rhoda is lazy. She doesn't want to learn."

With the arrival of a new worker, Mildred Chenault, in late 1939, Rhoda gained an ally. The older girls idolized the attractive well-dressed young widow who had just recently lost her husband in an auto accident. Rhoda felt especially drawn to this gentle woman with her soft wavy hair and ever-present smile who seemed to understand the young girl's painful search for identity.

As the children grew older, they were more sensitive to the lack of available funds for the niceties that others at the school enjoyed. Rhoda recalls how she mended and re-mended a pair of nylon stockings until they were so patched that she threw them away. In desperation, she prayed for a new pair of nylons before church the following Sunday. On Saturday afternoon, Miss Kaercher called the older girls into the office. As happened frequently, one of the local churches had sent in a box of used clothes for the children and this one contained a carton of brand new nylons - rare indeed in wartime!

The Second World War began to affect the Canadian economy and it became more and more difficult to find help to run Gowans Home. Mr. Otto Sherrick, a neighbor, often volunteered to repair leaky faucets and mend broken windows. Almost subconsciously looking for a surrogate father, Bob tagged after him to watch and ask questions and soon Otto began taking Bob along when he had jobs outside the Home. Bob credits this kindly neighbor with much of his practical know-how and ability to fix and improvise. As the oldest boy at Gowans, Bob not only helped Mr. Sherrick, but Miss Kaercher leaned on him more and more to do the "man's work". All winter, he stoked the three furnaces, keeping the fires going for warmth and hot water. Miss Kaercher also entrusted him to deliver payments to local merchants who supplied the home. At the Baptist church where Gowans' children attended, Bob became president of the youth group and, at 15, he preached his first sermon. For a time, he struggled between going into medical missions or going to seminary, but he finally reasoned he could both preach and practice medicine if he were a medical missionary.

With such a developing sense of duty and responsibility, it's no wonder that Bob seemed far more mature than his years. One of his contemporaries recalls that he was, even then, very intense. "I sometimes heard him talk in his sleep in French, or wake up shouting orders to his cadet company."

Bob graduated from high school in June of 1942 and went to work at the Collingwood shipyards to earn money for university that fall. He was assigned to the joiner's shop, working from seven at night to seven in the morning operating a planing machine. On the third night, his world crashed around him. Catching his fingers in the blade, he crushed the tips of two fingers on his left hand, leaving them a mangled, bleeding pulp.

Co-workers rushed him to the Anglican Church Sunday School hall, where a temporary ward had been set up after a fire at the Collingwood Hospital. In agony, Bob heard the nurses discuss amputation as they prepared him for immediate surgery. He couldn't believe this was happening to him. How could he ever become a doctor and perform surgery now?

Chapter 4

The Big Decisions

"Over the years I've come to realize that knowing God's will is not so much the problem. It's doing it. When you study the Scriptures, you find many people who didn't have any difficulty knowing what God wanted them to do, but doing it was never easy. Even the Lord Jesus who came to do the Father's will 'learned obedience by the things which he suffered.' In the Garden of Gethsemane, He struggled over his Father's will and 'his sweat became like great drops of blood falling down' as He wrestled with submitting to it.

"So it is in this life. In spite of the fact that I've walked in God's way for more than fifty years, it doesn't get easier. The tests that God brings just get tougher as He seeks to conform us to the image of His Son."

--- Dr. Robert Foster

****

Bob stared down at the two damaged fingers on his left hand. It still seemed strange to see them red and misshapen, without any fingernails. They were extremely sensitive to heat and cold and bumping them against anything sent lightning pain up his arm. But how grateful he was to the doctor who'd worked so tediously to repair the mangled stumps instead of amputating them as prudence would have dictated.

Indeed, God had performed a miracle so that Bob could continue to plan on becoming a doctor. But standing here in the registration line for university, he wondered how God was going to help him over the next hurdle. He shoved his hand gingerly into his empty pockets - reminding himself again that he had nothing toward his fees. Had he been able to work all summer, he would have felt a lot more confident standing in this registration line. He watched the fellows ahead of him put down their money and he tried to formulate some kind of acceptable explanation for his plight. Would they understand that God had clearly led him to the university so that he could be a medical missionary? Why his very acceptance in the light of more than eight hundred applicants should tell them that! Could they comprehend that if he could trust God to provide his needs, they could trust him?

Bob admitted that in spite of his injury, the summer had been good. Miss Kaercher had suggested he spend the rest of the time at the Canadian Keswick up in the lake country north of Toronto. Dr. Bingham had arranged a camp at this Christian conference center for the Gowans Home children.

Bob hadn't minded sleeping in a pup tent on the camp grounds, and since he had to restrict his activities, he made himself useful helping to care for the little children. He was like a big brother to them, and often read stories and helped them memorize Scripture back at Gowans Home. He recalled the problems the teenage counselor had in trying to discipline the little girls in her charge. It was obvious that Belva Mark didn't know how to handle them. But he didn't mind going down to the cabin after supper to help. He gathered two or three of the youngsters under each arm, and read story after story. Bob didn't know then that Belva thought he was a godsend in no uncertain terms. For her, the whole summer took on a better perspective.

Bob was not quite eighteen and had never had a girlfriend. Though he hardly admitted it to himself, the dark-eyed, soft-spoken young woman had attracted him back to the little girls' cabin as much as his desire to help. He'd learned Belva's father had a general store in Kinmount, Ontario, which had burned down a few months earlier. When Belva applied to be a counselor at Keswick, her parents refused to let her go because they needed her to help manage the store since staff was impossible to get during the war. But when the store burned to the ground, Belva re-applied for the job at the camp, though she had no experience working with children. Before the summer was over, Bob and Belva had become good friends and agreed to correspond with each other.

Now, as the line moved slowly forward, Bob put the summer's experience behind him and concentrated on the forthcoming interview. He could assure the university officer that he was personally well provided for. He'd had to leave Gowans Home and find a place in Toronto near the university. Earlier that year Mildred Chenault had remarried, and she and her husband, Graham Hay, were living in a large home in Toronto. They'd asked Bob to live with them so Bob worked for his room and board by shoveling snow and keeping the furnace going.

Everything seemed in order, except that Bob had nothing to pay his fees and books which amounted to about $450 a year. And he wouldn't have time to work future summers either. Because of the war, the medical program had been accelerated to five years by eliminating summer vacations.

At last Bob reached the head of the line. He was about to give a long explanation of his situation, when the registrar interrupted.

"What's your name?"

"Robert Livingstone Foster."

He watched her run her finger down a list of names, then stop and look up at him.

"Your bill has been paid. You won a scholarship from your final exams at high school and the money has already been credited to your account. All your fees have been taken care of for the year."

Bob left the registration line with an overwhelming sense of gratitude and wonder. There was no doubt in his mind that God had sent him to med school and He was going to pay the bills. In fact, in the years ahead, Bob saw such provision over and over again. Several years, he received scholarships for scholastic achievement and based on need. Three years after the accident, he received a call from Workmen's Compensation telling him they had made an award to him for permanent disability. The amount covered his whole year at med school. He recalls, "I got much more money out of the accident than I would have had if I had worked all summer. And it was when I was again desperate for money three years later, I received their call."

Since Bob couldn't take a summer job during his med school years, a friend in church asked him if he'd like to sell Fuller Brushes.

"I think you'll do all right," he encouraged.

So Bob began going door to door after classes or on Saturday, delivering his orders in a wagon he borrowed from neighbor kids.

"I loved selling," Bob recalls, "and I made enough money to pay for two years of university."

By 1943, Rhoda and Herb had joined Bob at the Hay's. There were now six young people living in the warm, hospitable atmosphere of the Hay's home. Missionaries and pastors frequently came to dinner and there were long hours of stimulating conversations and lively discussions around the table. Rhoda blossomed under Mildred Hay's love and training; they worked together in the kitchen baking bread and rolls, canning, cooking. Rhoda admired her attractive clothes and hairstyle, and tried to pattern herself as much as possible after her idol.

In 1944, ocean vessels could again travel the Atlantic without fear of German submarines and Charles and June Foster were finally able to return to North America. They'd been away seven years; not only was Robert in medical school, but Herbert was applying to study at LeTourneau college in Texas, and Rhoda was in high school. Their children were almost grown up.

As the time drew near, Rhoda became more and more depressed. She said little to Mrs. Hay, but Bob noticed her unwillingness to discuss plans about their parents' arrival and her disinterest in discussing furlough arrangements. Unable to contain her fears any longer, Rhoda confided to Bob that she really didn't want her parents to come back. She loved Mrs. Hay and wanted to keep on living with her. She could remember her own mother enough to know that she did not look or act like the typical

Canadian women she knew. Her mother wore sturdy walking shoes instead of stylish high heels; her clothes were unattractive and old-fashioned; her hair was pulled back in a bun. When she walked down the street, she "charged" ahead as though she were hiking through the bush instead of walking gracefully like other women.

Above all, Rhoda feared her mother's disapproval, knowing that the fads and fashions of her teenage life would not be acceptable to her mother's puritanical values. Bob tried to reassure her.

"Rhoda, if you knew our mother, you'd be so proud of her." He reminded her of the sacrificial ministry their parents were carrying on; that their father had put the Kaonde language into writing and had translated much of the New Testament. But Bob wasn't there to help ease the transition for Rhoda. After a few weeks at home, the senior Fosters moved to Chicago to be near relatives and supporting churches and took Rhoda and Herb with them. Rhoda recalls her embarrassment walking down the street behind her mother, and crying herself to sleep at night because she'd had to leave the Hay's home.

She still vividly remembers the hurt look in her mother's eyes the day she asked, "Rhoda, why don't you love me?"

"I'm sure I made her feel very unwanted. I probably did everything I could not to be with her and when I was, I probably wasn't friendly," she recalls.

But gradually Rhoda began to appreciate her parents, and in future years did everything she could to make it up to them. However, her fears that her relationship with the Hays would never be the same proved true. In 1945, they closed down the gracious home in Toronto and left for Ethiopia to serve with SIM. They arranged for Rhoda to move to a neighbor's house.

By now Herb was studying in the States, but Bob once again needed to find a place to live - a place he could afford. This time a fellow med student came to the rescue just hours before the Hays left.

The accelerated program at the medical school was demanding and left little time for personal life. But Bob managed to continue to squeeze in as many extracurricular activities as ever. Serving God was his driving force and he determined not to study on Sundays so he could teach Sunday School and be active in other church activities. While at the university, Bob read the story of Borden of Yale, the young American who died on his way to missionary service in Egypt. The story of this rich young man who gave up everything to serve Christ so impressed Bob, that he recommitted his life to the call of medical missions. China became the focus of his prayers and plans.

The University of Toronto had a vibrant InterVarsity chapter with three to four hundred students in its missions fellowship. One year, Bob served as chairman of this group and was active in organizing the first Urbana which was held in Toronto in December of 1946. About six hundred students attended the conference along with representatives from many missions.

Bob spoke to the China Inland Mission representative about his interest in going to China as a medical missionary. But he was told, "There's no use thinking of going under CIM to China. The Marxists are taking over and missionaries are leaving. By the time you get ready to go, you won't be able to get in. You'd better ask God if He doesn't want you in some other place."

History will record that God used the student commitment of the late 40's to prepare a massive missionary movement following the war. The zeal and enthusiasm for world missions in the Toronto chapter of IVCF was repeated in colleges and universities across the continent. Bob's disappointment over closing doors in China could not dampen his compelling urge to serve the Lord as a missionary. He influenced others in this direction. Two of his closest classmates were Robert Stephens and Paul Roberts. They were active in InterVarsity, and eventually formed themselves into the "Meds Gospel Team." Robert Stephens played gospel piano and Paul was an excellent cornet player. Bob sang and took turns preaching as the team visited churches and youth groups most weekends.

Both the Bobs were headed for the mission field and Paul admits they influenced his decision to become a missionary. He recalls listening to Clarence Jones at People's Church challenge the congregation to become involved in missions. He made a commitment to go to Latin America and became the founder of the Rimmer Memorial Hospital in Quito, Ecuador. Bob Stephens started a hospital in what was then the Belgian Congo.

The fellows on the gospel team often took their girlfriends along to the meetings. Among several whom Bob was dating was Belva Mark, who was now a scholarship student at the University of Toronto English department. Their summertime attraction of three years ago had waned and the correspondence had petered out. But they renewed their friendship at InterVarsity meetings, and though they dated others, they frequently enjoyed an evening together.

At first, Bob was just another good friend. Belva appreciated his good sense of humor, his vitality and his commitment to the Lord. She herself was now preparing for missionary service. She'd heard Tommy Titcombe, famous missionary to Nigeria speak, and felt God calling her to Africa.

In the summer of 1945, Belva had surgery for the removal of a cyst from her ovary. Between classes and selling Fuller Brushes, Bob found himself at the hospital every day. As a medical student, he had access to her charts and was aware that the doctors felt Belva had only a twenty-five per cent chance of bearing children because of the surgery. But though marriage was far from his mind at this time, he was definitely drawn to this delicate, gentle woman with skin like porcelain and a mischievous twinkle in her brown eyes - and above all, she shared the same love for the Lord and the same burden for missions as he did.

Over the next year, Bob and Belva spent more and more time together. Belva recalls, "I had never experienced as much freedom in any relationship as I did with him. I thought, 'If I don't win him, I won't win anybody! I'm not embarrassed, self-conscious or uptight.' That was the first time I'd ever felt that way."

But though attentive, Bob did not reveal his feelings. The years of independence, and having to make his own decisions without his family to guide him, had built up inner protections. Later, Bob would tell Belva that he had to be sure of her response before he could bare his heart to her. To protect her own emotions since she was unsure of Bob's real feelings, Belva kept him at "arm's length".

Finally in the summer of 1946, Belva could stand it no longer and spilled out her frustrations and insecurity to a friend. "We've got to talk about this and get it out in the open. I can't spend this kind of time with somebody and not know where I'm at. It's not fair!"

Bob had been doing some thinking too. He'd made a list of pro's and con's about his relationship with Belva. He had to face the fact that she might never have any children. But when word got back to him of Belva's frustrations and anger, he made up his mind and rushed back to Brantford where Belva was spending the summer, to tell her that he loved her. That Christmas he gave her a watch as a token of their relationship. But it wasn't until April, 1948, that they were officially engaged culminating six years of friendship.

Though Bob's personal life seemed to be coming together, he continued to seek guidance about his future place of service. In the spring of 1947, shortly before his graduation from med school, he attended the missions conference at People's Church in Toronto. Ezra Shank, the new Executive Director of the South Africa General Mission, had just returned from a visit to Africa, and Bob was interested in hearing his report and perhaps getting some news about his parents' work in Northern Rhodesia.

Shank didn't know Bob was in the audience but he gave an eloquent report of the work at Mukinge. He told of a meeting with all the pastors and church leaders of the area in which Pastor Ezekiel had made an impassioned plea for help.

"We've been praying for a doctor for twenty-seven years," he'd reminded the mission leader, "but the mission has never sent us a doctor. We just get sick and die and nobody cares. If you really mean business about wanting to help us here, send us a doctor."

As Bob heard those words, he knew in his own soul that God was speaking to him.

Bob shared this experience with Belva and she encouraged him to contact the SAGM for more information. Within a week, Bob received a letter from his parents. Though he knew they had been praying him into medical missions all the years of his life, they had never tried to influence him nor had they even suggested that he come to Mukinge. Yet without realizing that Bob had heard Ezra Shank's plea, Charles Foster wrote his son, "Robert, I know you're graduating soon. I don't know what you're going to do. I know you're interested in serving the Lord. Have you ever seriously considered serving the Lord in Northern Rhodesia. Your mother and I think that's something you ought to consider."

With a deep quiet conviction, Bob saw this letter as a further confirmation that God had called him to Africa to the very mission station his parents had founded and from which he'd left Africa almost twenty years ago.

Now that the decision was made, Bob could hardly wait for the time to pass. He began to dream of building a hospital, purchasing equipment, finding staff. But before all this could happen, he had to graduate from med school and write his exams for the Canadian Medical Council.

As the day for the exam drew near Bob did not have the $50 fee. God had so clearly provided all through medical school that he was confident the money would be provided someway. He raced to the mailbox the Saturday morning before the exam, only to come away disappointed. The next day the Meds Gospel Team had a service, and sometimes churches gave them a gift. But nothing came in. Bob's confidence began to wane.

The night before the exam Bob prayed, "Lord, You've provided all through school. Here I am ready to graduate. You certainly want me to write those exams so that I can practice medicine."

The morning of the exam, Bob woke with a deep sense of depression. Why bother getting up? He didn't have the $50 and there was no possible way to get it before the exam started this morning. For a moment, he was tempted to roll over and go back to sleep. But he couldn't give up so easily after all he'd been through. He dressed and decided to go to the examination room. Leaving the house later than usual, he met the mailman coming up the walk.

Hopefully he asked, "Do you have anything for me?"

Glancing through the letters in his hand, the mailman shook his head. Bob started to walk away when the mailman called him back.

"Yes, I do have a letter for you. I almost missed it."

The letter was postmarked Winnipeg, Canada with no return address. Inside was one single slip of paper - a check for $50. To this day Bob does not know who sent it.

October 16, 1948: It rained all day; a heavy, driving rain falling out of ominous grey skies. But it mattered little to Bob and Belva as they drove away from the church where they had just been married and headed for the General Brock Hotel at Niagara Falls.

After a year of residency in Toronto where he'd received only room and board, Bob had gone to Nashville, Tennessee for his second year. The hospital provided an apartment, all his meals and $300 a month. He felt he could now support a wife, and he could even take her to the finest hotel in Niagara. But the storm delayed their arrival and the hotel gave their room away. Disappointed that he could not give his bride the best on their wedding night, Bob drove on and found another room.

However, Bob's resources were still very limited. A friend in Tennessee lent him the car for the honeymoon and he'd planned a two-week trip through the northeast. Gasoline was much cheaper in the United States than it was in Canada so Bob wanted to fill up across the border. Halfway across the Rainbow Bridge, the car sputtered to a halt. It was empty. Fortunately, a friendly Tennessean just behind them pushed their car the rest of the way into the United States.

By now both Bob and Belva had individually applied to serve as missionaries with the SAGM and a few weeks after their wedding, they were officially accepted. While Bob completed his residency in a hospital which catered to poor southern blacks, Belva started to attend a local Bible school since she'd had no formal Bible training. For that matter, neither had Bob but with the excellent training at Gowans Home plus his own regular private study, he had a rich knowledge of the Word of God.

Two months after their marriage, Belva discovered she was pregnant. Although they had hoped to have the first year without children so they could concentrate on preparations for Africa, in reality both were delighted that the doctors' predictions had proven false.

"Bob was really very thankful," Belva recalls. "He wanted somebody else to deliver the first baby if he was going to deliver the rest out in the bush."

Stephen James Foster arrived on the 27th of August, 1949. In the years ahead, Bob did deliver their other six children in Africa.

At the end of his residency, Bob felt he needed a vacation - it was now seven years since his summer of enforced rest after his accident. So, he accepted the job as conference director of the Muskoka Baptist Bible conference, organizing daily programs, leading singing, planning games and other activities.

An unforeseen advantage of this "vacation" was the contact he made with the weekly conference speakers who came from all over the eastern states and Ontario. By the time the summer was over, Bob's fall deputation schedule was almost full. He saw this once again as God's providence, for outside of the local church in Nashville he and Belva attended, and their home churches in Ontario, he had almost no contact with other churches. However, the Bible Presbyterian Church of Nashville felt a special responsibility for this young doctor and his family. One Sunday morning, a deacon stood up in the service. "Pastor, I've got something I want to say," he announced. He went on to give a speech about how Bob needed a vehicle to take to Africa. He ended by saying, "I want to propose that our church family start a fund for a car as soon as possible."

Before that year was finished, they'd presented the Fosters with an ambulance to take to Africa.

Within eight months, God provided their personal support and everything needed to equip a forty-bed hospital in the bush. Beds, tables, drugs, surgical instruments - ten tons of supplies. When Bob visited his parents' church in Chicago, he challenged them with the need for a truck to haul supplies between Mukinge and the nearest town, still three hundred miles away. The church was not able to give him the $5000 immediately, but they suggested that the mission forward the money and they would repay in monthly installments. Ezra Shank willingly advanced the money - something the mission wouldn't do today.

Over the months, letters went back and forth between Bob and his father as needs and ideas crystallized. Bob's dad envisaged his son as a pioneer missionary, the sort who went out with a bag from village to village. Neither the Africans nor the missionaries visualized the modern hospital Bob was planning.

Charles Foster once wrote, "Robert, I think we can build a building and do what needs to be done if you bring $3000-5000." But that was not what his son had in mind. Bob had hoped to raise at least $25,000 to build the hospital. He'd drawn sketches and one of his friends built a three-dimensional model of his dream hospital. Another friend made little "hospital banks" which Bob left wherever he could - and later, he reminded people to "empty their banks" for the hospital building.

But when the Fosters left for Africa aboard a freighter in April, 1950, they had very little money for the hospital buildings and most of that was gone by the time they transported their goods and equipment from the port of Durban, South Africa to Mukinge Mission.

When one of the missionaries at Mukinge asked him point blank if he was going to build a hospital, Bob replied, "Yes, but I don't have any money. It's all gone."

If the older missionaries who had manned the station for many years with skeletal staff and limited finances felt this twenty-four-year-old seemed brash and over-confident, it was understandable. But Bob had no doubts at all - the Lord hadn't supplied all this equipment if He didn't mean for them to have a hospital.

Chapter 5

The End of an Era

"During the years we were building the hospital at Mukinge, there were a lot of questions and doubts about whether this was the right way to use our time in the mission. But the biggest evangelistic tool that we had at Mukinge has been the hospital. I don't think that any African or missionary who really looks at the facts and figures today would say the hospital has over-shadowed or destroyed the church. It certainly has been one of the biggest factors in contributing to the church.

"When we came to a conference after our first five years there, the pastor asked the conference how many had come to know the Lord at the hospital. The response was just staggering.

"The spiritual productiveness of any medical work is relative to the spiritual input of the staff at the hospital.

*If you're not making use of the opportunities, not
discipling, not evangelizing, not involved in the community, you will have precious little fruit."*

--- Dr. Robert Foster

****

What must it have been like, returning to the land of his birth,
to the people who'd known him as a child, to the very mission
station his parents had carved out of the bush when he was a
toddler? The house was the same one from which he'd left
as a four-year-old and many of the African children who
helped care for him were now leaders on the station.
Kyabasanga had been a ten-year-old orphan when Mrs. Foster
"adopted" her to help with the children in the house. She used
to haul Bob around on her back.

Bob himself had absolutely no recollection of people like
Kyabasanga - no sense of homecoming at all. His first memories
are of Gowans Home, and he came to Africa as green as any other
missionary. But many Africans remembered him. Some had carried the curly-headed boy on their shoulders or watched over him
while his mother was busy. They had often heard his parents pray
for their boy who was learning to be a doctor and one after
another, they came to welcome him back. The first morning after
Bob and Belva arrived at Mukinge, Sarai, the paramount chief's
first wife, appeared at the senior Foster's kitchen door, where Bob
and Belva were staying. She asked Mrs. Foster if she could speak
to the doctor. Mrs. Foster and Sarai had known each other for
many years, and had often prayed together about Sarai's desire for
a child. She had been married 25 years. The chief had several
younger wives who had all borne him children. On the verge of
tears, she begged Bob, "Can you help me? My husband doesn't
love me because I can't have children."

Bob listened sympathetically as his mother translated the
woman's plight. Infertility was difficult to treat at best, and this
woman was well into her forties. However, he encouraged her to
come back in a few months when his equipment would be unpacked and he could do a proper examination. Trying not to fan
unwarranted hopes, he reminded her that he was no magician. He

would do his best, but it was only God who could make his treatment succeed. Bob wouldn't have chosen to start his medical career in Africa with such a nebulous prognosis.

"I very well knew that in doing surgery in Africa, I had to pick operations that would be successful first," he explained. "I would never choose anything that I was doubtful I could do, or beyond my skill at that point, simply because I realized that the whole future of the work depended upon it."

But for now Bob could put off the problem. He'd barely settled Belva and Stephen into his parents' rambling home on top of Mukinge Hill and had seen that the equipment was safely stored in a shed on the station before he left for the mine hospital at Luansha where he would spend a month orienting himself to African diseases and treatments.

One morning before he left for Luansha, Bob was riding his bicycle across the station when he passed Kyabasanga walking along the road. He greeted her in the normal Kikaonde fashion and continued riding. Kyabasanga called out in Kikaonde, "Young man, stop!" Bob got off his bicycle and came back to her. "My boy," she said sternly, "I want to tell you something. You've got to learn how to greet people right. You don't say hello and go riding along on your bike. You've got to stop and do it in a proper way - especially to people like me."

Unlike most Africans who tended to address the missionaries with deference and found it difficult to reveal their true feelings about them, Kyabasanga felt free to speak her mind to this boy she'd known so long ago, and whom she looked upon as her child. She'd grown up in his parents home and accepted Christ through their teaching. After she became a Christian, she insisted against her uncles' wishes that she marry a Christian man. They threatened to put a curse on her, warning that she would never have any children.

In the following years Kyabasanga had one baby after another (nine in all) who never lived beyond two years of age. Mrs. Foster and Kyabasanga wept and prayed together time after time. There was little they could do about the bouts of malaria and dysentery which claimed more than half of all African babies. But they prayed that God would give victory over the perceived curse. Finally, Kyabasanga had three children who survived infancy, and were in school at the time Bob returned to Africa. One of her sons became the first Zambian hospital administrator.

Bob was grateful for this godly woman's reminder that he had come to be part of their culture so he could be Christ's servant to them. He must have been aware that he had stepped back into a different era. Physically, the missionaries still had few of the conveniences which would soon be standard on the most remote station. They still trekked on foot, wearing pith helmets and boots, sleeping under mosquito nets. Houseboys carried wood and water to heat baths taken in metal tubs outside on verandahs. Running water was an unheard of extravagance in the bush, as was electricity. But even more critical were the colonial attitudes which permeated African-missionary relationships.

Africans came to the back door of the missionary homes and were not invited for dinner. The day of intimate cross-cultural friendships had not yet arrived, nor were many missionaries feeling the need for such relationships.

There was often deep love and respect between the people and the missionaries. But as Mr. Foster told his son, "If you'd been here when we arrived and had seen what they've come from, you'd realize that they would have been embarrassed, and so would we, to invite them into our home for a meal."

Too engrossed in his drive to build and operate a hospital here in the heart of the African bush, Bob would not yet take time to think through the need for a new relationship between missionary and African. But his naturally outgoing personality and willingness to listen endeared him to the Africans even though much of the accepted protocol remained.

Belva found her life revolving around her family and learning how to manage a household in primitive circumstances. As she looks back on these early, sheltered experiences, she admits, "The people were warm and welcoming, but I didn't get close to them, except the cook."

Yet the adjustments must have been much more difficult for her than for Bob. She was now eight months pregnant and living with her in-laws whom she had met only briefly before she and Bob had developed a serious relationship. The Fosters had given up their huge bedroom, one of the three main rooms of the house. Belva could lie in bed looking up into the rafters disappearing into the darkness of the towering thatched ceiling, wondering what insect or creatures were crawling around in the grass above her, ready to drop down in the dark. She recalls that Mother Foster had prepared a wonderful dinner the night they arrived on the station. Belva commented on how tasty the chicken was. Mother humphed, "That was my best rabbit."

In order to give Belva time to do language study, Mother Foster supervised the cooking for the first six months. Belva must have stood in awe of her energetic and somewhat stern mother-in-law. She watched her manage the household with an iron routine. Every morning she blew an eland horn to call the workers on the station to morning prayers. She supervised the houseboys and those who worked in the garden. She herself spent hours in the garden, seeing that it was watered with bathwater, weeded, and harvested. She sorted the station mail religiously. She taught a women's Bible class and trekked out to the villages with her husband. And every spare moment, she read, edited and typed chapters of the Kikaonde Bible as her husband and his team of missionary and African translators completed them.

When Mr. Foster came home from a hunt, she saw to the cutting, cleaning and drying of meat. One time, Bob and his dad brought back five hartebeest. It was a feast for everyone on the station. But as Belva watched Mother Foster work with the houseboys to cut up the huge animals, cleaning out the innards (not very well Belva admitted) and prepare the meat for drying, Belva gave Bob an ultimatum. "If you're going to eat meat that you shoot, you're going to butcher it, because I will not touch it."

But Belva was very grateful for the orientation and help her mother-in-law gave her, and she determined then and there that when new missionaries came to the field, she would do the same for them. In the years ahead, every new missionary that came to Mukinge (and later Luampa and Cavango) would live in the Foster's home for several months.

There must have been a certain uneasiness during those early weeks, as the time for the baby's birth drew closer and Bob was still in Luansha, 300 miles away. Gratefully, Belva saw him return on a Saturday early in August. He plunged right into setting up a delivery room in a bedroom off the verandah, unpacking his delivery table, sterile drapings and instruments. The Irish nurse who had been the only medical person on the station till Bob came, watched in amazement at the elaborate preparations. She was used to treating hundreds of patients in a two-room, thatched clinic with little equipment. Patients too sick to return home slept on the dirt floor of a nearby grass hut.

Two days after Bob's return, Belva went into labor. As she paced up and down the long verandah, Bob was still hunting for the last pieces of equipment he needed for the delivery. Sharon June arrived August 9, 1950 in the specially prepared room in the Foster house. The nurse commented, "I've never seen such a sterile delivery in my life."

That didn't allay her suspicions of this American doctor who she felt was too ready with his scalpel after she saw him do an episiotomy on Belva. But Belva felt completely safe in Bob's experienced hands, and never wanted any other doctor to deliver her babies.

Word spread rapidly that the doctor had arrived at Mukinge, and long lines of Africans waited at the clinic down the hill from the Foster house. Bob set aside his mornings to study Kikaonde and was soon able to ask basic questions of the patients he treated every afternoon. He began performing simple surgery in one room of the clinic, handling emergencies like gunshot wounds, broken bones and crocodile bites. Within three months the "wards" of huts outside the clinic grew from three to fifty. Patient's families built them of "wattle and daub" sticks, mud and thatch, so they could stay with them and provide their meals while they recuperated. Bob was eager to set up his surgical equipment and do more complicated operations. But until a qualified surgical nurse arrived he could do only basic procedures. The urgency of this need came very close to home about three months after Sharon was born. Belva sent a messenger down to the clinic to ask Bob to come home to check on Sharon. She'd been crying frantically all day and Belva hadn't been able to stop her. As soon as Bob examined his tiny daughter, he knew they had an emergency on their hands. He had found an inguinal hernia in her groin at birth, and planned to operate on her when she was a little older. But now the hernia had strangulated and unless it was corrected immediately she would develop gangrene and die. The only facilities that could handle this delicate surgery were still that long three hundred miles away at the mine hospital at Luansha. Had this happened during the rainy season, there would have been no way to get the baby to the hospital in time.

There was only one road to the Copperbelt, a narrow track through the bush which became utterly impassable during the rains. Driving through the night, Bob and Belva could only praise the Lord for the dependable truck, for dry roads and for the friends Bob had made at the mine hospital whom they knew would do all they could to save Sharon's life. Instead of a three-week journey, as his parents had faced with Edgar, they were able to make the trip in just eight hours.

Bob recalls gratefully, "They did a good job. She was only nine or ten pounds. You could hardly find the patient for the bandages but she came through it fine, and has never had a problem since."

This experience just intensified Bob's desire to open his own surgery, and he counted the days until his surgical nurse would arrive.

When Bob had spoken at a missions conference at Tennessee Temple Bible college the year before, he had presented his vision of a hospital in Africa. He outlined his needs; a nurse to start the hospital, a surgical nurse and someone to start a nurse's training school. Frances Woods, a graduate nurse who was completing her Bible course at the school listened enthralled. She sought him out after the service at the SAGM booth. As they sat at a table, he pulled out a map and pointed out the location of Mukinge, "This is where we're going to work."

Frances recalls that from that moment, she had no doubt that was where God was calling her "even though it was 10,000 miles from where I'd been planning to go."

A year later, Fran found herself in Africa rattling down a bumpy dirt road in a panel van loaded precariously with table and chairs, medicines and supplies, and a terrified goat tied to the frame. Bob and his mother had driven to the Copperbelt to meet Frances and to bring her to Mukinge. It was a harrowing ride for the young missionary nurse. Whenever they met oncoming traffic, which wasn't very often, one of the vehicles had to get off the road to allow the other one to pass. In many places, the road was mired in mud because of heavy rains. When they came up behind an African on his bicycle, Bob blew his horn to warn him.

Unaccustomed to such a noise, the frightened African jumped off his bike and threw himself into the tall grass along the road. Bob couldn't help laughing at the comical sight.

Hour after hour, he and his mother harmonized on their favorite hymns. His deep baritone voice rose above the roar of the engine. "Like a river glorious is God's perfect peace." Frances watched this doctor she had come to work with in amazement. Right from the start, she recognized that here was a man of boundless energy and drive, with a passion to do God's work that nothing could deter.

She recalls, "When we arrived I felt very self-conscious. Everybody was watching me."

Indeed, the Africans were expecting her. The doctor had told them that when the nurse arrived, he would be able to do more operations that would remove their sickness. So, they lined the road into the station, clapping and singing to welcome her.

The mission houses were just about filled to capacity by the time Fran arrived. The staff now consisted of the Frosts, the Giffords, a nurse, a teacher, and the two Foster families in the big thatched house on the hill. Fran was billeted with the teacher in a house that had been condemned, where the ants were already busy eating away the mud walls. Fran quickly learned that mosquitoes and moths, candlelight and a "path" back of the house were to be her daily experience.

The very first morning, she also learned what working with Bob would be like, for he was there bright and early to take her to morning prayer meeting with the staff and patients and then off to the dispensary. He brushed aside her concerns about operating in this primitive mud and grass building without a proper sterilizer.

"No problem; no problem. We'll just do it." But Bob did want her to have a white uniform to appear professional and since her trunks hadn't arrived yet, he took her to an African trading store at the Boma to purchase some white material. He tried to describe what a surgical gown looked like to the African tailor operating his hand-run Singer sewing machine on the verandah of his shop.

"Just cut a hole for her neck and sew up the sides and leave just enough room for her arms to hang out," Bob tried to explain. It didn't make sense to the tailor so Bob did it. He folded the material, cut a hole in the neck and put pins to show where the armholes were to go. With two uniforms completed, Fran was ready to begin surgery.

What a contrast between Fran's impeccable Tennessee hospital, where they served breakfast with a pink rosebud on the tray and this primitive clinic. The wind blew through the openings between the thatch and mud-brick walls, bringing dust and insects down onto the operating table. Fran and Bob sewed together several sheets and hung them at the four corners of the room to catch the flying debris. Once in the middle of abdominal surgery, one corner fell, landing right on the patient.

In order to sterilize equipment, Bob had an "African kitchen" built outside the clinic, with a log-burning brick oven. For more than three years, they sterilized all their instruments outside although sometimes Fran would take them with her at night and put them into her oven at home.

Africans peeked into the windows to watch the surgery. Bob was really quite willing to have the people witness what he was doing. He made a point of displaying whatever he removed during surgery so they would understand that the cause of the illness was physical and not spiritual. This sometimes led to problems. One man went to June Foster to complain that the doctor was not acting like a Christian. He had promised to take out the sickness, and he refused to take out his wife's liver! Bob removed several massive tumors weighing between ten and fifteen pounds. It became a matter of pride to the relatives to be able to brag that "My wife's tumor was bigger than yours."

Though the Africans had asked for a doctor for many years, their concept of medicine was primitive. From their background of spirits and witchcraft came the common belief that illness was brought about by evil spirits and that the cause of the disease was more likely spiritual than physical.

"We knew the doctor would be able to cut something out when something was happening inside," Jesse Sandasanda explained. "He could take the bad thing out and throw it away." But in order to dispel the idea that surgery was some kind of magical trick, Bob invited Africans to observe what he was doing.

Jesse recalls the day Bob invited him, "Nkambo, let us go and see what I'm going to do today." Jesse was given a clean gown, and seated in the corner where he could see what was going on. "When I saw him cut with the knife, I was afraid that all the blood would fall out. But he touched every vein, stopping the blood to come out. That's the way that boy was doing."

It would be many years however, before Africans were willing to donate blood, fearing that they were giving away their lives. They also feared falling asleep under an anesthetic, believing that it was a state of death. Since Bob did not have qualified people to help him, most of the early surgery was done under local anesthetic.

Sarai, chief Kasempa's senior wife, was one of Bob's first patients after he and Fran were set up to do surgery. Examining the forty-year-old woman, he found she had cervical stenosis and he performed a dilatation and curettage. Once again, he tried to warn Sarai that there was no assurance she would get pregnant. He recognized that many people in the community were watching the outcome of the surgery and praying that day before the surgery as he did before every one he performed, he asked for God's intervention.

Dr. Jim Foulkes who later worked with Bob at Mukinge believes Bob not only was a gifted surgeon, but one whom God anointed with success in a special way. "We all get into things we're really not competent to do - often life and death matters. You just get the book out, the day or hour before - or sometimes have the book out while the belly is open in the operating room! The amazing thing is how good Bob came out smelling after some of the operations way beyond his knowledge or expertise. The Great Physician obviously guided his hand and made serious complications into nothing. It's a good lesson for me. When you really have to do it yourself, you have to expect divine care for the patients."

Bob was very much aware of the importance of establishing his credibility as a doctor with the Bakaonde. He knew the people were watching the results of his work, weighing his unknown treatments against their deeply held traditional dependence upon the witchdoctor and his power in the spirit world. Unless they truly trusted him, they would continue to go to the witchdoctor, coming to the hospital only as a last resort, when it was often too late to help them.

One day two months after her surgery, Sarai appeared at the clinic. All patients were screened by the nurse and only those whom she could not diagnose or treat were passed on to the doctor. But Sarai insisted on seeing the doctor. The outcome of her surgery had been of concern to Bob. He knew that news of her treatment had spread throughout Kaondeland. He could understand the people's skepticism; humanly speaking, it was unlikely she would bear a child. But Sarai was ecstatic that day. She was sure she had conceived. Knowing how easily her eagerness could deceive her, Bob agreed to examine her. Sarai was indeed pregnant!

Eight months later she delivered a strong healthy boy, whom she named Isaac after another child of his mother's old age. News of the birth filled the tribe with amazement. Bob's fame spread overnight and women began streaming into Mukinge looking for the same miracle. God had given Bob the credibility he needed to gain their confidence. The clinic could hardly cope with the success.

"Every woman in the tribe who'd never had a baby descended on me to see if I could perform the same magic," Bob recalled. His success was seen initially as "magic". The people considered Bob the greatest witchdoctor of all, greater than the famous Kahaya, a powerful witchdoctor who'd lived at the turn of the century. Some believed Dr. Foster was his reincarnation. So word spread that "Kahaya" had returned and people began flocking to Mukinge for treatment.

To this day Dr. Bob is lovingly referred to as "Kahaya" by all the people of the district, across Zambia, and even in Angola.

Chapter 6

Obstacles at Every Turn

"I can think of many times where God undertook for us in the hospital. Often, the patients we treated were beyond normal hope of recovery but genuine miracles were not necessary. Undoubtedly, however, God worked and answered prayer. All healing is God's. Sometimes He works in special ways but most often He uses ordinary means and people to effect a cure or surmount a problem. We have no right to dictate what He ought to do.

"The miraculous usually occurs when God wants to authenticate His Word or His work. God has proven Himself at the hospital. He provided the facilities, sent the staff, established His work and built the church."

--- Dr. Robert Foster

✳✳✳✳✳✳✳✳✳✳✳✳✳✳✳✳✳✳✳✳✳

One morning, an African man brought his young son to the clinic. The father wore a tattered, once-white jacket over his loin cloth; they had obviously come a long way on foot. Fran had never seen lesions like the ones on the boy's body, so she sent him to Bob. Bob recognized the classic symptoms of leprosy.

"Your son will have to stay here at the mission for a long time," he told the father who put a protective arm around his son as he heard the news. "You'll have to put up a hut for him to live in."

The father nodded his head, "I'll stay with him."

In a few days, the father and son had put up a strong little grass hut with a solid wood door in the area Bob had designated. This was the first hut in what would become "the leprosy village" with more than a hundred patients. Fortunately, medications were available to treat the dread disease so that the boy was never horribly disfigured as would have happened a few years earlier.

When the father headed back to his village to get his wife, he met her half way. Concerned, she had decided to follow her husband to find out what had happened. The whole family lived on the mission for many years; they all became Christians and the father became a leader in the Mukinge church.

But not all the stories of Bob's patients had happy endings. One little boy was brought in with a massive hernia in his groin, large enough for a football. Bob successfully repaired the hernia and the boy seemed to be getting along well. When he was discharged, he and his parents started the forty-mile journey back to their home village on foot. On the way, the repairs broke down and the boy died of a bowel obstruction before they could get him back to the hospital. With today's special reinforcements such surgery would be successful, but that failure set back other hernia operations for a long time.

Yet Bob did not back off the difficult cases if they were urgent. Fran recalls delicate surgeries where Bob would set his surgical book on the stand, and she'd turn the pages for him as he worked step by step through a new procedure. With the lack of up-to-date equipment and supplies, many times they had to improvise. Without blood available for transfusions, on several occasions Bob suctioned blood out of the abdomen and transfused it back into the patient. Even he admits it shouldn't have worked, but God seemed to infuse his very risk-taking methods with healing power in times of emergency.

With every such experience, the urgency of building a well-equipped hospital grew. From the first weeks after his arrival, finding the best place to build his hospital occupied much of Bob's time. Most of the thousand-acre station was still virgin territory, the hills covered with trees and bushes, the lower flat areas rich with waving elephant grass, and tropical plants.

Bob and his father tramped the station, looking for boundary markers that had long been covered with thick underbrush since Mr. Foster and Mr. Pirouet had staked out the station more than twenty-five years earlier. Bob's father suggested the south of the property might be suitable since there was a fast running stream. But Bob continued to explore the station every chance he could - sometimes alone in the early hours fresh from his morning time with God; sometimes with another missionary or African. If he was aware of the disgruntlement of some of the older missionaries who resented his grandiose plans and independent spirit, he never let on to them.

He was happy to discuss his plans with anyone who would listen, but their queries about whether such an ambitious project was necessary, or questions about its effect on the church, fell on deaf ears. The church leaders had already welcomed the idea of a hospital eagerly and assured him of their cooperation, and he was certain this was God's design.

At last, Bob found the ideal site for the hospital - on the northwest corner of the property where there were a number of springs which would provide pure water. He immediately set plans into motion to dig out a huge pond to catch the water so that they could use the overflow to operate a hydram. Bob had no experience with water but he had met a missionary while travelling on deputation who'd given him some ideas. Bob was never afraid to pick people's brains and to ask for help with projects new to him.

Clare Gifford, a missionary who had arrived at Mukinge a year earlier, was an experienced builder and handy man. Bob saw God's providential care in sending Clare to Mukinge. His very first project was to put in a fifteen foot dam wall to provide water for the hospital. It took four men almost two years of hand labor to clear the area of dense jungle and build the wall. They pulled down twenty-foot-high anthills and hauled the clay to make the core of the dam wall. Though it only cost about $1000 for the hydram and pipes, Bob didn't have even that much. But he wrote immediately about the need to friends and churches at home, and the money began coming in in "dribs and drabs."

Bob recalls, "I don't ever remember receiving a gift of $1,000. If we got $100 that was a terrific gift."

The very first Sunday Bob arrived, he organized an evangelistic service with the patients and their families who were staying in the huts around the clinic. He took it upon himself to go out early in the morning and invite them to come and hear the Gospel. But he got the shock of his life when he realized that they had absolutely no desire whatsoever to know.

"Come to the meeting to hear what God has to say," he invited.

"Has God spoken?" they asked.

"Yes, He has and I want to tell you what He said."

"Oh," was the usual response, "we've lived this way all these years and our fathers and forefathers lived this way. They never knew what God has to say. What difference does it make?"

Bob realized that Africans were just like the people next door back home in North America. "They don't care two hoots, either."

Puzzled, Bob talked with his father who knew the people so well. His father told him the Bakaonde called themselves the "people of God."

"Why would they call themselves that?" Bob wanted to know.

"Well, they called themselves that because they weren't as degraded in their heathen practices and in their worship of the occult as some of the other surrounding tribes. They considered themselves more tidy and clean," his father explained.

Later, when Bob was more conversant in Kikaonde, he often visited the villages trying to figure out how to talk to these people who had never heard the gospel. Though missionaries had been at Mukinge for over twenty-five years, there were only about 2,500 believers and many villages were completely untouched.

Bob knew the Bakaonde believed in a creator God, but they didn't worship him because he was good. They were fearful of the evil spirits whom they had to placate by making offerings to them. He began asking them about their sense of values. "Is it wrong to take another man's wife? Is it wrong to steal?" The answer was always in the affirmative. They admitted that they knew some things were right and wrong, but they couldn't help doing the things that were wrong.

When Bob tried to show them the message from Scripture that there was a way they could do right, they disagreed with him.

"You don't have to come here to tell us that there's a God. We know there's a God. You don't have to come here to tell us what's right and wrong. We know there are lots of things right and wrong. If that's all you've come here to tell us, then you're wasting your time, because we already know."

Though taken aback by these rebellious and hardened attitudes, Bob maintained his number one priority - to start each day at the clinic, and later at the hospital, with prayer and Bible teaching for the staff and all the patients. Each Sunday, he preached on the station or out in the villages.

Bob frequently went into the Boma, the government post three miles away, on medical business and matters concerning his building plans. He soon made friends with some of the young men in government offices; men who only had an eighth grade education but were so far ahead of their families in the villages that they were looked upon as "sophisticated, up-and-coming" young leaders. A number of these government employees had become Christians at Mukinge mission but Bob sensed their knowledge of the Bible was minimal and their commitment superficial.

Yet, when he offered to lead a Bible study with them one evening a week, up to a dozen showed up every Thursday. Bob continued this study every Thursday as long as he was at Mukinge. While most of his contacts with patients were short term and he could not follow up personally the growth of those who had made decisions in the hospital, this little core of believers continued faithful over the years.

"Most of them have gone on to be leaders and elders in local churches. God gave me a tremendous opportunity to train and disciple these men," Bob acknowledges. Thirty years later, he still delights to spend time with some of these men, to chat with them about things of the Lord and to hear what they are doing and how they're involved in the work of the Lord. There must be thousands living for Christ because of contact with Bob in the clinics and hospitals but this little group of men is particularly encouraging to him as he saw the seed he'd sown bear fruit in their lives over so many years.

As Bob moved from one government office to another, he learned that the Rhodesian government had matching funds available to build hospitals in needy areas. And since there wasn't another hospital within three hundred miles in any direction, it seemed a logical request. In order to qualify for the grants, the medical department told Bob he would have to present a set of plans for approval so Bob returned to Mukinge to begin a task completely foreign to him - drawing detailed building plans.

He also continued to write faithfully to his supporters and churches, and to contribute articles to the mission magazine, "The Pioneer," and some money for the hospital began dribbling in.

One day, Bob received a letter from Highland Park Baptist Church in Chattanooga where Frances was a member. One of the leaders of the youth group wrote, "We believe God wants us to do something to help you with the hospital. We've been thinking about raising funds to buy an X-ray machine for the hospital.

Bob quickly wrote to thank them but urged them to re-think their project. "We don't have any building; we don't have electricity. It seems a bit queer to be thinking about buying an X-ray if we don't have any of the things to make it work."

He encouraged them to raise funds for the hospital instead. But the young person wrote back, "We're praying that God will send you help in other ways, provide in other ways. But we'd like to take on the project of raising funds for an X-ray."

Bob recognized that the Lord had His hand in what the young people were doing and wrote to tell them to get on with it and he would trust the Lord for funds from other sources.

Meanwhile, Clare Gifford organized teams of Africans to make bricks and crush tons of rock by hand for concrete. There was no sand on the station so it had to be hauled six or seven miles to the site. Bob spent his evenings drawing and re-drawing plans, only to have them rejected.

While the Senior Fosters were home on furlough, Bob had hoped to build his own house so they could live on their own when his parents returned. Belva was now expecting their third child and he would have liked her to have the conveniences of indoor plumbing and freedom from the inevitable tensions when three generations live together. But the hospital ran into so many snags that he could not get to planning his own house.

Then early in 1952, Fran came down with an undiagnosed problem. For weeks, she was so weak that Bob had to pick her up with the van to drive her to the clinic so she could help him in surgery. Dave and Elwanda Fields, another couple he had recruited even before he came to Africa, were to arrive in late May so there would be another nurse on the station. By now the Irish nurse had been transferred and Bob was pretty well on his own.

Though Belva seldom complained that Bob was too busy, other missionaries believed he was driving himself and those around him too hard. Another SAGM missionary, Dr. Alex Henderson, and his wife came for a visit from Angola, just about the time that Belva's third child was due. In fact, Alex and Blanche helped at the delivery of Sheila Joan but Blanche took Alex aside to voice her concerns about the long hours Bob put in at the clinic. She felt Belva needed more consideration and urged her husband to speak to Bob about his coming home late for meals, then working long into the night at correspondence.

Yet Bob's effervescent energy never seemed to dim. When Fran was reported to be gravely ill after surgery in Luansha, he jumped into his jeep and drove those long miles to see what he could do.

Fran remembers, "It was really embarrassing because he thought I would be lying there half dead and by the time he arrived, I was feeling quite better."

It was this concern for his staff that endeared him to their hearts and made them willing to do almost anything for him. A few weeks later Bob again made the long trip to Ndola to pick up the Fields. Bouncy and full of energy, Elwanda added a new sparkle to the team. The Africans nicknamed her Lusekelo (Joy) for her ever-present smile and cheerful disposition.

In July 1952, the senior Fosters arrived back from furlough to find Bob and Belva and their three children still living in the big house on the hill. Naturally, Belva was well ensconced as mistress of the house with her things in the cupboards and closets and the staff following her orders. It must have been very difficult for both women, though each very graciously tried to defer to the other. Belva had almost more than she could cope with, running the big house where dust settled everywhere, insects and snakes a constant battle, no indoor plumbing and a staff of Africans to supervise. She admits she wasn't as frugal as Mother Foster had been nor did she spend time keeping up the garden as her mother-in-law had done.

One day, Mother Foster blew up about the mangoes rotting on the trees. Belva encouraged her to get a houseboy to pick them. "But," complained Mrs. Foster, "he doesn't work for me; he works for you. I can't tell him to do that."

Belva recognized the dimensions of the problem and began urging Bob to move ahead more rapidly to get them into their own house. Bob realized that the strain on his independent and frugal mother, and on his wife whose energies were drained by three small children and coping with inconveniences, could damage their otherwise good relationship. When his father also took him aside to speak to him about getting his house built, he knew he had to take action.

He had selected an ideal spot down the hill at the north end of the station, right next to the hospital site. So while he continued to work on the hospital plans, he designed his own house, the first on the station to have indoor plumbing and running water.

Drawing the hospital plans had become a source of deep frustration. Bob could sense that some of his colleagues were laughing behind his back. How could this man think he could build and run a hospital if he couldn't even get the plans passed? For almost a year he worked on plans, sending them in to the Department of Health, only to have them rejected. Bob studied the Public Health Act which detailed the number of windows per cubic feet of space for each bed, the height of ceilings, etc. But there was no one to whom he could turn who knew anything about drawing plans and he had never drawn any himself. Finally, after almost a year of rejections, Bob received word that his seventh plan had been accepted. In faith he'd gone ahead with preparation of the site and by that time, the pump had been installed and they had water there. Tons of rock for concrete had been hauled to the mission and crushed by hand. Foundations for the first building were dug, and some funds had begun coming in. Bob was elated! With a matching grant from the government, it looked as though the Kaonde Hospital would become a reality at last.

With three nurses, the clinic was handling hundreds of patients a day. The hospital couldn't open a day too soon. But problems continued to plague the project. There was no cement available anywhere in the country and the building was again at a standstill.

One day, Mr. Foster senior received word that the Governor of Northern Rhodesia, Sir Gilbert Rennie, was coming to visit Mukinge. Everyone on the station was excited at the honor. Mrs. Foster prepared an elaborate afternoon tea to which she invited all the mission staff. During his visit, Sir Gilbert and Bob fell into conversation.

"I understand you're wanting to build a hospital," the governor said, "Where are you going to build it?"

Without hesitation, Bob offered to show him around. When the Governor saw the tons of crushed rock, the sand and the trenches already dug, he asked somewhat perplexed, "Well, why aren't you getting on with it?"

Bob explained that they had looked all over the country for cement, but there was none to be had anywhere in Northern Rhodesia. The governor listened thoughtfully. Before he left that Saturday afternoon he told Bob to send his truck to Lusaka the next Monday. "I'll see that you get five to ten tons of cement. We have quite a bit in government storage."

What a sense of excitement and wonder at God's provision when they received not only all the cement they needed, but at no cost to the mission! Now Bob was in his glory! Checking up on the progress of the building every spare moment he could get, watching the administration block and first ward rising before his eyes just as he'd dreamed. At the same time, their house was also progressing, and Bob and Belva planned to move in a few months.

Then one morning, Bob awoke with abdominal pains and nausea. He tried to joke that it was the peanuts and coke he'd had the night before, but as the hours wore on and the severity of the pain increased, he had no doubt about the diagnosis. Appendicitis.

The worried medical staff stood around his bed. None of them would dare operate on Bob. Even the young visiting intern fresh out of medical school had no surgical experience and, even if he had offered, Bob would not have entrusted his life into his hands. There was nothing to do but drive three hundred miles to Luansha again.

A messenger was sent to the Boma to dispatch a telegram to the mine hospital to prepare for surgery late that night. Belva packed for what would probably be at least a week's stay. She had not driven since she'd come to Northern Rhodesia and did not feel she could handle the children and Bob alone on that long rough journey. So Brian, the young intern, offered to drive the jeep. At least there would be some medical care available in an emergency on that desolate road. Bob was given a mild sedative and settled as comfortably as possible.

Trying to avoid the bumps and ruts, Brian drove as cautiously as he could. Instead of arriving at the hospital by midnight as planned, it was dawn before the jeep pulled into Luansha, not any too soon. The surgeons removed a red-hot appendix which was about to burst. True to form, Bob brought it back to Mukinge to show the Africans "the sickness the doctors took out."

With every obstacle God seemed to provide another answer to prayer so that everyone involved in the hospital became aware of the "coincidences of God" which were inexorably moving the hospital into reality.

During the building phase, Bob received another letter from the young people in Chattanooga Tennessee. In two years, they had raised the $5,000 for the X-ray equipment and wrote Bob that he should go ahead and order it.

But Bob replied, "Your faith is bigger than mine. Although we have set aside a place for the X-ray and darkroom, we have no electricity, no motor, no generator and no funds."

The determined young people responded, "Go ahead and order it. God's given us this money and we believe God will provide the electricity."

So, rather humbled by their faith, Bob sent the order for the equipment which would take a good many months to arrive at the mission.

It became a Sunday afternoon ritual for all the staff at the mission with their children and dogs, to walk down to the building site following afternoon tea for a tour. As the hospital rose out of the tropical bush, the staff began making plans for a gala opening on July 25, 1953, and the pressure was on to have everything completed by that time.

Late on a winter afternoon in June, Dave Fields headed down to the dispensary looking for Bob. The dispensary was closed for the day, but he knew Bob was still working. He wanted Bob to stop by to see their sick baby, one-month-old daughter, Barbara Sue. Outside the dispensary, he saw an unfamiliar Landrover parked and a group of Africans talking seriously with each other. Inside, he found Bob working over a gruesome sight. Bob looked up from his injured patient and greeted Dave, "Ah Dave, come help me with this."

As Dave came closer to the operating table his stomach turned. A four-inch piece of wood protruded out of the man's shattered forehead; blood covered his lacerated face.

"He was hunting with his muzzle-loading gun," Bob explained as he worked. "It went off and the butt of the gun disintegrated in the explosion. It exploded with such force that fragments flew smack through the frontal part of his cranium and penetrated his brain."

Dave watched Bob study the injury carefully. "When I pull this piece of wood out, I'm going to pull part of his brain out." He shook his head - this was a tough one. He explained that he'd already told the family that he didn't expect to be able to save the man. Even under the best of circumstances such an injury would be fatal. Once he pulled the wood out of the brain, he would have to fish for bits of bone. There would be loss of cerebrospinal fluid and blood and certain brain damage.

Because of the nature of the injury Bob had just given the hunter a mild sedative and no anesthetic. Fortunately, the frontal lobe of the brain doesn't feel pain. Feeling faint and unable to watch the surgery any longer, Dave excused himself.

Bob continued to work by the light of a tilly lamp well into the evening painstakingly fishing bits and chips of bone out of the brain, finally sewing up the dura and the wound itself. All he could do then was order massive doses of antibiotics and pray for God's touch.

A week later, the wound was healed and the man walked out of the dispensary, seemingly none the worse for the experience. Bob was amazed he didn't get meningitis or encephalitis. He concluded that God simply had mercy on the man, perhaps just so he and his family would come into the hospital and hear the Gospel.

But while the hunter's wounds healed, Bob began feeling tired and weak. There was so much to do in the final work on the hospital. It seemed impossible that all the construction would be completed, the walls and frames painted, the furniture and equipment he'd brought three years earlier unpacked and assembled - everything ready in just over a month.

At first he attributed his lack of energy to these pressures but it became evident that something more serious had occurred when his skin began turning yellow. And when it was confirmed that he had hepatitis, Bob knew that while everyone else was pushing to complete the hospital before the opening, he would be on the sidelines, flat in bed.

Chapter 7

Provision, Protection and Priorities

"One of the big opportunities I had was to disciple the hospital staff. First thing every morning, I met with them to read and discuss a few verses of Scripture and have a time of prayer together before we went to work. I did that consistently over the years in every hospital. I have read completely through the entire Bible several times in each place.

"We tried to employ people who were Christians. Invariably you find that some are true believers and some are believers in name only. But starting from the point that they professed to be Christians, I involved them in this regular Bible reading and devotion each morning. I found this was a very significant part of my ministry."

--- Dr. Robert Foster

✸✸✸✸✸✸✸✸✸✸✸✸✸✸✸✸✸✸✸✸✸

An outsider observing preparations for opening the hospital those four weeks must have felt like he was watching a fast forward video. Everyone on the station was involved. Alan Huntingford came over from the Luampa mission, two hundred miles away, to supervise the final completion in Bob's place. Every morning, he met with Bob who was lying in the living room of his house, too weak to get up but still able to talk. Each morning, he gave Alan instructions about what should be done for the day. Alan supervised one hundred African workmen, many of whom who were unskilled and untrained, and whose language he could not speak.

The Foster children loved having their father home all day to play games with them. They thought it was wonderful having such a captive audience. Eileen Greenwood, a nurse who had recently come from Canada, and Elwanda kept the dispensary running. Though they tried to avoid it, they had to bring their seriously-ill patients up to the Foster house, and the doctor diagnosed from his bedside.

Fran spent every moment she could setting up the hospital. Everyone on the staff put in extra hours painting window sills, washing windows grubby from construction - at last making up the sixty beds with quilts given by Christians overseas. The night before the opening, Fran and Alan spent hours on their hands and knees waxing and polishing the tiled entrance floor. "We walked around in our stocking feet so it would look good," she recalls, "Five seconds after we opened that ribbon, it didn't show at all. I don't know what we were thinking! We worked so hard."

What a thrill to see the gleaming hospital with its white-painted beds, colorful quilts, clean sheets and shining equipment. What a difference from the dozens of grass huts that had made up the wards around the old clinic. No longer would Fran have to bend her six-foot frame to crawl through the doorway into the windowless huts crowded with the patient and all the relatives settled in for the duration of the illness.

No longer would nurses have to give injections to patients lying on the dirt floor, using a flashlight to see what they were doing. Bob had unwillingly, but wisely, remained in bed for four weeks. His skin was no longer the color of a carrot, but it took all the strength he could muster to get up for the dedication ceremonies. What a sense of satisfaction must have poured over him as he toured the completed hospital-each bed and piece of equipment exactly where he had planned it. To walk through the new operating room, bright and sunny with windows on two sides must have seemed like a miracle! Even without electricity, it must have seemed like everything he had dreamed about.

Belva hardly had time to appreciate the transformation as she prepared an elaborate dinner for twenty-seven special guests and dignitaries served on the verandah of their home. That afternoon the missionary women helped to serve a high tea for more than a hundred local chiefs and European guests after they took a tour of the hospital.

Missionaries from all the Rhodesian stations came, including Herb and Elenore Foster who had joined SAGM the year before. More than a thousand guests, including seventeen Bakaonde chiefs attended the dedication ceremony. Bob seemed to have some of his old energy back as he took charge of the service, his strong baritone leading the crowd in a song that sprang from their hearts - *"Praise, my soul, the King of heaven."*

Because of Bob's weakness and the limited nursing staff, they had planned to begin using the new hospital gradually, limiting the patients only to serious emergencies. But the first night, one of the local headmen was brought in with a broken hip that had to be put in traction - an impossibility on a mud floor. He had never been on a bed before. When the nurses returned to check on him, he was lying rigid, too afraid to move for fear he might fall off.

That same night, a woman with tetanus was brought in in a comatose condition, and put into the hospital. By the end of the week all sixty beds were full. Before the end of the year, the hospital would serve over eleven hundred patients, and Bob would perform two hundred operations.

Though the people were thrilled with the new hospital, they really didn't quite know how to enjoy its conveniences. The nurses often found many of the patients sleeping on the floor under the bed with the rest of their relatives. Teaching new patients to take a shower before putting them in bed, took patience. Many showered with their clothes on, and wouldn't use the towel because they didn't want to get it dirty. One morning, Fran heard a swishing sound as she began making rounds in the female ward.

She found a woman sitting up in bed, the four corners of her rubber sheet tied so it held water. She was having "a good old bath" just like in a bathtub.

The biggest problem with training patients, however, was teaching them how to take medicine as instructed. Bob had given one man a prescription to last three days. Surprised to see him back at the out-patient clinic the next day, he asked him why he'd come. He explained that he was out of medicine.

"What do you mean, you're out of medicine?" Bob asked in his booming voice so everyone in clinic could hear.

"I've taken it all," the man replied.

"But you were supposed to take it when the sun is here, and here, and here," Bob reminded him, using his hand to show the sun's position.

Uncomprehending, the African shook his head, "Kahaya, I thought if I took it faster, I'd get better faster, so I took it all."

Demanding of himself and those who worked with him, Bob had amazing patience with the Africans whose experience and background had not prepared them for the twentieth century, in this, he endeared himself to them. He spoke with candor and force, if he thought they had deliberately broken the rules, but his buoyant sense of humor and personal concern for them and their families won their hearts. Of course, they still looked upon him as a miracle worker. His fame spread even across the border into Angola that he could help barren women have babies, and enable the blind to see. Removing cataracts was one of the most gratifying surgeries he performed.

One morning, an elderly woman came to the out-patients' department leading her blind husband with a stick. She explained that he had been blind for many years, "But I have brought my husband to you, Kahaya, because we hear you can make blind people see." Examination revealed cataracts on both eyes. Bob scheduled surgery. For several days following the operation, the old village headman lay motionless on his bed, his head held firmly between two bricks. When the bandages were removed, his face filled with wonder and astonishment as he looked around the room, exclaiming, "I can see, I can see." Then he looked at his faithful wife who had served as his eyes for so many years. Tears were streaming down her cheeks as she knelt on the floor before Dr. Bob to thank him for the miracle.

Bob had collected old glasses for just such an occasion. As he put a pair on the headman's nose, even greater wonder filled his face, "With these little windows, I can see the door, the people outside; I can even see you, Kahaya."

Many patients and relatives who had known of the old man's blindness crowded into the room, watching the procedure with awe and marvelling at the miracle of sight. But Bob reminded them that he had not performed a miracle. God had given him the strength and knowledge to do the surgery. When the old couple left the hospital, they took with them their new-found faith in the One who is truly the Great Physician.

There was often the fear of losing a patient, for so many came in with conditions that were almost beyond hope. One of the most deadly diseases in this region infected with the Tsetse fly was sleeping sickness. Most Africans had developed some immunity to the disease, and generally ignored the early signs of fever, loss of weight and lethargy. By the time the characteristic which gives the disease its name occurs, there was little that could be done.

One day, a white overseer brought his whole crew of laborers into the hospital. They had been working out in an infected area, and he wanted blood tests done. The tests revealed that three men had the trypanosomes in their blood, though they showed no outward symptoms. Bob insisted they go right to bed. One of the workers refused to believe he was ill even though both Bob and the foreman tried to convince him of the seriousness of his condition. During the night he slipped out of the hospital and ran away. Three months later, he was brought into the hospital beyond hope. The disease had followed its inexorable path.

It seemed death was also inevitable for Seya, a young boy whom his family brought by hammock six days' journey from the mission. His skeletal form lay limp and lifeless, unable to talk or eat. When the blood test revealed sleeping sickness, Bob and the nurses felt the case was hopeless. They'd never seen anyone recover from such an advanced case. Once again they explained to the family that they had no magic cure, and that the disease had taken such hold of the boy that they offered little hope. Yet each day when they came to Seya's bed to give him his injection, they

saw slight signs of improvement. Soon he was taking nourish-
ment, then sitting up in bed. The day came when Seya could join
the rest of the patients for morning devotions outside on the lawn.
He sat right in the front row, taking in every word - listening to
the story of God's love for him, but never showing a sign of
response.

Then one morning his grandmother, the only family member
who'd remained with him during his recovery, stood up at the end
of the service to accept Christ. Yet there was no move from Seya,
who by this time was well enough to return home. That afternoon, Seya turned up in the out-patient department, wanting to
talk with one of the nurses.

"I want Jesus to come into my heart and make me clean," he
said.

After seeing this young boy pulled back from death's door,
everyone on the staff had a special interest in him, and word
spread quickly that Seya had accepted the Lord. The next morning as he and his granny began the six day journey back to their
village, the whole medical staff was there to send them off. Would
they ever hear from Seya again? Would the rest of his family listen gladly as he and his granny told them of Christ? Or would
they ridicule their conversion and write it off to pressure by the
missionaries? As far as anyone knew there were no other Christians in the village, and no one to send along to preach the Gospel.
But while there were no evangelists or even Christians out in the
villages, the spiritual power of the witchdoctor still held great
sway. Many patients came to the hospital only after the witchdoctor had exercised his craft and failed.

One day, a family arrived with the body of a woman who had
died right after taking some medicine given to her by the
witchdoctor. Bob was required to report the cause of death and
perform an autopsy if necessary. He demanded that the witchdoctor come to the hospital and bring some of the medicine with him,
threatening to turn the matter over to the authorities if he didn't
come.

A few days later, a heavy-set man wearing the beads and skins
of a witchdoctor arrived at the hospital to see Kahaya. Bob asked
him for the medicine he'd given the dead woman. When Bob
took it, he asked sharply, "What is this?" The man just stared at

him without a word. So Bob asked Elwanda, "Bring me a spoon."
He poured some of the medicine into the spoon and handed
it to the witchdoctor, "Here, you drink some." When the man
paled and backed off, Bob knew this was a case for the
authorities.

The witchdoctor was so entrenched in the African culture that
some Christians continued to respect his power. He was like an
insurance policy - just in case God didn't work! Though the mission tried to hire Christians to work in the hospital, they often
proved to be Christians in name only. Thus Bob took his daily
time of Bible study and prayer with the staff very seriously. But
he also believed that the small church at Mukinge had a responsibility to evangelize and deal personally with patients and their
relatives who often stayed at the mission for many months. The
local Christians seemed to feel that evangelism was the responsibility of the missionary or the pastor.

Bob began by challenging the church to appoint a full-time
pastor/evangelist who could live near the hospital, readily available to the patients. Within a short time, the church appointed
Pastor Munguya who committed the next twenty-five years to
ministering to the patients.

After a time, Bob spoke to the church leaders about
hospital evangelism again, "This is the responsibility of all the
people in the church - not just of a few."

He encouraged them to start a system whereby some of the
leading lay people in the church would become involved. Soon
the church leaders had set up a roster where women took services
in the women's and children's wards; others came one night a
week to read Scriptures and pray with the patients. Eventually the
evening devotional service in each ward was led by a lay person
from the church. By the time Bob and Belva left for furlough in
1955, more than two thousand people had come to the Lord
through the hospital ministry.

While Bob made time to minister not only to the hospital staff
and patients but also in the church and community, Belva found
her time almost completely taken up with the care of her family.
A few months after Stephen's fourth birthday, Stacey John arrived, giving her four children under five years of age. Belva had
never had the inexhaustible energy of her husband, and she

learned she had to pace herself if she was going to be able to spend time with him when he came home from the hospital.

Bob was a night person, staying up late working on plans, preparations or correspondence. But he also got up early in the morning for his personal Bible study and prayer before anyone in the family was awake. The only way Belva could find the energy to spend the evenings with him was to get a rest in the afternoon.

Some of the missionaries criticized her for not getting involved in the ministry, but never once did Bob intimate that she was shirking her duty. Belva believes that their relationship has been an encouragement to others who worked with Bob.

"I've often said that the thing that made Bob more acceptable to other people was that he didn't marry somebody that was also capable of doing so many things. I was very ordinary or less, and didn't have nearly the energy he did. When other people saw that he didn't expect me to keep up with him, it was easier for them to realize that he would accept them."

Bob knew her inner strengths and the refinement of her nature that provided a peaceful core to the whirl of activities around him. Many saw her as a dignified lady and mistress of a gracious home. But he saw disciplined strength to cope with inconveniences, constant demands of people and the heavy responsibility of raising children in a foreign land. He appreciated the fact that "she could cut me down to size."

The Foster home had a constant flow of guests. Any missionaries who came to have a baby or needed medical attention, used the special guest room at the Fosters'. That often meant the whole family came to stay. New missionaries lived with Bob and Belva for several months before going to their own quarters. Government officials who passed through were entertained at the doctor's house. Those who observed Bob and Belva's relationship saw the clear line of demarcation in their roles, and that Belva was very comfortable in hers. But in the earlier years she struggled with her inability to take part in active ministry.

"I can remember going home on my first furlough thinking I was the biggest failure as a missionary that ever existed," she admitted, "I had done no 'missionary work.' I discounted totally all the hospitality I had given which enabled other people to come for treatment and have their babies."

In spite of his heavy load, Bob felt it was important that he take his responsibilities as a father seriously. He often took one or two of the children with him when he went to the Boma in the jeep or down to the gardens below the dam. The land was so rich the gardens produced eight hundred pounds of vegetables a month for the hospital and missionaries. The children loved to help by bringing back armloads of carrots, corn, and other fresh produce.

But nothing could match the times when Bob would get down on the floor to play with them. They screamed with delight as they wrestled him to the ground or climbed on his back as he crawled around the house on his hands and knees. His own boisterous laughter could often be heard outside.

Bob also managed to help Belva with some of the time-consuming tasks of living on an isolated mission station. The canner they'd brought from home was put to good use for meat was available only when someone came back from Lusaka or Ndola, or after a hunt. Since there was still no electricity on the station, meat did not keep unless salted and dried or canned.

Late one afternoon, Bob was helping Belva store a batch of canned meat in a shed outside the garage. He'd made a game out of the job as Stephen ran to fetch cans of meat and hand them to his father. All of a sudden Stephen began screaming and frantically rubbing his eyes. Bob turned to see a cobra slithering under the house. In an instant, he grabbed the screaming child and raced to the kitchen, shouting for Belva to bring some milk. Over and over he washed the snake's poisonous venom out of Stephen's eyes with milk until he was sure the danger was over.

Electricity was high on the prayer list at the mission, not only for the convenience of the missionaries, but even more so for the hospital. But it would be a major expense to purchase a diesel generator and all the wiring needed to electrify the station. Completing the hospital had drained all the funds. Just about the time of the hospital opening, Bob received word that the X-ray equipment he'd ordered months ago was on its way, and would be arriving before the end of the year. A room at the hospital was ready and waiting for the much needed equipment. How much easier it would be to be treat fractures and diagnose lung conditions, if that machine were in place! But an X-ray machine without electricity was useless.

The very week Bob received word of the equipment's imminent arrival, he also received a letter from the government asking whether the hospital had any projects which needed funding. There were some excess funds available for medical programs if the Kaonde hospital needed them. Within a week after Bob turned in a request for funds for the electrical system, the check was in his hands. This provision came as no surprise to Bob who had seen God bring the hospital to reality with His timely acts of grace. Yet there was still one more hurdle - who would put in the extensive electrical system? Neither Bob nor Clare Gifford had any knowledge or experience in electrical work.

About this time Bob made one of his many trips to Luansha, and as he frequently did, he spoke on a Sunday morning in a local church, telling the congregation about the latest developments at Mukinge and the need for someone to install the electrical system. After the service, a young Englishman who worked on the mines as an electrician came up to Bob and introduced himself as Ken Askey.

"I would be interested in going out there and helping you sometime."

"When do you think you could come?" Bob asked.

"I've got some vacation coming up, and I'll use that to do the job for you."

In the weeks ahead, Ken came out to the mission and figured out all the wiring, switches, fuses and other supplies needed. In the meantime, Bob purchased the powerplant and had it installed. By the time Ken came everything was ready for wiring. He had hoped to complete the job in two weeks, but even by working from early morning until late at night, there was still a lot left to do when his vacation ended.

When he left, he told Bob he would try to get some extra time off from the mine and come back to finish the job. What a surprise to see him back the next week, free to take all the time he needed to complete the job.

Again God had providentially intervened. Some weeks earlier while Bob had been in Luansha on business, he was invited to dinner at the home of Dr. Hanford, one of the doctors at the mine hospital. Several other guests were invited, including the personnel manager of the mine. The guests listened with interest as Bob, in his inimitable entertaining way, told them about life in the bush. He'd recounted the latest developments and how one of electricians from the mine had come out on his holidays to install the electrical system.

Later when Ken asked the personnel manager for time off to go back to Mukinge, the manager asked him, "Is that where Dr. Foster is?"

Upon hearing that Ken was the electrician Bob had been talking about, the personnel manager told him to take whatever time he needed to finish the job, and the mine would pay his salary. Ken and his wife Ada came back to complete the installation, and through this experience felt God calling them to missionary work with the SAGM. Bob is described as a "man's man" and God often used his charismatic personality to influence others to help him in his ministry. But just as often, it seemed God moved upon others to continually remind Bob and his co-workers where their resources came from.

One such provision is remembered by everyone who worked at Mukinge at the time. Hospitals use a lot of cotton swabs to clean wounds, to sterilize skin for injections, to stanch blood, in surgery, etc. When supplies began to run low, an order for more was included with the next trip to town. But there was no cotton in town, none to be had anywhere. Everyone tried to be very careful not to waste cotton, trying to stretch the dwindling supplies as far as possible. Yet one morning in staff time, Bob announced that they had come to the end of their cotton. As so often occurs in missionary staff meetings, they discussed at some length all the options and possible solutions, until someone suggested they stop then and there and pray about it. It did not seem incongruous at all to ask the Almighty, Eternal and Omnipotent God for cotton to help them heal Africans' wounds.

But neither was there any great expectation of an immediate reply. Each returned to his work, trying to figure out how to make the best of the situation.

Later that morning, a woman came to the Foster's back door, carrying an enormous load on her head. She had walked many miles and wondered if there was anyone at the mission who would like to buy her cotton. There was enough raw cotton to last until the next shipment arrived in town. Never before or since has anyone offered to sell cotton to the hospital.

It was such provision that reinforced Bob's confidence that God would keep His word to provide "all your needs." So, when the Fosters left for their first furlough in 1955, Bob gave his car to one of the missionaries on the station who didn't have one, confident that God would provide another.

Before the Fosters left for furlough, Dr. Enid McRuer and her pharmacist husband, Bob, arrived. By that time, seven additional buildings were completed at the hospital, including three dormitories and a classroom block for thirty-six student nurses. When Clare Gifford went on furlough, Bob was also responsible for the building program. Many Africans remember Kahaya using a hammer and laying bricks. But the nurses sometimes found it exasperating that he was away when they needed him. Besides frequent trips into town on mission business, he made regular trips to Luampa, an SAGM station southwest of Mukinge where there was no doctor. Even when he was at Mukinge, Bob often slipped away unnoticed and they didn't know where to find him.

One day, Fran had prepped a patient for a scheduled surgery and was scrubbed up ready for Bob to come. She waited and waited, not wanting to leave the operating room and have to begin sterilization all over again. She sent several nurses to tell Bob he was past due in surgery. When no one could find him, she stormed out of the operating room herself and headed for the building site, calling Bob's name. Then she heard his familiar chuckle and she shouted again, "Bob, where are you?"

"I'm up the chimney," he laughed. Sure enough, he had crawled up the chimney of the unfinished kitchen to do some mysterious work that only doctors up chimneys can do. Even Fran's annoyance could not rush him.

"It'll take me about thirty minutes to finish this," he promised. When he emerged, his hands black and grubby, he looked like anything but a doctor.

Just as often as Bob could be found on the building site, he would be found in the wards with the patients. He was unwilling to leave all the spiritual ministry to others and was particularly concerned about patients in serious condition who might not have another opportunity to hear the Gospel.

One Friday night, just such a patient was brought into the hospital. Several days earlier, Wilson had been wandering through the bush on his way home from a party and fell in a drunken stupor in the tall grass. As he lay there a grass fire roared through the bush, enveloping him in flames. When he didn't arrive home the next morning, his family sent out a search party for him, and found his charred and nearly lifeless body. By the time they brought Wilson to Kaonde Hospital, he was in a state of shock from loss of blood serum. His face was so badly burned that his eyes and mouth were just black holes in the raw skin.

Bob and his team worked for more than three hours to treat the burns, wrapping him in dressings so that he looked like a mummy lying on his hospital bed. He was given little hope for recovery.

On Sunday morning, one of the missionaries needed to find Bob, and Belva directed him to the hospital. Bob made it a rule never to do routine surgery or see patients on a Sunday unless it was an emergency. Usually he preached in the Boma or out in one of the villages in the mornings, and participated in a Bible study at the house for the missionary staff in the evening. So he seldom went to the hospital on Sunday unless there was a crisis.

On this morning, as the missionary wandered along the verandah of the men's ward, he heard Bob's voice and he peeked through an open window. He saw Bob bending over Wilson's bandage-swathed face, reading to him from the Bible. The missionary decided his request could wait until a more appropriate time. That evening at the missionary Bible study Bob told those gathered that Wilson had once followed the Christian faith but had grown far away from God as he grew older. Bob had been able to lead him in a prayer of repentance and faith, and for the preservation of his life, if God so willed.

Once again God chose to spare a precious life through the ministrations of His servant.

Chapter 8

We Need You, Kahaya!

"From the year of our marriage, Belva and I have always read the Scriptures and prayed together at the breakfast table. I was a bit of a disciplinarian by saying that everybody had to get up and eat breakfast together because that's when we read the Bible and prayed together before we began the day.

"In the early days, because there wasn't any electricity or many vehicles, people didn't move around at night because they were afraid of evil spirits or wild animals. As a result, following our supper, we always gathered together as a family to sing a chorus or two, to memorize a verse of Scripture and to discuss the meaning of it.

"That was one of the great blessings as far as our family was concerned. It was far easier to regulate time with the family in Africa than it ever would have been

at home. As the kids grew older, we had opportunity to talk about things, not only the verse of Scripture we were memorizing but the problems of the day and what God has to say about them. Then we prayed together and the kids learned to pray by taking turns praying at family devotions"

--- Dr. Robert Foster

****

One Tuesday night after supper, Bob went out to the garage behind the house to take care of five hundred pounds of dried fish he'd ordered for the hospital. The fish had to be treated with a chemical preservative to destroy any insects that got into it. All of a sudden, he heard terrible squawking coming from his chicken house. In recent days, chickens had been disappearing and he and Belva suspected a two-legged thief. He dashed out to the chicken house but by the time he opened the door the chickens were sitting quietly on their roosts. There was no sign of an intruder.

Bob noticed one hen sitting in the corner on her nest, and as he bent down to check on her, he felt something hit the back of his neck. Reaching up he discovered his neck was wet. As he straightened up and turned around he found himself staring right into the eyes of a cobra coiled on top of the rafter. "So this is the chicken thief," he thought.

Since it was quite dark by this time, he called Ken Askey who was working at the hospital next door to come and hold the flashlight while he attempted to kill the snake. When the two men returned to the coop, they caught the snake in the act of biting one of the fowls on the head and watched it fall dead from its perch.

Bob quickly disposed of the snake and put it into a box so he could display his chicken thief to others in the morning. Then he returned to finish up his fish preservation in the garage. He had been working by the light of a hurricane lantern. As he finished his task, he unhooked the lantern from the ceiling and set it down on the floor. In seconds, a shimmering blue flame emanated from the top of the lantern. Intuitively, Bob dashed for the door just as a powerful explosion destroyed the garage behind him and everything in it.

Patients and staff came running from the hospital and soon a crowd of Africans gathered, their astonished faces mirroring their curiosity and fright.

"What happened, Kahaya? Are you all right?"

Still shaking from his close brush with death, Bob explained what he now realized had transpired. The heavy fumes from the chemical had settled near the floor and when he put the lantern down, the flames ignited the gasses.

"But that's just half the story," he explained as he opened the box to show them the cobra. The "dead" serpent reared up to attack, bringing forth screams of terror before Bob slammed the lid down.

"Yo-yo-yo," one African bystander shook his head in wonder. "If you'd been an African, Kahaya, you would have been dead twice." It seemed only natural to praise the Lord together before each one drifted back to the hospital or to their homes.

Two weeks later, Bob received a letter from Mrs. Hart, a woman he'd met while doing deputation before coming to Africa. Mrs. Hart had been bedridden for more than ten years. Her bedroom was literally papered with pictures of missionaries for whom she prayed. Even the ceiling was covered with prayer cards. When Bob visited her, she'd told him, "I promise to pray for you every day."

Now she wrote to say, "Bob, what happened to you last Tuesday? That day as I was praying, God said to me, 'I really want you to pray for Bob Foster.' I want to know what happened. I've had such an urgency to pray for missionaries before and I usually find out they had a special need."

When the Fosters were home on furlough Bob went to visit Mrs. Hart. They talked about the need Bob had had for prayer and how God had used her to intervene on his behalf. She told him of other experiences she'd had when God gave her an urgency to pray for a particular missionary.

That night Bob had a one hundred mile drive back to Toronto and part way home, he ran into a heavy snow storm. It was a literal "white-out." At one point, he slid off the road; at another, he missed a corner because he couldn't see the turn. It was one A.M. before he made it safely home.

The next morning at eight Mrs. Hart phoned him, "What in the world happened to you last night Bob?"

Bob marvelled at her closeness to God and her ability to be sensitive to the prodding of the Holy Spirit to intercede for someone in a time of crisis. He realized that such a prayer partner was a very special gift from God. He would never know how much of the success of his ministry in Africa related directly to the faithfulness of Mrs. Hart and others who meant it when they said, "I'll pray for you."

Bob and Belva must have come back from their furlough in 1956 with the comfortable feeling of "coming home." The major buildings at the Kaonde Hospital were complete. The outpatient department was seeing 300-400 patients a day; 165 leprosy patients were under care, and hospital beds had expanded to 125. Bob never seemed to find it difficult to attract new staff to his team. On this furlough he'd been able to recruit a doctor, a lab technician and several nurses who would be coming out to join the staff in the next two years.

But they also returned to face a painful separation. Seven-year-old Stephen was ready for school; in fact, he was eager to join Marilyn Gifford, the only child on the station older than he, who was already attending the Sakeji school for missionary children in the northwestern corner of Zambia. He would come home twice a year - six weeks at Christmas and ten weeks between June and September. Sharon was also ready for kindergarten but Belva was secretly relieved to learn that the school could not take her yet and she would be staying home one more year.

The whole family drove three hundred miles to Sakeji to take Stephen. Everything went smoothly until Bob and Belva and the children got in the car to leave for home. Suddenly, Stephen burst into tears. The full impact of their departure came over him; he would not see his family until Christmas. Belva remembers that as one of the most difficult moments of her life. She was tempted to ask Bob to turn around and go back but he stepped on the gas and spun away in the dust. The next year, Sharon joined Stephen eagerly but, once there, became very homesick. Every time she went back to school it was harder. Not that Sakeji wasn't an outstanding school. The children received excellent training, both academically and spiritually, but it was very regimented and it wasn't home.

The Foster children's memories of home are warm and positive. Sheila recalls the wonderful holidays when her parents would make every day special. Even though Bob was away all day, suppertimes were fun as they memorized Scripture and discussed the meaning of the verses. Sometimes the children put on a Bible skit and they always sang choruses.

But even during holidays, Bob exercised his authority. If a child disobeyed while at the table, Bob sent him or her to stand in the corner until an apology was forthcoming. A visitor to the Foster home recalls when four-year-old Stacey refused to learn to tie his shoes. After a week of cajoling and teaching, Bob simply sent him to his room and wouldn't allow him to come to breakfast until he'd tied his shoes.

Sunday afternoons, Bob often took the children with him when he visited African farmers who lived around Mukinge. They looked over the crops and visited the pigs. Then sitting properly on a mat on the ground, they relished the hot, sweet tea served in the best mugs or tin cups the woman of the house had to offer. Sometimes, they received a much-coveted piece of sugar cane which they chewed contentedly the rest of the afternoon.

Another special Sunday afternoon activity was tea at Grandma and Grandpa Foster's house up on the hill when all the missionaries gathered. In those days it didn't seem strange to anyone that there were only white faces at these gatherings which served as a ritual outlet from the routine of the week.

Though most missionary kids "adopt" the missionaries on the station as aunts and uncles, the Foster children had a real uncle and aunt living just a hundred miles away at Chizera mission. Herb and Elenore and their children occasionally visited Mukinge. Sheila remembers how she envied them because they could "run wild without any shoes on," and they "could speak Kikaonde like Africans." The fact that they played freely with the African children at Chizera added to their linguistic prowess. Mukinge MK's were discouraged from mixing so freely, ostensibly to prevent exposure to the many kinds of disease prevalent around a mission hospital.

Bob held regular clinics at Chizera and sometimes took Stephen along. One of Stephen's most vivid memories is of going hunting with Uncle Herb who was a superb shot, and bringing home a roan antelope.

"Uncle Herb used to carry one of those canvas water cooler sacks - the kind where you poured boiling water into it and let it evaporate on the front of the truck. Uncle Herb could swig one of those completely in one fell swoop."

At that time, the children were too young to realize that their uncle was considered the best Kikaonde speaker in the mission. He'd grown up on the mission station until he was ten years old, and by that time had picked up the idioms and intonations that never left him. He first taught at the Chizera Bible School and later moved to open a new work in Kaindu, a completely unreached area under the control of a powerful witchdoctor. Bob proudly watched his "little brother" develop into a highly effective pioneer missionary.

Even though the three Foster sons were now on the same continent, they had not been together for twenty years. Bob had visited Harold on his farm in southern Rhodesia but it was only when Harold came to pick up Mother and Dad Foster to take them to Salisbury on their way home for furlough, that the three brothers came together. Little did they realize it would be the only time.

Besides visiting Chizera from the very first year, Bob had also been visiting Luampa every six months to provide medical help. There was only a nurse-staffed clinic on the station and no hospital in the whole district.

His first trip to Luampa had been a nightmare. He travelled in December, taking several missionary kids home from Sakeji. The rains had turned the narrow dirt trail into a quagmire. Then, as they neared Luampa the terrain became sandy where the Kalahari Desert extended into the southwestern corner of the country. Without four-wheel drive, the tires of Bob's vehicle churned deeper and deeper into the unforgiving sand. They spent two nights in the bush, digging themselves out over and over again.

When Bob visited Luampa after he returned from his furlough, the African people there began asking in earnest for a hospital for themselves. Pastor Benjamani and Pastor Jehosophat (who was also a local chief) had been hinting at this need for several years but now the church formally requested a hospital. Whenever Bob came, he took seriously ill patients or those needing surgery back to Mukinge. But in between, the patients found it almost impossible to get to the hospital. Buses were irregular and expensive for people who had very little cash income. To walk took between ten days and two weeks over the rough terrain, difficult for a healthy person; a nightmare for someone seriously ill. Bob's first reaction was negative.

He admits, "After having built a hospital and getting some facilities and an operating room and lab, an X-ray machine and a training school, it wasn't easy to think of leaving it and starting all over again with nothing."

But the Africans were persistent. Bob said he'd give them six months to think about it and when he came back the next time, they should come up with a plan as to what they could do to get a hospital started. Six months later, Bob again met with the people in the Luampa church; three to five hundred people were gathered in the thatch roofed, cross-shaped mud brick building. For hours, Bob listened as one after another, the people stood to their feet to explain their urgent need. Some recounted stories of how they'd lost family members because there had been no medical help. Some testified how their lives had been spared because Kahaya had come just when they needed him. Many referred to their poverty and lack of education, to make sure Kahaya understood they couldn't do it without him.

By the time the lengthy meeting was over, it was decided the Africans would be responsible for making burnt bricks and for cutting timber from the forest for rafters and door frames. They proposed that Kahaya should be responsible to buy cement, roofing and steel windows.

Though impressed with their sincerity and determination, Bob was still hesitant. They needed government approval and assistance if anything as big as a hospital could take shape. But even more, he told them, "I can't leave Mukinge if there aren't doctors to take my place. It's not right to build a hospital and leave it unstaffed. If God wants us to proceed with this, then you'll have to pray with me that He will provide the medical staff needed at Mukinge. And," he added, "the church and the missionaries at Mukinge have to agree."

In the meantime, Bob approached the Federation of Rhodesia government to see if he could get approval for a hospital at Luampa. But the answer was negative. Officials had been attempting to start a small hospital at a government post in Mankoya, about an hour's drive from Luampa. But as Bob delved deeper into the problem, he realized the Catholic provincial medical officer wanted to direct available funds to building a Catholic hospital in the district. So, the project seemed to have come to a standstill.

Nothing was standing still at Mukinge, however. An air of excitement pervaded the station - romance was in the air, as Fran Woods became engaged to an English railway engineer, Michael Warburton, working in Ndola. Mike was deeply interested in missions and as the months passed, it became clear to him that he should apply to serve with the SAGM.

Bob and Belva couldn't have been happier even though it was likely that they would lose Fran at the hospital. The Lord provided for that need, too, for in 1957, three nurses, Ellen Groh, Phyllis Spahr and Lillian Brannon joined the staff. Just months before, Corrie Hubert, an experienced lab technician had arrived. So by the time of Fran's wedding scheduled for August, 1957, the hospital and nurse's training school were well staffed. And Bob and Belva threw themselves into the preparations as though it were their own daughter.

The logistics of planning a wedding several hundred miles into the bush was just the kind of challenge Bob enjoyed. When Mike arrived with uncooked ham instead of the cooked and sliced ham Belva had ordered, Fran panicked. But Bob in his inimitable way soothed her, "Don't worry, we'll just cook it." And down to the hospital kitchens he went, instructing the cook to empty the huge meat pot so he could cook the ham and then supervised the slicing.

Fran's mother could not come to the wedding but she sent a beautiful wedding dress for Fran and Belva's mother sent a lovely beige outfit for her as she was standing in for Mrs. Woods. On the day of the wedding Bob seemed to be everywhere, vacuuming the living room, supervising the pressing of the dresses, shooing Mike out of the way.

Not only was a mission wedding a big function for the whole community, but Bob must have felt a special responsibility to launch Fran well. He had, after all, been the human instrument to bring her out to Africa and she, in turn, had helped him launch his surgical career in Kaondeland. Within a few months after Fran left Mukinge, Dr. Jim Foulkes, whom Bob had contacted on his furlough, arrived to bring the number of doctors at Kaonde Hospital to three. Because of its competent staff and modern facilities, the sparse European community also came for medical help. With the prevailing white-black attitudes and the vast difference in standard of living, the mission did not feel it could put white patients in the same ward with the Africans. So, whenever they needed treatment, the Foster home became an extension of the hospital and Belva had the care of patients to add to her family responsibilities.

When the annual mission conference was held at Mukinge, everyone on the staff joined in to house the extra families from other SAGM stations in Northern Rhodesia. The host station was also responsible for cooking for the week-long conference. It was not unusual to find Bob in the kitchen supervising food preparation, cutting meat and serving food.

For the 1958 conference, the missionaries met in the nurse's classrooms behind the Foster house. One afternoon a frantically blaring horn broke into their deliberations as a jeep squealed to a stop in front of the hospital. Bob recognized it as belonging to the local game warden, Paul Reid, who had become a good friend. Paul jumped out and ran towards the hospital, holding his left hand in a viselike grip.

As Bob raced after him, Paul shouted he'd been bitten by a mamba just five minutes earlier. The black mamba is Southern Africa's most deadly snake, its bite usually fatal within ten or fifteen minutes as it attacks the red blood cells and paralyzes the respiratory system. There wasn't a minute to lose. One of the nurses raced for the anti-venom serum kept under refrigeration while Bob applied a tourniquet. As Paul slipped into unconsciousness, he mumbled that he tried to cut off his ring finger where he'd been struck.

Paul was carried over to the Foster home and the nurses set up a 'round the clock watch. Within a few hours, Paul had gone into convulsions; then his breathing stopped. Lillian Brannon who was watching him at this point called loudly to him, "Paul, you've got to breathe!" and he took a shuddering breath. Even after he regained consciousness, the pain was excruciating but Bob could give him no relief for fear of depressing the respiratory system.

It would be many months before Paul was completely well but he could thank the Lord that he was only minutes away from the hospital when the mamba attacked.

But when Bob needed Paul, he was away.

One morning at breakfast, a messenger came running from the senior Foster's house. The workmen refused to work. A wounded leopard was loose on the station. During the night, gun-traps which had been set by the local game wardens in the senior Foster's goat and sheep pen had gone off, injuring a leopard in the hindquarters. There is probably nothing more dangerous in the African bush than a wounded leopard and Bob knew the station would come to a standstill until it was killed. Grabbing his gun, he jumped into his jeep, agreeing to Stephen and Sharon's insistence that they could come along, and he drove over to pick up Dave Fields and Clarence Gifford. The two men agreed they needed help from the game wardens so they sent word over to the Boma, three miles away, to pick up two African wardens. Unfortunately, Paul was away but an African warden came.

The leopard's trail led into the tall elephant grass at the bottom of the station - grass so tall that Bob's six-foot height disappeared in it. With the children safely stowed in the back of the jeep well out of the action, Dave climbed a tree to serve as a lookout while Bob and several others beat the long grass down with poles so they could see their prey.

Dave thought he saw movement in the grass and then a tawny form sprang into view. "Bob, he's charging. Get out of there!" he screamed. Instantly, Bob hoisted himself up into a nearby tree. The rifle slipped into the tall grass as he pulled himself as high as he could on the precariously thin branches. An uninjured cat would have attacked him with one leap but this enraged animal could only claw at his feet, snarling and foaming at the mouth. The two African game wardens disappeared, along with other spectators who had stood at a safe distance watching the excitement.

Dave called out, "I can see him, but I don't know if I should try to get him from here."

"Don't shoot. You might hit me." Bob was aware that the smallest error could send the spray of bullets from Dave's shotgun into his body which was just a foot above the roaring animal. Out of the corner of his eye Bob could see some of the Africans, including his truck driver, inching back to see what had happened. An idea struck him.

"Kibale," he called, "crawl around behind the tree in the deep grass and pick up my gun. I'll keep teasing him so he won't notice you." To prove his point, Bob broke a piece of a branch off and began poking it into the leopard's face. He could almost feel the hot slobbery breath as the infuriated cat strained his powerful muscles to get at his tormenter. Kibale shook his head and started to back off. But as Bob tantalized the leopard, he shouted again to Kibale to come and help him.

From his lookout, Dave joined in, promising to cover Kibale if the leopard made a move toward him. Slowly and cautiously, the driver edged himself into the tall grass behind the tree, trying not to make a move that would attract the animal. Gingerly, he picked up the rifle and tossed it up to Bob. In an instant, Bob pointed the barrel of the rifle down the throat of the snarling animal and pulled the trigger. As the patients recounted the story over and over that day, they shook their heads and marvelled. Was there anything that Kahaya could not do?

Chapter 9

Lip Service

"If there's any legacy I'll remember from my mother and dad, it's the enthusiasm of believing God and history. They taught me, 'Don't make your God so small that He can't do anything. Take your hands off; become part of what God wants to do.'"

--- Dr. Stephen James Foster

"I've lived my life on the basis that the Word of God is absolutely trustworthy. I take God at His Word; trust Him, and ask Him to prove it. One thing I can say, we've proved the trustworthiness of the Lord's Word in our lives."

--- Dr. Robert Foster

✳✳✳✳✳✳✳✳✳✳✳✳✳✳✳✳✳✳✳✳

Every day in the hospital brought a new challenge. One afternoon, Paul Reid drove his pickup in from the Boma with an

African messenger in the back. Kungarisi served as a sort of policeman for the British Commissioner's office, but today his usually impressive blue and red uniform was covered with blood. Paul jumped out of the truck and rushed into the outpatient's department where Bob was working.

"Can you fix up this fellow's lip? My dog has just bitten it off." Paul seemed almost embarrassed as he pushed the dazed Kungarisi towards Bob. Bob removed the rag which had been tied around the lower half of Kungarisi's face. Sure enough, about three-quarters of the bottom lip was gone. As they took Kungarisi into the operating room Paul explained what had happened.

He'd been at the local trader's store at the Boma to pick up a bag of mealie meal (cornmeal), leaving his faithful German Shepherd sniffing around the truck, but with an ever-watchful eye on his master.

Kungarisi, a six foot giant of a man, came out of the store and greeted Paul cheerfully. He offered to help load the heavy bag but Paul shook him off, saying he could manage. Playfully, Kungarisi pushed him aside to grab the mealie meal himself. At that moment, the German Shepherd let out an angry growl and flew at Kungarisi's face, snapping at his lip.

Bob listened as he cleaned the ugly wound. "It would be so much easier to sew his lip back on rather than make a new lip," he explained to Paul. "Do you think you could find his lip?"

Paul agreed to go back to the scene of the accident to see and within a half hour he returned, gingerly holding the filthy piece of flesh rolled in a leaf between his finger and thumb. Bob instructed the orderly to wash it in a saline solution while he explained to Kungarisi what he was planning to do.

"I'm going to have to give you a little anesthetic. I can sew your lip back in. I think it will take. It's only been out half an hour or so and I think it will work."

But the terrified patient shook his head. "I don't want any anesthetic."

"How am I going to sew this back in if you won't let me give you some anesthetic?"

"No, no anesthetic. I'm afraid."

"There's nothing to be afraid of," Bob reassured him. But he knew that Africans were deathly afraid. They believed a person actually died and came to life again under anesthetic.

"You don't have to go to sleep for this," Bob explained. "I'll give you a local anesthetic and we can sew this in easily."

But Kungarisi refused and after doing all he could to persuade him, Bob admitted defeat. He simply cleaned up the wound and dressed it as best he could. When Kungarisi arrived home his third and favorite wife took one look at him in shock.

"What happened to you?" she cried.

He told her the whole story including Bob's offer to sew the lip back on. His wife was furious. "You go back there and get your lip sewed on. I don't want to live with a man without a lip."

So after lunch, Kungarisi turned up at the hospital to tell Bob he was willing for the surgery. Anticipating that Kungarisi might change his mind, Bob had left the sterilized lip in a normal saline solution on the mayo stand in the operating room. Once more he and his assistant scrubbed up and were ready to proceed with the operation when Bob looked at the mayo stand to find it empty.

"Where's this guy's lip?" he shouted. "It's not on the mayo stand."

The nurse was dumbfounded. "I don't know. We left it there before lunch." She checked with several African nurses and then the cleaning man admitted that he'd thrown it out into the rubbish because he thought the man didn't want to have it sewn back on.

"Well, this fellow's come back here now and he wants his lip so you go out and find it," Bob ordered.

About ten minutes later, the cleaning man came in with the lip wrapped in the same gauze it had been thrown out in. So once more Bob cleaned it up. But now he was dubious about the outcome.

"I don't know if this will take after all this time and all this lip has been through," he warned Kungarisi. "But we'll try."

He sewed the lip back on, but Bob fully expected that when the man returned in five days to have the sutures removed the whole thing would slough off. But when Kungarisi returned even Bob couldn't believe his eyes. The lip had healed well enough so Kungarisi could use it and in time he even got back full feeling.

About a month later, Kungarisi came back to thank Bob for what he had done for him.

Bob reminded him, "You really shouldn't have a lip.   Ordinarily, there's no way you would have one. This is a miracle. God's been good to you and you need to thank Him."

"How does a man thank God?" the huge African asked.

Bob explained that men in Scripture had asked that same question and he quoted from Psalm 116, "What shall I render unto the Lord for all of his goodness to me?"

"The man who wrote that many years ago said if we really want to thank God, the first thing we do is to take the salvation God offers us," Bob explained. As they continued speaking, Kungarisi's once-mangled lips broke into a smile of comprehension and before they had finished, his lips offered the sacrifice of praise. For many years to come, he would follow after the Lord, offering Him far more than lip service.

For Bob such an experience fulfilled his deepest desire, that his medical work would not only bring physical healing but spiritual life to his patients. He enjoyed preaching and his week wasn't complete if he hadn't preached several times on Sunday. One of his regular commitments was at the relative's compound where several hundred people lived in temporary quarters until they could take their family member home.

Though he was an avid student of the Word, reading and studying each day before he began his hospital rounds, Bob also knew how to distill the best from others. Dr. Stephen Olford, who became a friend of the family, could be heard over missionary radio at 9 A.M. on Sunday mornings. Often Bob would make a few notes from his radio message, then go out to the compound and preach. His creative energy affected everything he touched. He began pushing Sunday School at the Mukinge church and even got Dad Foster involved. At first Mr. Foster felt it would never work for adults in Africa but after Bob continued to urge him to try, he promised, "If you get me twelve men, I'll do it." In fact, Mr. Foster never had less than sixty in his class and the Sunday school grew to over eight hundred by 1958.

By 1959, the pressure from the Luampa church for a hospital had become ever more urgent and the situation had to be resolved. Bob and Jim continued to make regular visits to Luampa, working in the dark grass hut which everyone called the "Black hole of Calcutta." Nurse Ruth Kingston recalls Bob operating in one corner, while she was delivering a baby in another.

The staff at Luampa was effectively caring for over four hundred leprosy patients on the station and another fifteen hundred registered at out-station clinics. Mrs. P. G. Watson received an MBE (Member of the British Empire) from the Queen of England for her heroic pioneering ministry. But there seemed to be little enthusiasm among the missionaries to have a hospital on the station though the Africans were willing to make almost any sacrifice to see it happen. There were so many stories of needless deaths and unimaginable suffering because of the distance from a hospital.

Ruth Kingston tells of one patient with a strangulated hernia. The only vehicle on the station had burned up so she had him carried on a stretcher to the road at the edge of the station. The roads were "just a mud bath" and the huge trucks which did come by infrequently got bogged down over and over. Ruth and her patient waited by the side of the road for six hours until a heavily-loaded truck stopped. The driver was willing to hoist the patient on top of his load but he refused to take Ruth. Sixteen agonizing hours later the truck arrived at the hospital in Mungu, 114 miles away, only to find that the doctor had gone to Livingstone for a conference.

Though the patient survived the trip, he was in deep shock from the pain of the hernia and the terrible bouncing on the road. He died shortly after arriving in Mungu. When the Africans learned that Mukinge now had three doctors, they reminded Kahaya that one of his major obstacles had been overcome.

Yet Bob still needed the approval of the Mukinge church and the missionaries before he felt free to accept their call. At one point, he asked Jim Foulkes if he would be willing to start a new hospital in Luampa but Jim refused.

"That wasn't the kind of situation I flourish in - bucking the missionary staff and raising a quarter of a million dollars! I knew it would be a lot easier for Bob."

So Bob asked the Mukinge church to call a special meeting. No one really thought the African church would approve. They had waited so long for the hospital and they had seen Bob bring it into being over the last ten years. The meeting went on for many hours; some said "Yes", others, "No".

"But when they finally came down to it," Bob remembers, "they gave me their blessing and said we believe God wants you to do it."

What a confirmation this was to Bob and to the rest of the missionaries. When they met for their annual conference in 1959, they gave their approval and blessing.

The Luampa congregation wasted no time. More than three hundred, including forty-two village headmen, turned up on the day set to make a start. Ruth Kingston remembers hundreds of Africans filing by her window, carrying hoes and shovels and singing joyfully. Bob visited Luampa regularly to check on the progress of the work. The enormity of the task of starting over and raising funds for another hospital didn't seem to phase him but Belva admits to some hesitation.

She was now expecting their fifth child. She'd heard so many stories of the isolation of Luampa; Bob often said it seemed much farther away than 185 miles because of the bad roads. The station itself was situated in a flat, sandy region, much hotter than Mukinge. She admitted that it was hard to think of starting all over again to learn a new language, and care for her growing family under primitive conditions. The few buildings at Luampa were very old and, of course, they had no electricity or running water.

However, once it became clear that God was directing them to Luampa, Belva was able to write their prayer partners, "We feel assured that this is the Lord's will for us on our return to the field."

It was decided that Bob and Belva would go home on furlough in 1960, a year earlier than planned, so they could start the new term at Luampa. In the meantime, Bob continued to visit other clinics besides Luampa including the Mutanda station a hundred miles away where Fran and Mike were now living.

Dr. Sam Kasonso, who later became the head of the Zambia Evangelical Church, was headmaster of the Mutanda school. He recalls, "When Dr. Foster was there, you could hear his laughter across the station. He was just delightful. He laughed; he had joy. He wasn't afraid or unsure of himself. He was confident of what he was doing. This was a big help to the patients."

During one visit to Mutanda, Bob's self-confidence was tested to the point of death. He had arrived at the station about noon and after lunch at the Warburton's, he went over to begin examining patients whom Fran had already determined needed more attention than she could give. There were several hundred people sitting out in the hot African sun and a hundred patients lined up to see him. Bob began examining the first woman. Suddenly she sat up on the table, pulled her cloth around her and started to get off.

"I have to leave."

"But I'm not finished yet."

"No! I want to leave."

Bob continued to listen to her heart and realized it was racing wildly. What was going on?

The woman jumped off the table. As soon as she got to the door, she began shouting, "Don't anybody go into the clinic. There's a big snake in there."

Bob turned to look around. He didn't see any snake. He came back out to ask the woman, "Where is this snake? I don't see anything."

"Kahaya, when I was lying down on your examining table, I looked up at the rafters and there was a big black mamba right above your head."

Sure enough, when Bob looked up into the thatched roof of the clinic, he could see a mamba as thick as his arm, at least eight feet long, lying on the rafter at the gable end of the roof. He knew no patients would go into that room again - nor would he for that matter - until that snake was killed. So he returned to the crowd outside and asked, "Who will help me kill the snake?"

There was a deathly silence; not a soul volunteered. Again Bob asked, "We've got to kill it. We can't work as long as it's in there. Who will help me?"

No one responded. Finally the pastor who had come to hold a meeting with the patients while they waited, replied, "Kahaya, you go. We'll pray."

Taken aback for a moment, Bob agreed. "All right. If you'll really pray I'll go. Does anyone have a gun?"

They shook their heads. Then one man came forward with a six foot long spear, "You can fight the mamba with this." Another fellow gave him a cane. So armed with spear and cane, Bob stepped back into the dark empty clinic - empty but for that slithering mass of death, now watching him menacingly. Bob knew if he came within reach, the snake would bury his deadly fangs in him instantly and he'd never make it back to Mukinge alive. Someone had brought a step ladder so that Bob could get near enough to the snake to strike him with the spear.

Bob analyzed his chances. "If I get him speared against the wall, I can hit him with the cane," he thought.

He called out to the people, "OK, now you pray!"

With a crescendo of prayer outside, Bob struck the mamba in the middle of its body, pinning it to the wall. In a flash, the venomous head attacked him, missing him by inches. With his right hand, Bob lashed out with the heavy cane, intending to strike the snake's head. But the creature struck out so quickly, the cane missed. Over and over again, Bob and the serpent struck at each other. Each time the snake could not reach far enough because his body was held by the spear; each time the deadly head ducked Bob's blow.

The prayers outside the window continued unabated but Bob was fast losing strength. It could have been an hour that the man and snake held each other at bay. Bob's arm holding the spear was so tired, he couldn't continue. With a jerk, he pulled the spear towards him, throwing the snake to the ground. It disappeared behind a cupboard. Gingerly Bob got down from the ladder and stepped outside. Everyone's eyes were on him, hoping he'd been successful.

"Look," he pled, "I'm tired; the snake's tired. It's gone behind the cupboard. I need some help to finish him off."

Out of all the people standing around, a wizened old man with a crippled leg came forward to help. He was so short he fit under Bob's arm. The two of them returned to the scene of battle. Bob explained that when they pushed the cupboard against the wall, the snake would try to dart out. If he got out, it would be the end of them. But if they held the cupboard tightly against the wall, the snake would be stuck part way out.

At Bob's shout, the two slammed the cupboard against the wall and the deadly head emerged. But just as Bob predicted, the mamba could get no further and with a few mighty wallops, Bob finished it off.

Bob was so worn out that he could not continue with the clinic that afternoon. He drove back to Mukinge, praising the Lord all the way for His protection. In the days ahead, Bob often drew a parallel between the story and missionary work. "People say to me, 'Bob, you go; we'll pray.' And I go on to say that if they really pray, God will work." But he had found, too, that when it comes to volunteering for difficult ministry, it's often the old and decrepit who are willing while the youthful and seemingly strong-hearted hold back.

While tragedy was averted in the snake experience, other traumatic events tested the faith of the missionaries. In September, 1959, Jim and Marilyn Foulkes' two-year-old son died of complications from tracheo-bronchitis. A few months later, Mike Warburton fell seriously ill. Bob and an orthopedic surgeon who was visiting from Canada stopped by Mutanda late one night on their way back to Mukinge. Bob hadn't planned to stop since it was already one A.M. but at the last minute, they turned off the main road to go the two miles to Mutanda. He was sure Frances wouldn't mind giving them a cup of coffee before they continued their journey.

Frances was overjoyed to see them. Mike had come down with a high fever several days earlier but she was worried about symptoms that were not typical of the usual malaria. The doctors checked Mike but were unable to diagnose the problem. They suggested that Mike come to Mukinge in a few days when their seminar was over and they'd give him a more thorough check-up.

However, by the next day Mike was experiencing numbness in his feet and Fran decided to drive him to Mukinge herself. There, a spinal test revealed the first indications of encephalitis. In the next few days, his condition deteriorated and Bob feared the ascending paralysis would soon affect his breathing. He drove Fran and Michael three hundred miles to Kitwe where there was a respirator. Mike stood to his feet for the last time on the eight-hour drive to Kitwe. For the next few days, his condition was critical but as the missionaries and Africans prayed, the drugs began to take effect and the paralysis ceased. Though the iron lung stood outside Mike's door, it never had to be used.

It would be two years before Mike could return to Mutanda, this time in a wheelchair. But his handicap opened new doors and relationships as he served God among the African people. In 1974, the mission appointed Mike as Assistant to the International Director and he and Fran moved to the international office of what was by then known as the Africa Evangelical Fellowship. They were there waiting for Bob and Belva when Bob became International Director in 1981.

Mike's near brush with death was just one more indication to Bob that the mission needed better communication and transportation. In fact, he had been urging the conference of missionaries to consider radio communications between the stations. It took several years before they were convinced that this was not just some luxurious gadget and agreed to let him purchase an intercom system. Ever since he'd visited the Mseleni Mission in South Africa, another SAGM station, Bob had been dreaming of a mission air service. He'd seen how much more could be accomplished with an airplane to cut down on the long hours of travel between isolated stations. Instead of eight bone-wearying hours of driving over rugged roads, he could go back and forth in less than an hour. Seriously ill patients could be picked up and brought into the hospital within hours of their diagnosis instead of taking days to make the trip. Doctors could visit clinics more frequently; evangelists could accompany the doctors and nurses so that each clinic would have more regular teaching.

By the end of 1959, the mission finally agreed that an air service would be a practical addition to the hospital work and Bob made arrangements to take flying lessons.

Chapter 10

Presumption or Faith?

"In preaching and in public, I try not to make a pitch for money. But I have always felt in my ministry that if I preach the Word, God will touch people's hearts. God will move them to take the initiative and say, 'Bob is there something you need?' I believe it's better to ask for more than less; to challenge a person to give by faith and make it a spiritual experience.

"I don't usually go to a place praying, 'Lord, today I have to have a certain amount of money.' But I do say, 'Lord, is there someone here who should help me? Have him come and talk to me.' Then I just preach the Word and trust God to speak."

--- Dr. Robert Foster

****

Once the approval for a plane for Mukinge was given, Bob wasted no time in making arrangements to take flying lessons. A fellow SAGM missionary in South Africa made contact with a South African doctor also wanting to learn to fly. Since "two could learn cheaper together," Dr. Robertson arranged for himself and Bob to stay with Dr. Paul Bremer, a Christian gynecologist in Pretoria. The Bremers were a staunch Dutch Reformed family of Afrikaans background. Traditionally Afrikaners are very family oriented and hospitable, and Paul and Elfrida welcomed the two missionary doctors warmly.

Those who knew Bob well often remarked at his candor and ability to make himself at home. One missionary remarked, "Nothing is too much trouble if he thinks there's a way he can help. But in the same way he's not afraid to ask other people to do things for him. If he comes to your house and has dirty laundry, he's not afraid to ask you to do it. He knows how to give and receive."

Initially, Elfrida was a bit taken aback by this forthright, self-assured American. Two days after Bob arrived, he came back after his flying lesson to find Elfrida canning peaches. Stopping in the kitchen to chat, he looked into the pots and remarked, "These are too soft. You can't bottle them. You'd better turn those into jam."

Speechless, Elfrida watched Bob pour off some of the water and add sugar for jam. "Before I knew it, I had five bottles of peach jam, which we don't even eat!" she recalls laughingly.

Over the weeks, Elfrida learned something of Bob's background and varied abilities, and she learned how to parley his frankness with her own. After a special occasion for a number of guests, Bob remarked, "That's the first decent cup of coffee I've had at your house since I've come to stay with you."

Intrigued, Elfrida asked him why. "Because it was brewed and had cream in it," was his reply.

She retorted, "Well, you're not having another decent cup until we have guests again. You're part of this household."

And that Bob had become; roughhousing with the Bremer's daughters, teaching them Scripture at the table, entering into long discussions about medical missions with Paul, and enjoying the verbal exchanges with Elfrida.

This was the first of many visits Bob, and later Belva, made to the gracious home in Pretoria. At one time, the entire family stayed two weeks along with Elfrida's sister's family. The children totaled fourteen!

Elfrida remembers, "It all went off very smoothly."

She also remembers how Bob began "nagging" her to start teaching a Bible study. "Bob has a very winning and encouraging way about him, without flattering. He just started out saying, 'There you are with a maid and everything running on oiled wheels. You have lots of time, lots of friends. You should start a Bible study.'"

At the Dutch Reformed Church, the Dominee (pastor) did all the teaching. The thought of a lay person, particularly a woman, leading a Bible study was against all tradition. Still, Bob continued to urge Elfrida to teach, and even offered to lead the first Bible study to show her what to do. Reluctantly, Elfrida agreed, and today, almost thirty years later, her original group of doctors' wives has grown to over three thousand Afrikaans Bible studies with more than thirty thousand women enrolled.

Elfrida began translating materials into Afrikaans and then writing her own. She employs two people full time just to fill orders for her materials.

This ability to see a need and challenge others to be risk takers for God has marked Bob's ministry over the years. When others said, "It can't be done," he would respond that "God can do it. Just trust Him, believe Him, put His Word to the test."

Most of the time, Bob led the way himself and men and women eagerly followed his lead, putting their lives and their futures on the line for God. But often, as was the case with Elfrida Bremer, he saw a need and did not hesitate to urge others to take up the task if he believed this was what they ought to do.

While Bob was at the Bremers taking flying lessons, he began looking into the kind of plane he should get for the medical work. Elfrida remembers him sitting at the coffee table with a colorful brochure about a Cessna spread out before him.

He explained its advantages to her. "This is the one I want," he said as he looked at the picture admiringly. "I want black and silver trimmings just like that."

Elfrida remembers thinking, "Wow, I can understand that he needs a plane to get around when he can't get through by road, but to say, 'Lord, I want black and silver trim,' that's a bit of a cheek."

Two years later, when Bob and Belva returned from furlough, they came through South Africa to pick up the plane. He invited Paul and Elfrida out to the airport for a flip.

"And you know," Elfrida marvelled, "Bob came with the exact model he'd shown me in the lounge, and it had black and silver trim!"

Even before Bob had any funds to purchase his own plane, he was asked by mission headquarters to fly to Angola with missionary Harold Stevens to study the needs of the medical work there. SAGM pioneers had been working in Angola since 1912, and two of the five stations operated medical programs. However, tensions between the Portuguese colonists and African nationalist groups were developing. Though Portuguese officials were helpful in their "red-tape way," restrictions against Protestant missionaries were already in force. Bob and Harold saw tremendous needs and opportunities in Angola, but they could not know that it would be another ten years before new missionary visas would be granted. Once missionaries working in Angola left the country, they were not permitted to return, and a number of SAGM missionaries stayed on without a furlough for eleven years.

The "winds of change" sweeping across Africa were also stirring in Northern Rhodesia. African leaders had objected to the Federation of Northern and Southern Rhodesia and Nyasaland from its inception in 1953. They felt the move would strengthen Southern Rhodesia's racial policy and deprive Africans of all rights. Indeed, the gap between the white and black population widened. Salisbury had become the capital and the British labelled African protesters as "agitators." Kenneth Kaunda was one of those arrested in 1955 after a mine strike on the copperbelt which had forced black laborers out of the union.

With Kaunda's imprisonment, fragmented black parties began uniting, and when he was freed in 1960 he was given the leadership of the United Nationalist Independence Party (UNIP). Realizing that independence was bound to come, Bob had initiated charging nominal fees at the hospital in preparation for the time when the hospital would have to be self-supporting. But as political demonstrations in other parts of the country increased, some political leaders threatened the mission, angry at the imposition of charges.

Bob and Belva's last prayer letter before furlough commented, "The sword that has dropped in the Congo, that is hanging by a thread in Nyasaland, is swaying back and forth here, dividing the loyalties of men."

Over the next few years, several mission houses were set on fire, but the mission generally escaped the effects of demonstrations and sabotage experienced in the urban areas.

Bob was more concerned about how to feed the hundreds of patients and their families who relied on the hospital for food. He initiated a number of schemes. One Sunday was "potato Sunday" when people donated potatoes to the church which the hospital then bought. The proceeds were used to help build a new church at the Boma.

He was also concerned about Herbert on whom he'd operated for appendicitis earlier in the year. During the surgery, he noticed some growths he didn't like, and had sent a specimen to Lusaka for analysis. The report came back negative, which was a great relief to Herb although not entirely satisfactory to Bob. Six months later, while Bob and Belva were on furlough, they received word that Herb had died of cancer, leaving Elenore who was pregnant with their seventh child.

There was so much to do to get ready for furlough since this was not an ordinary furlough. It meant closing up the house and the ministry at Mukinge, for they would not be returning here to live. Bob planned to take a refresher course at the University of Toronto Medical School while home, and just weeks before they were to arrive there, they learned the promise of a house had fallen through. For Belva these must have been difficult days. Stuart Jeremy was less than eight months old; taking five children on furlough with the inevitable deputation, staying in people's homes and travelling long distances by car would test her endurance. Bob would be away for weeks at a time, leaving her with the heavy responsibilities of the family alone. And leaving Mukinge, rich in friendships and memories, for the isolation and primitive conditions of Luampa was wrenching. But her letters to friends and relatives at home expressed a serene confidence that God was in control.

"Last week we learned that the house is no longer available. As Bob said, 'It was certainly merciful of the Lord to put our minds at rest all these months, thinking that the accommodation problem was settled.' Now we only have to face it for a few weeks, and we cannot doubt that He has something just as perfect for our needs as the former provision would have been."

Though only ten years old at the time, Sharon recalls, "We returned in late summer and only had about ten days till school started to find a house in Toronto. I'll never forget hearing conversations that we had to find a place and get settled, and there was nothing available, but I also recall that within that one week a furnished house was provided so we were moved in and ready to start by the first day of school. Bob and Ruth Stephens had moved within a few blocks and their kids were going to the same school."

Bob had some clear goals for this furlough: buy a plane, find a pilot (the missionaries had decided that Bob had too many other pressures to also pilot his own plane), raise funds for the building of Luampa Hospital, buy all the needed equipment, take a refresher course and visit all his supporting churches.

In February of 1961, Bob was in Florida for meetings. One Sunday morning in a small church a man came up to him and offered him $3000 to purchase a Piper Cub which is what Bob had in mind at the time.

Rejoicing in this provision, Bob went on to a missions conference in Fort Lauderdale where he would be speaking all week. At the conference a woman came to him and said, "I'll give you $10,000 to buy a Cessna 180. Someone has told me that a Piper Cub would not be adequate for you."

In the months previous, Bob had met Don Amborski, a young pilot from the Korean War who applied to SAGM to go to Africa to work with Bob. Bob called him and asked him to see if he could find a plane for $10,000. Within a week Don called and said, "I've found a good Cessna 180 for just under $10,000."

The wealthy owner had it outfitted with every known gadget, but after a short time decided it was too small for him. So he sold it to Bob for a very reduced price. When Bob called the gentleman who had offered $3000 for a plane, he suggested that he could use that money to transport the plane to South Africa. The man gladly agreed. For the remaining months of furlough, Don and Bob used the Cessna with the black and silver markings to get around to do their deputation, and Bob continued to see God provide in remarkable ways for the Luampa project.

By the time they were ready to return to Africa, Bob had most of the equipment he needed for the hospital. A medical relief association provided him with about $25,000 worth of drugs. When he took the drugs to the boat to ship with their goods to Africa, Bob learned that it would cost $300. That night at a church supper in Brooklyn, New York, a lady came up and gave him the needed $300.

During that furlough the Lord provided an airplane and pilot, several nurses, funds for the hospital, several tons of drugs and equipment and a vehicle. Bob simply provided the opportunity for people to get involved in a need in Africa. He was personally just as ready to respond to a need when the Spirit of God prompted him.

He recalls a time when he met another missionary during a conference where they were both speaking, and the Lord seemed to say, "Give him $50." Bob's initial response was, "Lord I only have $50 in my pocket, and I still have expenses to get me home."

But all that night he couldn't sleep. Even though he'd never met this missionary before, there was that haunting sense that he needed to do something for him. So the next day, Bob pulled the last $50 out of his pocket and gave it to the missionary.

He hadn't mentioned the incident to anyone, not even Belva. That night after the service a man came up to him and said, "The Lord told me to give you this," and he pressed $50 into Bob's hand.

"I've learned in life that if the Lord impresses upon you to do something, you'd better do it," Bob observes. "If the Lord can use you to bless somebody else, He'll bless somebody else by getting them to help you. It's been a tremendous experience for me to see how God works. We can be so tightfisted. Even if we don't have what we think we need, if we're prepared to share it, it's exciting to see how God provides. He doesn't always do it the same day, but the Lord is no man's debtor. Time and time again, we've had experiences with helping people, and how God pays us back - sometimes even through the government."

While Bob gave freely when he saw a need, he in turn expected God's people to give freely when he presented a need. Paul Bremer had opportunity to learn that firsthand when Bob returned from his furlough.

Bob had been speaking to Christian medical students in five medical schools in South Africa before heading north to Luampa. One day, Paul took him to the airport to visit another school and on the way he suggested, "Bob, we would like to give you a present from our Christian Medical Fellowship. Is there anything you still need?"

Bob quickly responded, "We've got most things, but we don't have the means to get it up north."

Paul wondered if Bob was referring to rental of a truck for the three-thousand-mile journey. "What do you have in mind?"

"Well, a Mercedes is the best," Bob responded offhandedly. It dawned on Paul that Bob was talking about a seven-ton truck. When he hesitated to respond Bob urged, "Go back to your colleagues and talk about it. When I come back from this conference, you can tell me what you've decided."

Upon Bob's return, he took Paul to the Mercedes Benz dealer in town. While Bob asked questions about horsepower, tons and fuel consumption, Paul was feeling farther and farther from reality. When the dealer finally quoted an astronomical price, Paul felt faint.

"Any delay in delivery?" Bob asked.

Bob was realistic enough to realize the cost was too high and suggested they go look at a six-ton Bedford. Paul took out a loan, and then let his colleagues know what had been done. Since there was not a good medical insurance program for doctors, they worked for each other without a specific charge, accepting whatever gratuity their colleagues wanted to give. Paul explained that these donations would go to pay for Bob's truck and within three years the loan was paid back.

Did Paul feel that Bob had taken advantage of his friendship?

"Not in the least. One feels a loyalty to Bob and the effect on one is that Bob was expecting something quite in the realm of possibility."

In fact, during the three years Paul was paying off the loan his income and gratuities increased as never before or since. When he later told that to Bob, Bob responded, "Well Paul, you'd better step out in faith and do it again sometime."

Elfrida quips, "We've learned not to say, 'We want to give you a present, what do you want?'"

Chapter 11

Starting Over

"There was a whole generation of African men that God raised up that were taught by P.V. Watson and some of the older missionaries at Luampa. Some of those men were exceedingly fine, godly men who were involved in teaching and preaching the Word of God - men like Pastors Benjamini and Jehosophat, who were two of the great leaders of the church. They knew the Scriptures and were able to teach the Scriptures far better than anybody at Kasempa. These older men were able to work together in spite of the rivalries and jealousies of the various tribes in the area. They prayed together. Their differences didn't stop them from preaching and working."

--- Dr. Robert Foster

❋❋❋❋❋❋❋❋❋❋❋❋❋❋❋❋❋❋❋❋❋

Northern Rhodesia had been a haven for Angolan Africans since the sixteenth century. The Portuguese had found their greatest source of wealth in slavery and some of the African tribes had joined in the lucrative trade, waging raiding parties on villages of other tribes and turning their hapless victims over to the Portuguese. It is estimated that a third of all slaves taken from Africa passed through Angolan ports.

Though the slave trade had virtually stopped by the mid-nineteenth century, the Portuguese settlers found other ways to "enslave" the Africans in the territory. They demanded six months of enforced labor every year, so thousands fled into the neighboring countries of Northern Rhodesia (now known as Zambia) and the former Congo. Africans who became Protestant Christians faced the added oppression of a Catholic hierarchy that persecuted those who strayed from the mother church. Thus, thousands of Angolan Africans had settled in the Luampa area, including Pastor Benjamani who had been invited by Mr. Jakeman, the founder of the station, to come and preach to the refugees.

Pastor Benjamani was saved through the love and care of a Christian nurse at a mission station in Angola. He'd been deathly afraid to go to a "missionary" who had been described to him as "a semi-human who sleeps in the river at night and has all the color washed out of him." None-the-less, after the witchdoctor threatened to cut off his leg infected from stepping on a thorn, Benjamani decided to take a chance with the terrifying missionary. There for the first time in his life he heard of the love of Jesus and saw it demonstrated in the lives of those who treated him. After his conversion, he grew under the teaching of the Word of God, and was more than ready to follow Mr. Jakeman to the Luampa area to work with his fellow Luchazis who'd fled there.

There were not only Luchazis, but Mbundas and Chokwes from Angola along with the Luvales, Lozis and native Bankoyas. This mixture of tribes and languages was always a potential source of tension. But by the time the church began approaching Bob to come to Luampa, these groups had learned to work and worship together in the church. Much of the credit was due to Pastor Jehosophat, who was also a local chief, and Pastor Benjamani.

When it became clear that the government would neither approve nor finance the hospital, church leaders sent letters to all the local chiefs asking for their approval and assistance. At one time, they took Bob to visit the paramount chief who had been educated in England and could speak English. Paramount Chief Musanaweni set the example by giving one thousand kwacha towards the hospital. Without exception, the chiefs welcomed the proposed hospital, and most sent gifts to help with the construction. Much of the early work on the hospital was provided by hundreds of volunteers. Men cut timber; they formed bricks of mud and baked them in a kiln they had built. When the summer rains washed the kiln away, they started all over again. Women carried calabashes filled with water on their heads from the river to the kiln, and carried stacks of bricks on their head to the building site.

Though some of the enthusiasm and energy would wane as the months dragged into years, the African Christians succeeded in putting up the first men's ward, and had foundations in for a second by the time Bob and his family returned from furlough. No doubt, Bob knew that, though the African church was willing to do almost anything to have a hospital at Luampa, the missionaries on the station were not convinced. One missionary recalls, "I remember sitting around in staff meeting wondering what we were going to do with Bob Foster when he comes with all his ideas."

They'd seen the changes he'd brought at Mukinge and some felt the "hospital would over-balance the spiritual work." They knew, too, that when Bob came the work on the station would double and they wondered who would do the work, and where the staff would come from. Some openly scoffed at the idea that the Africans would accomplish what they said they'd do - and particularly to do it for nothing! Now Bob was coming not only to build a hospital, but bringing an airplane! To some this was wasteful and even unspiritual. Yet Bob had sent word that a plane and pilot had been provided and he instructed the church to start on the airstrip he had laid out behind the hospital site.

In April 1962, Bob and his pilot, Don Amborski, flew the plane to Luampa district for the first time. They landed on an airstrip at Mankoya, a government post just a few miles from Luampa. As Bob alighted from the plane that April morning, he was surprised to see a European man dressed in white coming out on the apron to meet him. He introduced himself as the new provincial medical officer.

"I want to be the first one to greet you on your arrival here in the Western Province and to let you know that the government has changed its policy. We welcome your coming and we want you to go ahead and open this hospital."

Though the man hastened to add that there were no available funds at present, Bob rejoiced in this welcome news, and saw it as God's encouragement in the formidable task ahead.

It had been a long journey since they'd left New York on the Robin Grey in January. Bob had just completed a tour of South African medical schools, speaking to the Christian medical students. During this time Belva had taken the four older children to Sakeji. She and Stuart had arrived at Luampa on the truck with their goods just the day before Bob flew in. There was no house for them to live in, but how good it was to be together again after seven long weeks.

Initially they stayed with the Donalds, a missionary couple from Belva's home church, and stored all their furniture and belongings in a garage on the station. About five o'clock on that first morning, Bob was awakened by a tap on his window. One of the nurses, Pauline Connet, called, "Bob can you come down to the dispensary?"

Bob dressed quickly and ran down to find a man with serious knife wounds he'd sustained in a drunken brawl. His relatives had carried him through the night in a hammock. His stomach had been slashed and his intestines were hanging out, wrapped up in a filthy T-shirt.

Bob looked around the sparsely stocked clinic, "Pauline, what do you have that we can use to help this man? We can't move him anywhere in this condition. I'll have to operate."

Pauline confirmed there were no sutures, needles, sterile towels, or instruments of any kind. They did have some syringes and needles for injections, some medicines to put the patient out, and chloroform - which Bob hadn't used for years.

"They didn't even have a pair of gloves, say nothing of sterile gloves," Bob recalls.

Leaving Pauline to treat Savindindo for shock as best she could, Bob made the rounds of the missionary homes. "Do you have darning needles, cotton thread, or scissors?" he pled. Pauline found a couple of forceps, but there was no "needle driver" so Bob borrowed a pair of pliers to pull the needle through the tissue. Without scalpels, he settled for a sharp razor blade.

It took several hours to gather these motley supplies and sterilize them in boiling water. When they were finally ready, Bob told Pauline, "I'll put Savindindo to sleep with the chloroform, and then you'll have to keep him asleep while I clean him up, wash out the debris and get his intestines back in."

As Bob worked, he found punctures in two places which he sewed up using a darning needle and pulling it through with the sterilized pliers. When he finally closed up the wound and inserted drains, he thought to himself, "This fellow will never live."

Bob had already warned Don Amborski to radio ahead to Mukinge that he would be flying the patient in to Kasempa, which had a government airstrip about three miles from the hospital.

"This was the Lord's mercy and miraculous healing power," Bob recounts. "One week later, Savindindo was discharged from Mukinge and flew back to Luampa. He got out of the plane, feeling fine, pounding his tummy. Everybody had been convinced that he was going to die. As a result, the tale got around the countryside about this fellow who was dead and who was brought back to life. I'm sure the Lord did this to authenticate our work right from the start."

For Belva, the new start was less exciting. Ann and Keith did all they could to make them comfortable. Bob and Belva and Stuart slept on a mattress on the living room floor and moved the mattresses outside during the day.

"It was so hot, we could have slept outside," Belva explained, "except for mosquitoes, snakes, and other unwelcome visitors in the African night. The Luampa sand got into everything and living conditions were much more primitive than at Mukinge. "Just physical survival took a tremendous amount of effort," she recalls.

Finding a private place was almost impossible. Keith Donald recalls finding Bob sitting out in the car early in the morning having his devotions. Belva had known there'd be a new language to learn, but how she missed being able to converse in Kikaonde, especially trying to give instructions to a houseboy, or an African visiting at the back door.

However, Belva was not one to dwell on the negatives and she looked forward to settling into the quonset hut being put up near the hospital site, so she would have a place to welcome the four school age children when they came home from Sakeji in June. She wrote friends at home, "The quonset hut is quick, cheap and will make a good garage/storehouse when we move to larger quarters. Meanwhile it will be like summer-cottage living but basically adequate and a lot of fun."

Was it fun when the temperature underneath the curved corrugated asbestos roof reached 110 degrees?

... when she cooked outside in a thatched "African kitchen"?

...when every drop of water the family used had to be hauled from the river a quarter of a mile away?

...when the flies buzzed incessantly around her head and invaded the privacy of everything she touched?

Not only flies, but more sinister creatures were visitors. One night, she and Bob awoke, inexplicably, in the middle of the night. Bob shone his flashlight over to Stuart's crib. On the wall behind the crib was a pulsating column of army ants; in minutes they would cover the crib and the sleeping two-and-a-half year old. Army ants devour anything in their path and have been known to kill chickens and even sheep. Bob snatched Stuart out of their way, and then spent the rest of the night burning them out with blazing kerosene.

At least Belva knew the quonset wasn't permanent. This time Bob started work on their own house within a few months after arriving at Luampa. Belva insisted it be ready by Christmas when the children would come home again. Besides, Grandma and Grandpa Foster and Elenore's four oldest children would be coming to spend Christmas at Luampa. Elenore had taken her three youngest, including the son born after Herb's death, to Canada on furlough, leaving the four older ones in school at Sakeji.

Just a few days before they arrived, Bob and Stephen were still laying parquet tiles in the living room, and red and white tiles down the long hallway to the four bedrooms. The house was just a hundred yards from the hospital so Bob could supervise the building there while he put the finishing touches on his home.

Even before Bob arrived at Luampa, he had decided to learn one of the Angolan languages spoken in the area, "Just in case God ever gives me the opportunity to go to Angola." There were enough similarities between Kikaonde and Luchazi that he could use his old grammar book and write in new meanings. Kenneth Malula, a teacher on the mission came over mornings to talk in Luchazi and interpret for Bob. Within six months he was able to preach in Luchazi.

Malula remembers one morning while he and Bob were studying, a leper came to the Foster door, mutilated, dressed in filthy rags, covered with flies. Belva tried to tactfully suggest that Bob should see him outside. But Malula recalls him saying, "No, no my wife, that's why I've come to Africa," and he invited him in to sit on a chair while he talked to him.

"He loved the people as his own children. He worked very hard; sometimes his tea became cold," Malula explains in his colorful African idiom.

The Africans seemed to understand Bob's sense of humor too, even when the laugh was on them. His booming laughter could be heard through the wards of the hospital as he joked with them when he made rounds. Somehow even in matters that ordinarily would be taken to the chief for reparations, Bob's good humor could turn the situation around.

In one instance, as he rode across the station followed by his dog, the large animal attacked an African passing through, and ripped the seat of his trousers. Instead of going to the chief with his complaint, the African ended up following Bob home, where he was given a needle and thread to sew up his trousers.

Bob worked very closely with the African church and encouraged them to form a hospital committee. Jeremiah Makai, one of the early evangelists, believes Dr. Kahaya inherited his love for the people from his parents. He found him ready to listen to the church leaders who tutored him in the ways of the tribal people of the area - such as how to greet people, and how to treat a chief with respect. Pastors Benjamani and Jehosaphat continually struggled to bring the tribal groups into a harmonious unity in the church, but this was always a tenuous liaison at best and they wanted Bob to understand these tensions and how to avoid misunderstandings.

Very soon after he arrived at Luampa, Bob began holding services with the outpatients and their families on Sunday afternoons.

Belva wrote, "Three or four adults, often elderly, have made decisions every week that Bob has been able to be there."

The outpatient department became the first hospital building to be completed and put to use. The Luampa area was much more densely populated than around Mukinge and right after Bob arrived the number of outpatients rose to over three hundred a day. The grass-thatched building which had served as the only clinic for years, sat right in the middle of the station. One room had five or six beds for emergency cases; the other two rooms were used as a dressing room and one to examine and treat patients.

Sprawled around this building was a compound where the patients lived while under treatment. Soon after Bob arrived, seventy in-patients and their families were staying in temporary facilities around the dispensary in dismal, unsanitary conditions. There was no running water; some pit latrines had been built but many didn't know how to use them and the air was fetid. Flies swarmed everywhere, spreading disease.

It was a great encouragement in that time of need to receive a gift of almost $10,000 from the Beit Trust, a philanthropic foundation established by one of Rhodesia's pioneers. Funds for the hospital had run out, and the new grant enabled them to complete the outpatient building. With extra missionary help and other financial gifts it looked as though the buildings could be completed.

They needed equipment, though - beds, bedside tables, mayo stands, etc. - to make it operative. These items could not be purchased in Lusaka, and had to be made to order. Bob knew it would take many months to complete the equipment yet he had no funds to place an order.

One day, on one of his trips to Lusaka, he went to see the owner of the Alpha Steel company. He explained to the owner what his needs were and asked how long it would take to make these items. The man estimated it would probably take eight to ten months plus transportation out to the mission, "I'd say you better allow a year."

"Well, I need to order now then," Bob replied, "but I have no money on hand."

"How did you pay for what you've got?" the businessman responded. Knowing the owner of the business was not a Christian, Bob explained how, in answer to prayer, God had provided all they had acquired over the past two to three years - the plane, medical equipment, drugs, the truck.

The man listened intently and when Bob had finished his story, he responded, "If what you say is true, I believe that God will provide this for you too and that you'll pay me."

"Are you willing to take my order on that basis?" Bob asked.

"Don't worry about it," the owner replied. "You don't have to pay me until next year when you take delivery."

So Bob left him with an order of equipment three typewritten pages long, and their confidence in God's I.O.U.

Chapter 12

Tough Love

"Last Sunday at Sakeji, I was asked to speak to the Sunday School. Before me were our orphaned nieces and nephews and another family of our mission whose daddy was expected to pass on at any time (he did on Monday). The only verse I could talk about was, 'The Lord will perfect that which concerneth me' - Psalm 138:8.

"With a new year approaching, I cannot give you a better one, whether your circumstances be tragic or triumphant. Let us allow Him to do His perfect work in us."

---Dr. Robert Foster
Prayer letter, December 1963

****

With the completion of airstrips at Mukinge and Luampa and several other smaller stations, Bob was able to be "on the go" more than ever. Whether flying to Sakeji to pick up children for the school holidays, taking a pastor to an outstation for special meetings or off to the mission field council, Bob still managed to maintain a superhuman schedule back at Luampa.

The supervision of the building program fell upon him when the missionary builder resigned. Keeping in touch with donors and thanking people for gifts was a relentless responsibility, and each evening long after most people on the station were in bed, Bob wrote countless letters. Seldom did he reveal any discouragement or doubt about God's provision.

His son Stephen explains, "Dad has a sense of the bigness of God and His generosity and willingness to bless those who live by faith. He believed God is as big as you are willing to let Him be in your life, in His ability to provide for your needs and provide for the task at hand."

Though he was confident that God would supply his needs, it must have been disconcerting to find the building balance down to $30. Each time he went in to Lusaka, he visited Alpha Steel to check on the progress of his order and each time, he had to say he still had no funds for the equipment.

Without an adequate operating room at Luampa, every two weeks Bob took patients to the government hospital at Mankoya (now Kaoma) where they had an operating room, but no surgeon. Bob operated on his own patients and any critical cases at Kaoma. Nurses who travelled with him recall the long days - leaving at daybreak, operating all day into the dark, then returning to Luampa still to do rounds, sterilize equipment in their pressure cookers or stoves at home, and be up and ready for prayers early the next morning.

There was no surgeon at Mukinge at the time, so Bob regularly flew over to do surgery there as well. One morning, he and Don left to go to a church conference at a smaller station. Just as they were ready to take off, they realized they'd almost forgotten the two-way radio so that the hospital could contact them in an emergency.

The next morning at the outstation, they tuned into the regular eight o'clock call. They learned that a young woman in labor at

Mukinge could not deliver because her pelvis was too small. There was no surgeon at Mukinge to do a Caesarian and they desperately needed Dr. Bob. Within an hour and a half of the radio message, the plane had landed at Mukinge and Bob performed the C-section before returning to the church conference.

This was not an easy era for the staff at Luampa. Belva asked for prayer in a letter to donors. "Everyone is overworked. There are only three nurses to care for almost four hundred outpatients and seventy in-hospital patients, daily."

Bob neither spared himself, nor his nurses. One nurse remembers that if you complained that you weren't feeling well to Bob, he would say, "Take two aspirins and come back to work."

There were frustrations. A nurse wrote in her diary, "Working with Bob is difficult. Yesterday, he said he would see certain patients but today he got so involved, he couldn't see the ones I'd set aside for him."

The single nurses, especially, found Bob's expectations hard to cope with. Though he never demanded more of them than he did of himself, they felt he didn't take into account that they didn't have someone at home to do their laundry, clean house and cook meals.

Yet, they were fiercely loyal. Dr. Alex Henderson, who later worked at Luampa recalls, "I think the people he worked with idolized him. He was a terrific worker but the nurses found it hard."

When the children came home from school, Bob and Belva made time for special family activities in spite of his heavy schedule. Sharon recalls that Bob took the four oldest on a camping trip, sleeping on the ground, and pointing out the stars by name. He showed them how to bake a chicken by putting hot coals into a hole, then burying the foil-wrapped chicken in the sand until morning.

Holiday breakfasts became precious nuggets of time to invest in the children's lives. In a personal letter to friends, Bob recounted one such special morning.

"At our family devotions, we read of the apostles who on the day of Pentecost spoke in many different languages the wonderful works of God. We paused for a few minutes as we went around the circle and each one recounted some work of God this past year for which we should give special thanks.

"Stephen spoke of how the Lord had helped him catch up in his school work. Sheila mentioned our safe trip back to Northern Rhodesia. Another thanked the Lord for good health we've all enjoyed. Our house was another cause for thanksgiving. One of the children said we ought to thank God for the Lord Jesus, for His Word and for those who have come to trust Him. Then we took turns praying, praising and thanking the Lord for His goodness."

Evenings were times to play games - the new ones the children received for Christmas and the old favorites like Pit, with Bob shouting "Two, two" or "Three, three" louder than any of them. It was during school breaks after the hospital was completed at Luampa that Bob began to invite the older children to come up to the hospital to observe and help where they could. In the earlier years the hospital had been "off limits," partly because of the danger of infection and disease. But once the children were old enough to understand these dangers, and if they showed any interest at all in medicine, Bob gave them every opportunity to learn all they could.

Steve began hanging around the operating room when he was in his early teens. There never was a question in his mind that he would follow in his father's footsteps. Once when Bob was away at a conference, thirteen-year-old Steve assisted a medical student who was filling in for Bob. A woman began hemorrhaging and Steve helped him take her to find a blood donor at Mankoya in the middle of the night.

Sharon and Sheila were only ten and twelve when they first scrubbed so they could help during surgery, getting things Bob needed, listening to him explain what he was doing. Since there was no nursing school at Luampa, Bob trained all his African assistants in the same way. Though Bob never pressured any of the children to go into medicine, he gave them every opportunity to develop a love for it.

One Sunday afternoon, there was no staff available to help Bob do a C-section. He went back to the house to ask Sharon and Sheila, then in their early teens, to come and help him.

"I scrubbed and Sheila circulated and I was so thrilled when we delivered the baby," Sharon recalls.

But these family times had to end when the children returned to school and the family prepared to be separated for another five months.

"Just before going back to school, we always had a special supper," Sheila recalls. "The boys would hunt pigeons with their BB guns and by the end of the holiday we had enough to make pigeon pie. We all dressed up for that dinner."

In January 1963, the children returned to Sakeji just hours before their brother Stirling Jeffrey was born, bringing the number of Foster "SJ's" to six. Though Bob and Belva welcomed each life as a precious gift from God, they were bewildered about how to limit Belva's constant pregnancies.

"I was resentful, I'm sure, for many years. Each pregnancy left me feeling dragged out and burdened, never really on top of it."

Because of physical problems, Belva was not supposed to have more children after Stuart was born. Bob was concerned about the dangers to Belva's health, and was particularly upset when his medical judgments were contravened by a specialist to whom he'd sent Belva.

When she became pregnant for the seventh time in 1965, Belva says "he was devastated". Looking back from the vantage point of years however, they admit that the two "tail enders" - Stirling and Shelley - were the greatest blessing in their lives, and greatly contributed to their sanity in the difficult years in Angola.

In the same letter announcing Stirling's birth, Belva also announced encouraging news about the hospital. Additional funds for building had come in and the powerhouse, surgical block and administration units were all under construction. At the same time, Nurse Ruth Kingston returned from furlough and a woman doctor had been accepted to work at Luampa.

These encouragements were offset by rumblings of discontent and black-white tensions as the wheels of independence began to churn faster. When Bob started charging sixpence for each outpatient visit, local UNIP members complained. One day, a group of UNIP men came to the outpatients department. Bob went out to meet with them. They accused Nurse Nancy Reist of being hard on the patients and not loving them. They said they didn't like having a woman tell them what to do. Bob spent hours patiently listening to their complaints. He also tried to explain why he'd levied charges for services. He feared that if government funds were cut off after independence, the hospital could not continue offering free care. After a long discussion, the men withdrew their charges but this action left the missionaries with an uneasy feeling as to where the next accusation would come from and what reprisals might be taken.

On the Copperbelt, the cities had experienced demonstrations, arson and strikes. Generally, however, there was little tension in the rural areas as the British dissolved the Federation at the end of 1963, and Dr. Kenneth Kaunda was elected prime minister of the first African-dominated cabinet in January 1964. Independence celebrations were set for October, 1964 when the new nation would be known as Zambia. Dr. Kaunda made it clear from the start that Zambianization would not exclude Europeans who were committed to the country as citizens, and there were high hopes that the nation would avoid the bloodshed experienced in Kenya and the Congo just a few years earlier.

Though their funds were once again at almost zero, the staff set an opening date for a few days after Independence in October, 1964, which would make the Luampa Hospital the first new hospital in the new nation. The very next day after their decision, a large gift arrived for the buildings but there were still no funds to pay Alpha Steel for the beds and equipment. A month before the hospital opening, Bob went empty handed to Lusaka once again. The owner knew of the opening date so he suggested that Bob begin to haul some of the equipment out to the hospital. It would take at least three loads. Bob collected the first eight tons and hauled them over the three hundred miles of corrugated dirt roads.

When he returned the second time, the owner asked if he had received any money. The bill amounted to about $7,500.

"Nope," Bob responded, "but we'll get it."

Bob admits he was getting a bit nervous by this time but yet his confidence in God's promise to provide remained. He returned to Lusaka for the third load still without any money. Before going to Alpha Steel, he picked up the mail and, in a letter from a supporting church, was a check for $5,000. By the time of the hospital opening, the balance of the funds had been paid, a timely tribute to God's faithfulness.

1964 marked several major milestones. The South African General Mission changed its name to the Africa Evangelical Fellowship to better describe its far-reaching ministry. The country celebrated a peaceful transition to an independent African nation, and the Luampa hospital was opened.

To the African Christians the dedication of the hospital was a special joy, as they saw the fulfillment of their dream of many years, and the results of their labors. By this time, the church had appointed a hospital evangelist, Luka Sachingumbe, and Bob had established his routine of evangelism, ward ministry and discipling the staff.

As had happened at Mukinge Hospital (renamed after Independence) many Africans formerly untouched or unresponsive to the message of Christ, became Christians through the hospital ministry. Masona, a male nurse, was one who flourished under Bob's discipleship. One day, he came to Bob to ask a question. He'd read an article about tithing and had been studying Bible references to giving.

He asked, "Kahaya, is this something a Christian should do?"

"Well," Bob responded, "the Lord tells us that we should give as He's blessed us. In the Old Testament days tithing was required, but gifts were to be given in addition."

Masona listened thoughtfully, thanked Bob and left. Two days later he came back.

"I'm going to start tithing." He gave Bob some money which was the equivalent to a tithe of a year's salary. When Bob expressed surprise, Masona responded, "I've got a lot of catching up to do."

Masona later left nursing to become an evangelist.

Busy weeks and months passed. Bob was instrumental in getting a hostel established in Lusaka for missionary children of high school age, since Sakeji only went through grade nine. As medical supervisor for the Africa Evangelical Fellowship (AEF) and member of the international field council, he made periodic trips to South Africa. When the Zambian missionary conference was to be held at Luampa, Bob took over the kitchen, cooking for almost a hundred and twenty people.

He and Belva began planning a celebration for his parents' fiftieth anniversary in Africa and made secret arrangements for Rhoda and her husband to visit - her first since she'd left Africa at eight years of age.

But Bob found himself facing one of the most difficult decisions of his career. Allan Habbick, chairman of the US council of AEF came on a special visit to see him. He brought the disturbing request that the board would like Bob to become the next executive secretary of the American office when Ezra Shank retired. AEF was a mission ready for change. The African continent was in upheaval, with twenty-five countries gaining independence during the 50's and 60's. Churches established by missions expected a new kind of servant leadership from missionaries. Some even called for a moratorium, believing the Africans had to flex their own spiritual muscles without the aid of western leadership.

In this climate of change, the American headquarters of AEF needed new strategies and directions and dynamic leadership. If the mission was to expand, it needed aggressive recruitment that would attract the right quality of young missionaries.

The council members were convinced that Dr. Bob Foster had these qualifications. They knew he was highly respected not only by the missionaries, but by the African church as well. His vision, energy, ability to plan, to pull a team together, and to trust God for what seemed impossible goals pointed to him as their key choice. As they prayed over the issue for many months, the confirmation grew and they sent Allan Habbick to present their case.

Though Bob listened carefully and asked insightful questions, everything within him rejected the plan. God had called him to Zambia as a medical missionary; this was his place of service and there was still so much he wanted to do. The thought of taking a desk job in New Jersey left him cold.

After lengthy discussions, Allan suggested that Bob talk it over with Belva and pray about it and they could continue their talk the next day. When they resumed their discussion, Bob reiterated that he'd been born in Zambia and planned to die in Zambia.

"I intend to serve the rest of my life here," he concluded.

Allan returned to New York, his mission a failure but he left a strangely unsettled doctor behind, not at all sure that he'd been totally honest with himself or God. What really kept him from accepting this appointment? Was it his lifelong commitment to serve God in Africa or was it his intense love for medicine?

Chapter 13

Medicine or Mission?

"Speak, Lord, in the stillness while we wait on Thee,
   Hushed my soul to listen in expectancy
Speak, O blessed Master, in this quiet hour,
   Let me see thy face, Lord, feel thy touch of power.
For the words Thou speakest, 'They are Life,' indeed.
   Living Bread from heaven, now my spirit feed.
All to Thee is yielded, I am not my own.
   All to Thee is yielded, I am Thine alone.
Fill me with the knowledge of Thy glorious will.
   All Thine own good pleasure in Thy child fulfill."

--- E. May Grimes
Pioneer SAGM missionary
South Africa
1894-1901

"Suddenly, jolting us out of our lethargy and our routine, come experiences that change the course of life. How wonderful they may be, and yet sometimes how utterly devastating and traumatic. Whatever comes, our confidence as children of God is that all things work together for good to them that love God."

--- Dr. Robert Foster

****

For days, Bob fought against the thought of accepting the invitation to become executive secretary of the American office. Though he had told Allan Habbick he could not leave Zambia, he had no peace within his own heart that the decision was final. Bob always discussed matters which affected the family with Belva. He respected her judgment and knew she would be objective in her suggestions.

They spent many hours discussing the question and in the end, as usual, he made the decision. As he battled things out with the Lord, it became obvious to him that what was really keeping him from seriously considering the invitation, was the thought of leaving medicine, and particularly surgery. Once he recognized that his own personal love of medicine might be keeping him from doing the Lord's will, he began to look at the offer more objectively, and to understand the council's dilemma.

Indeed, AEF was in a rut; few new missionaries were applying and no new fields had been opened in years. The call from the American council had been unanimous. Bob placed high priority on the advice and opinions of the body of Christ - whether the African church, the local mission conference or the council. Their request could not easily be ignored.

He did not feel ready to give up medicine, especially as he recalled the miraculous ways in which God had provided his training. But at that point, the Lord seemed to be showing him that a detour at this point in his life might be in order. Finally, he and Belva agreed that if certain requirements were met, they would be willing to go for three years. They felt it necessary that

God would supply a replacement and that the African Church and the missionaries would agree to his accepting the invitation. Once again, Bob approached the missionaries for their blessing on this move. Though many expressed bewilderment and dismay, in the end they agreed that he should go. Dr. Alex Henderson, a former medical missionary in Angola, now serving at Mukinge, volunteered to take Bob's place at Luampa. He already knew Luchazi from his Angolan days.

By 1966, Luampa Hospital had grown to a hundred and twenty beds, so Bob assured Alex that one of his first priorities would be to recruit a second doctor to help him. With the blessing of the African church, Bob and Belva began their preparations to leave Zambia. Every item accumulated over sixteen years in Africa had to be sorted: Give this away; sell that; pack this in the drums to ship. The children still remember Bob standing on top of a barrel auctioning off their household goods. They kept only five drums of things to take to the USA with them and a hundred and twenty cartons of books.

"The rest we disposed of down to the last can-opener," Belva wrote.

Once the family was settled in the new mission headquarters' residence in Glen Ridge, New Jersey, Bob wasted no time in making the changes he saw were necessary. His goals were to reorganize the American office, put AEF on the map in the United States and recruit a hundred new missionaries.

Bob was away from home at least half of the time, visiting churches and mission conferences all over the eastern half of the United States. The adjustments for the family were not easy.

Stephen had left Zambia to complete high school in Canada several months before the family move but the other teenagers struggled to fit into the American culture of the 60's.

Sheila recalls, "High school adjustment was difficult. I came into the 11th grade as a stranger and it was hard to make friends. Sharon was in 12th grade and it was even worse. If we hadn't had the same lunch hour to encourage each other, I don't think we would have survived."

The girls invited some of the Christian young people they met at school to a Bible study at the mission and when Bob was home he taught it. "The kids loved to come when Dad was home,"

Sheila remembers.   "But church was a disaster in terms of friendships. Except for the other missionary kids in the area, only one girl was friendly."

No wonder thirteen-year-old Stacey (who was small for his age and very sensitive) just shriveled up inside. The whole culture - the music, TV, the anger over Vietnam - was bewildering and threatening to a boy who'd grown up in the unsophisticated climate of colonial Africa.

Belva didn't have time to develop intimate friendships either, nor did the more reserved culture of the eastern seaboard make it easy. She was busier than ever as hostess for the missionaries coming and going and, with Bob away so much of the time, she had the full responsibility of caring for and guiding six children bombarded by new and uncertain values.

Within nine months after their arrival, twenty-five candidates had either been accepted or were in the orientation process through Bob's recruitment efforts. He developed the mission's first candidate school and brought several men into the office to help with deputation and business administration.

"Bob didn't spare himself at all," one co-worker in the office observed. "He put himself under the yoke of a most exacting program. He served as medical director, worked at the office and spoke at conference after conference. It was a very pressurized time."

Bob was also deeply interested in expanding the mission's outreach into other countries. Not since 1936 when a work was established in Mozambique, had the AEF entered a new country. Now the mission wanted to expand into areas where no other mission was working, among people who were truly unreached.

As Bob made inquiries he learned that the island of Mauritius, almost two thousand miles off the eastern coast of Africa, had no Protestant mission work for a population of eight hundred thousand Indians and Creoles. In 1968, he flew to Mauritius to research the possibilities of AEF expansion. When he stepped out of the airport, one driver more aggressive than the rest offered to take him to a hotel. Bob had arrived without a single contact person or reservation so he accepted the offer.

On the way, he asked the driver if he knew of a church in the area. "Roman Catholic or a Hindu temple?" the driver asked.

When Bob explained he was looking for a Protestant church, the driver shook his head. He didn't know of any; however, he did offer to show Bob the island. For the next three days, the cab driver showed him all around the coast and into every city and town of the island which is only seven hundred ninety square miles, thirty-five miles at its widest point.

As they were driving into the capital of Port Louis, Bob asked if there was any way he could meet the governor general.

"No problem," was his driver's response. He drove up to the guards at the gate who greeted him cheerfully. Within a short time, Bob found himself seated in the governor general's office. However, when he explained his interest in starting mission work on the island, the governor disapproved. "We've got enough religion on this island. I don't think anybody here will agree to your sending any missionaries to start a new religion."

But not wanting to seem ungracious, he suggested that Bob go to see the Minister of Immigration. Once again, Bob took advantage of his driver who seemed to know everybody that was worth knowing on the island. The driver took him right to the government building and requested an audience with the Minister for an important American visitor.

The Minister of Immigration was not quite so blunt in refusing Bob's request. He did indicate that AEF would have to have an invitation from a local church for a missionary. So Bob was back to his original quest - the elusive evangelical church.

Trying another tactic, he asked if there were an office of the Bible Society on the island. The Minister directed him to the town of Rose Hill.

The taxi driver was untiring in his quest, following up every lead until they found the man working for the Bible Society at his home. When Bob asked about an evangelical church, the man said there really wasn't an evangelical church, as such, but there was an elderly British lady who ran a Sunday School in Rose Belle.

Once again Bob and his driver were off. This time they headed for the local police station asking for Miss Groom. The officer directed the driver to a house, but when they arrived it was all closed up. Asking neighbors, they learned that Miss Groom was sick and had gone down to the coast to stay with a friend. Undaunted, the driver headed down to the coast where they finally found the home of Miss Groom's friend.

After Bob introduced himself and his purpose, Miss Groom's face lit up. "Miss Minton and I have just been praying here this morning that God would send somebody to this island to take over the work that we've been doing. To think that God has sent you this very afternoon."

In the months that followed, Bob was able to make arrangements with Miss Groom's mission in Britain and in 1970 Wilfred and Marie Green, who had just retired as general director of the AEF, went as the first AEF missionaries to Mauritius.

But even beyond the thrill of establishing a beachhead in a new country, Bob marvels, "It was a wonderful experience to see how out of the hundreds of taxi drivers there in Mauritius, God brought the one to me who knew the people, who had the contacts, and was able to get around and help me see everybody that I needed to see."

No sooner had Bob returned from Mauritius than he was back on the speaking trail again. Disturbing news from Africa added to his burden. Several missionaries, including the only doctor at Luampa, Gordon Jones, were desperately ill with sleeping sickness. They needed a temporary replacement urgently. One night Bob spoke at Ben Lippen Conference. He often spoke at this well known east coast conference center where his old friend, Stephen Olford, Pastor of Calvary Baptist Church in New York, was co-director. Olford describes Bob as "an able preacher and expositor of God's Word. The people fell in love with him."

That night, Bob asked the people to pray for the missionaries at Luampa and, in particular, for a doctor to step into the breach as Gordon recuperated. After the meeting, a woman came up to Bob and asked, "Have you thought that you might be the answer to your own prayer?"

She gave Bob the money for his airfare and in a few days, he was on his way. The telegram announcing his arrival hadn't had time to reach Luampa, but he received a tumultuous welcome as he arrived. In two weeks, he performed twenty-two major surgeries, visited his parents at Mukinge and attended the Zambian church conference.

By the time he came back to New Jersey, his appetite was thoroughly whetted to return to Africa. In fact, he and Belva had decided that when the three-year contract with AEF was over in 1969, they would return to Africa. To stay on any longer in the States would mean completely leaving medicine. Bob had many offers in the USA to join a clinic, run a hospital, go into partnership with other doctors.

"People badgered me. I had all kinds of opportunities if I wanted to stay but it was in our bones that our place was on the mission field. Other people weren't willing to go, so we would go."

As they began to pray about their return, the mission suggested they consider Rusitu in Southern Rhodesia. Early in 1969, Dr. Rudolph Brechet, a Swiss doctor whom Bob had met at Sakeji when both men came to bring their children to school, came to the United States. Dr. Brechet had been working for many years in Angola at the Kalukembe Hospital run by the Swiss Evangelical Missionary Alliance. Brechet reopened the interest in Angola Bob had first had when he visited there with Harold Stevens eight years earlier. For eleven years the doors to Protestant missionaries in Angola had been shut. The Portuguese government blamed the Protestants for stirring up the terrorist movement against them. The Catholic government funded only Catholic schools and hospitals, but there were very few. Now with a change in leadership, the new government seemed less repressive, more interested in developing schools and hospitals and more open to Protestants.

Brechet urged Bob, "If you are thinking about going back to Africa, why don't you think about coming to Angola? The situation is improving. The government has assured me they are now open to new missionaries, especially Protestants."

There was no doubt in Bob's mind that it was time to return to Africa. By the end of 1968, he had recruited sixty of the goal of new missionaries. The office was well staffed. Allan Habbick himself had responded to Bob's challenge to serve with AEF and had resigned his engineering job to come on board full time. The council appointed him as the new administrative secretary, and Dr. Terry Hulburt as executive director.

As Bob surveyed God's provision for the headquarters - he and his secretary had been the only full-time staff three years earlier - he assured the council, "You don't need me in this office any longer. There are enough people to run it two or three times over. Let me go back to Africa."

The council agreed that Bob could return to Angola, if a visa should be granted; if not, to Rusitu.

In September 1969, Bob applied for a visa, fully expecting he would receive no reply for three to four months. To his surprise he received a letter from the consulate in three weeks, saying his visa had been granted and he would have to enter the country within ninety days.

Bob was stunned. How could they get ready in three months? Arrangements had to be made for Sharon and Sheila who would be staying behind to attend university. With the economic conditions in Angola, it would be necessary to take not only drugs and equipment but household furnishings and supplies with them. He would need funds since Catota hospital had been operating without a doctor or improvements for over eight years. With mixed emotions he drove to Newark to see the Portuguese consulate to get his visa.

When he met with the consul he pled, "Can't you possibly give us another thirty days?" He explained how difficult it would be to close down the house, arrange for the family and make necessary purchases before Christmas. The consul hemmed and hawed but finally extended the visa to the 21st of January.

What a whirlwind of activity followed in the next four months! Bob made a trip to all their supporting churches to present the challenge of Angola and the opportunity to resurrect the hospital at Catota. Christians generously responded and thousands of dollars were received for equipment and other needs. Dr. Brechet suggested that Bob bring as much furniture and household goods with him as he could because manufactured goods were difficult to obtain. Alan Habbick built crates and Bob packed a couch, rug, stove and washer, plus drugs and medical supplies. In order for the family to arrive within the deadline, they had to fly, but Bob put ten tons of supplies and equipment on the ship to Lobito.

For the first time, they left three of their children behind - Steve in med school and the two girls in Rutgers. The emotional drain of leaving the family escalated until those final moments when they lifted off from Kennedy Airport, heading once again for Africa. It was a relief to be on the way after the pressures of the past months. Little did they realize they would have a long time to rest up.

Chapter 14

A Caged Lion

"After being three years in the American office, I remember the tremendous thrill it was to get involved in grassroots evangelism and church planting, getting things started there again. Abiding in Him is the secret of eternal life which begins now and has a quality of reality, timelessness and meaning that impart 'a savor of life' to even menial tasks.

"Do continue to uphold us in prayer as we tackle this new opportunity virtually single-handed. It is the greatest challenge to faith we've ever had."

--- Dr. Robert Foster
Prayer letter, 1970

✸✸✸✸✸✸✸✸✸✸✸✸✸✸✸✸✸✸

The police officer looked sharply up at Bob from the papers on his desk.

"How did you get this visa?"

Just a day earlier Bob and the family had arrived here in Sa da Bandeira (now Lubango), Angola, and he'd come, as instructed, to get his residence permit from the local police. Bob turned to his interpreter, Don Lutes, who had been a missionary in Angola for many years, for an explanation. For a few minutes Don and the police officer talked back and forth rapidly in Portuguese. Then Don explained that the police had no record of his visa and that Bob was here in Angola illegally.

Shocked, Bob tried to explain through his interpreter that he'd applied for the visa through normal channels in Newark and had even been to the consulate in person to discuss an extension. But the officer closed the file in front of him with all the Foster passports inside and fired rapid instructions at Don. As they left the office, Don explained that the officer would make further investigations and Bob should come back in a month. In the meantime, he made it very clear that Bob was not to leave the city, not even to visit Catota, and he was NOT to practice medicine. Don assured him this was typical Portuguese bureaucracy and everything would sort itself out.

Bob and the family had planned to spend six months here in Sa da Bandeira to study Portuguese, anyway, so he would just get on with it. In the past, missionaries had gone to Portugal for a year of language study before coming to Angola, but with the difficulty of getting visas and the urgent need for a missionary doctor, Bob had decided to come ahead and study in the country. He purchased a fifty-lesson language course on cassettes and barricaded himself in the living room each morning to study.

The family lived in a large vacant manse next to the Portuguese Mission Church. The Lutes found a few pieces of furniture - a bed, some camp cots, a table and chairs, and essential cooking equipment. Their goods coming by ship were expected in a few months so until then, they would manage living out of their suitcases. Located about five thousand feet up the escarpment, Sa da Bandeira was a city of about thirty thousand people, mostly Portuguese with black squatter areas on the outskirts. Portuguese colonialism took advantage of African labor, forcing

them to work six months of the year on roads and other government projects. Unlike some of the other colonial powers, Portugal
bled its colonies for all it could get out of them and did little to
raise living standards for the Africans. If an African could get an
education, learn Portuguese and adopt Portuguese culture and the
Christian faith, he could become an "assimilado" and a Portuguese citizen. Few Africans were able to acquire that status and,
even if they did, still suffered discrimination.

By 1970, when the Fosters arrived in Angola, the terrorist
movement for freedom from colonial rule had accelerated and the
Portuguese government was finding it difficult to control the
various factions. The MPLA led by Augustino Neto, the FNLA
by Holden Roberto, and the UNITA led by Jonas Savimbi,
carried on limited guerrilla warfare, fighting both the Portuguese forces and each other. In retaliation, the Portuguese
military carried out reprisals and increased its harsh treatment of
the people.

Yet at the same time, the officials had indicated that medical
missionaries were welcome and Bob was confident that the
bureaucratic delays would be untangled.

But in February when he returned to the police, he was told
"Come back next month." He got the same response in March. It
was especially difficult for Belva to run her household of six with
so few amenities, worsened by her inability to communicate in the
shops and neighborhood.

Bob had to take time from his language studies to re-do the
sewer system because roots had broken pipes. Though she was
barely five years old, Shelley remembers the cold barn-like house
with cement floors and the fact that they were often without running water.

"I remember that we used to draw a big tub full of water in the
morning or whenever it was available, so we would have water
for the next few days," she remembers. But gradually the family
settled down to a routine. The children made friends in the church
and neighborhood and picked up Portuguese faster than their
parents.

Stacey studied by correspondence to finish high school but the
three younger ones began attending the local Portuguese
schools.

"We went to the Portuguese school of the black aprons. We had to wear a black dress that covered us and it had a little white collar," Shelley remembers.

When their goods arrived at the port of Lubito, Bob made a special appeal to be allowed to get them out of customs and deliver them to Catota, about three hundred miles east of Sa da Bandeira. The authorities grudgingly gave permission, but he was NOT to open any of the crates or unpack any of the goods, ostensibly so that they could be shipped back to the USA if the visa application were ultimately denied.

The trip to Catota was a nightmare. The truck driver refused to go further than Silva Porto because of possible guerrilla activity and Bob had to unload the heavy crates and re-load them on another truck. Arriving at Catota was a bittersweet experience; hundreds of Africans welcomed the "doctor" who could not treat them. The run down dispensary and ward cried out for attention and the overworked missionary nurses plied Bob with questions. Bob was able to look over the station, particularly searching for possible sources of water.

What frustration to leave the crates behind unopened, knowing how much easier life would be for Belva if she had some of the linens and dishes, if the children had some of their books and toys - and if only he could get his hands on some of his tools! But he had to drive the weary miles back to Sa da Bandeira empty handed.

Then the inconceivable happened. The authorities refused Bob's request to work as a doctor in Angola! Shattered, he immediately drafted an SOS to his friends back home, "Yesterday a tidalwave hit us. We received a letter from the director of Health Service stating that he had received word from Lisbon that my request for permission to practice missionary medicine had been denied."

In their desperation and despair Bob and Belva turned to God's Word, their faithful source of comfort and guidance. Bob was reminded of Hezekiah who went into the temple after receiving bad news and "spread it out before the Lord." Isaiah's words to Hezekiah in II Kings 19:6 struck him forcibly, *"Be not afraid of the words which thou has heard."*

Don Lutes tried to assure Bob that this was a ploy of the government to get him to leave voluntarily so that he couldn't say he'd been put out. Whatever the purpose, Bob and Belva knew that only God could resolve the rapidly deteriorating situation. Daily Bob cried to God - one moment confident that God had brought them here so he could practice medicine at Catota, the next questioning why God would bring them this far and slam the door shut in their faces.

There was nothing else he could do. His fate seemed to lie in the hands of capricious government officials - and he couldn't even speak their language! Bob felt like a caged lion - his effervescent energy bouncing off the walls of the house that had become his prison. The people in the church, however, comforted him. As their Portuguese improved, Bob and Belva found love and spiritual strength in their fellowship.

One morning, a young Swiss couple came to their home. Siegfried and Verena Schurch served with the Swiss Evangelical Mission. In broken English and simple Portuguese, they offered a gift to Bob and Belva. They would like to come and pray with them for about fifteen minutes every morning until God answered their prayer. They were confident that God had brought the Fosters to Angola to serve Him. So, over the next nine months, the two couples met. Siegfried and Verena prayed in German - which Bob and Belva couldn't understand - and Bob and Belva prayed in English - which the Schurchs didn't understand.

Each month, Bob returned to the police only to be told once again that they had received no word. By June, Bob was speaking Portuguese fluently enough to preach in the local church. When Willy Brandle, another AEF missionary, left for a few weeks' ministry in another part of Angola, Bob was able to go out to his station in an outlying district and preach to the primitive Huila tribe. Under the old comity rules, the Huilas had been an AEF target for many years, but the tribe proved so resistant to the preaching of the Gospel, that results were meagre. Yet even this brief contact stirred up Bob's impatient longings to be out among the people, evangelizing and healing. That's what he had come for. How long would he have to wait?

Finally in October, Dr. Brechet went to Luanda, the capital, to speak with the Governor General of Angola. He reminded him of how urgently Angola needed doctors and pointed to Bob's excellent record in Zambia. The governor promised that he, himself, would look into the problem. When Dr. Brechet returned to the governor in November, he was assured the case was being resolved but he had a few disturbing questions: Why had Dr. Foster learned an Angolan language when he worked in Zambia? And why hadn't he returned to Zambia?

The implication was that Bob had some kind of subtle political motivation in coming to Angola. Might he have loyalties to the terrorists? Though the governor did not openly state these reservations, he suggested that Bob write an "exposition" explaining his purposes fully. When Brechet returned with the dissertation, he was assured that the case would be resolved soon. He warned, even then, that Bob might not be allowed to go to Catota because of the delicate political balance of the area.

On December 15, 1970, almost one year after he'd left New Jersey, Bob received a telegram: "You are granted residence permit under two conditions:

1. You cannot go to Catota

2. You must practice only religious medicine."

Whatever religious medicine meant, it was the kind Bob practiced - medicine not for profit but for the healing of soul and body. Bob had no problem with that restriction. The news about Catota was not unexpected, but was a disappointment, nevertheless. He knew how much the staff there had been waiting for a doctor and all the improvements a hospital would bring. The immense relief and jubilation of being allowed to stay and work in Angola tempered the pain. Dr. Brechet had already suggested that Bob go to the Cavango Mission, a leprosarium operated jointly by several missions working in Angola. AEF missionary, Dr. Regina Brandle, Willy's wife, had practiced there until her marriage nine years previously but now it was doomed to close. There had been no doctor on the station for over nine years, and no other missionaries for the past four years. The subsidies of the American Leprosy Mission were to be withdrawn at the end of the month, and the leprosarium would have to be disbanded.

It was not an AEF station; hospital facilities were rundown and inadequate; there was no other medical personnel. But when Dr. Brechet put the offer before him, Bob knew what his answer should be, "God has brought us here. Of course we'll go!"

Chapter 15

Bonding With Africans

"We really appreciated the fact that there were no whites at Cavango when we arrived. As a result, we bonded with the people there in a way that we were never bonded at Mukinge or Luampa. We were thrown in at the deep end and it was sink or swim but the relationship that God gave us with those Africans was something special, far surpassing anything we had ever known before."

--- Dr. Robert Foster

****

What joy and excitement filled their hearts as the little caravan neared Cavango. It had been eleven years since Bob had paid a brief visit here. For nine years, the leprosarium had not had a resident doctor and the last missionary nurse had left four years earlier. The Brechets drove ahead the day before to ready one of the four missionary houses for the Fosters and to alert the African staff caring for the leprosy patients that God had granted them a reprieve. They would not have to close their doors at the end of the month. God was sending them a doctor!

Belva had never seen the station, but she tried not to think of the deterioration that must have set in. Her philosophy to "Never borrow joy and never borrow trouble" probably stood her in good stead as she once again faced starting up a home in unknown and primitive conditions.

Someone once asked Bob, "How many women would be willing to start over from the bottom as many times as Belva has?" Bob just grinned and said, "It only takes one."

Yet any qualms they might have felt were certainly eased as they approached the mission. A hastily constructed sign of banana leaves said it all, "Bem Vindo - you are very welcome." Indeed, the smiling black faces radiated joy as hundreds of leprosy patients from the village pressed forward, singing and waving their hands. The women, dressed in brightly colored turbans and print skirts, danced in the road ahead of them. Some waved crutches as they hobbled on deformed feet; others grimaced out of misshapen faces, or clapped hands with knobs for fingers. Many of the patients' families lived on the compound so a bevy of children raced back and forth, not fully understanding what these white strangers were all about but entering into the rare festive occasion with abandon.

As the two vans loaded with an accumulation of a year's living in Sa da Bandeira neared the mission buildings, Belva must have felt encouraged. The sunbaked brick buildings looked sturdy enough from the outside; the walkways were swept clean and the African staff members were standing erect and beaming in front of the clinic radiating confidence and happy anticipation.

When the cars stopped, the staff came forward to "officially" welcome the doctor and his family. Bob's hand joined in a firm handclasp as Israel Canjila introduced himself in a warmly resonant voice. Did Bob sense an inner tug of response? He could not know then that here would be a brother, friend, partner and co-worker who would stand with him through danger and heartache. As each of the staff came forward and introduced themselves, Bob appreciated that these men had kept this mission running and intact these years with very little outside help and no resident medical personnel. From the very first moment, he realized that working with them would be a new experience.

Dr. Brechet led the caravan down to the mission houses and stopped in front of the smallest of the four. He explained that the missionary physiotherapist, Grace Wilson, had left six years ago expecting to return after furlough so she'd left her furniture, linens and dishes behind. Except for a rare visitor, it had remained unused and untouched all those years. There were only two bedrooms but the three boys could crowd into one, and Shelley could sleep in the passage for the time being.

Before dinner was served, Bob reconnoitered the other houses standing in their overgrown gardens like a ghost town in a movie set. The empty rooms were thick with dust and invaded by termites which had built their cone shaped edifices inside. He announced at dinner that he would renovate one of the larger houses for the family. Mrs. Brechet remembers that he even paced off the living room to see if their rug would fit.

Then suddenly, the Brechets and Schurchs, who'd brought a load of things in their truck, were gone and Bob and Belva and the children were all alone in the Angolan wilderness - except, of course, for two hundred and fifty leprosy patients, their families and the African staff they'd met that afternoon.

With its higher altitude, the weather at Cavango was pleasant, even in the heat of December. The terrain resembled Mukinge with rolling hills and rich foliage. In the first few days as Bob tramped thousands of acres with one of the African staff, he caught a glimpse of wildlife and his African partner told him about herds of antelope and smaller bush buck and dyker which roamed through the mission. It was a hunter's paradise, and seventeen-year-old Stacey could hunt to his heart's delight. He would provide much of the meat for the family table in the next year.

A fast flowing river formed the boundary of the station about a mile from the clinic. The postcard beauty of the falls and rapids were a delight to the eye, but Bob's practical mind was already wondering how he could harness it for hydroelectric power. Of course, the first job was to reactivate the medical work. In times past Cavango had been primarily a leprosarium with room for forty beds crowded into a dark mud-brick building for acutely ill patients. Bob looked over the run down buildings. Almost immediately, he began drawing up plans for an expanded, modern hospital. His experience at Mukinge and Luampa shaped his planning and he was sure this would end up being one of the finest mission hospitals on the continent. Close beside him each day was Senhor Israel, a man of integrity and faithfulness who had acted as liaison with the American Leprosy Mission in this end-of-the-world outpost. The leprosarium had deliberately been established in a remote area back in the 50's when patients with leprosy were still isolated from the rest of the population.

Bob talked every decision over with Israel and the rest of the African staff, taking their advice seriously. He found Israel extremely competent and was happy to leave the handling of finances and personnel completely in his hands. The people marvelled that Bob spoke Luchazi and could communicate with them right from the start. Most white people in their experience hadn't bothered to learn their language. But Bob's choice of language at Luampa proved right, for Luchazi and Ngangela, a sister language, were spoken predominantly in this area. The very first Sunday, he preached at the leprosy compound, a practice which was to continue as long as he worked at Cavango.

Bob discovered that though the staff were regular churchgoers, they really knew very little about the Bible nor did it seem they really understood what it meant to have a personal relationship with Christ. He began meeting with the eight men each morning for Bible study and on Sunday evenings, he invited them and their wives to the house. It was in these times of study and prayer, as they talked about the problems of the hospital and their country, they opened up in a way Bob had never experienced with Africans before.

"We were the only whites on the station for a year and a half so we bonded with those Africans in a way we never bonded to any other group. The long and the short of it was, we needed them just as much as they needed us."

One day, two burly Portuguese secret service men visited Cavango. Stern and businesslike, they did not try to hide their dislike of the new developments.

"What are you?" one asked Bob skeptically.

"We thought we were getting a doctor, and here we find you're a preacher."

"I'm doing medical work and rebuilding a hospital, but I'm also a preacher and as long as I'm here, I'm going to preach and teach the Word of God along with my medical work," Bob explained forthrightly.

He was somewhat amazed at the way in which the staff stood with him, and spoke up to the officials. He was just beginning to realize a major difference between his role in Zambia and his new role in Angola. In Zambia, missionaries were part of the colonial establishment and the things the Africans resented about the government, they resented about the missionaries. Because of the large number of missionaries on a station, patterns of behavior and relationships were set and new missionaries almost automatically fell into them. But here, Protestant missionaries had been under attack by the Portuguese Catholic government and they were just as much under surveillance by the authorities as the Africans were. The same restrictions and problems applied to both so Africans felt missionaries were on their side of the fence.

"They knew we were there for only one reason," Belva explained, "because we loved them. They knew there would be no other reason for us to tolerate the kind of treatment we received."

While Bob supervised the building of the new ward, Belva and the children established a routine of school every morning. In renovating the new house, Bob built an addition for a separate study and a room permanently set up as a classroom.

"It was difficult to get visas in and out of Angola in those days, as it was later under the Marxists. So we got into the home schooling thing and it worked well for us," Belva reported. "I took that as my morning commitment. Later on when other missionaries came along, I had five children and five grades. Every morning, Darryl Hockersmith came and helped with sports. They played volleyball for 15 minutes."

Shelley remembers that "Dad taught science and sometimes math when Mom got stuck. She was always fine in history, literature and geography." Stacey finished his high school by correspondence and then returned to go to college in the United States. Except for the few months at the Portuguese school in Sa da Bandeira, the three younger children never attended a formal school after they came to Angola. Stuart went on to graduate from Harvard and Gordon Conwell Seminary; Shelley earned a degree in nursing from the University of North   Carolina, Greensboro; and Stirling earned a Bachelor of Science degree in animal science at North Carolina State in Raleigh.

"The younger ones believe they had the best experience," Belva explains. "In those days, there wasn't anyone who opted for home schooling if Sakeji was available but now some of the younger couples have strong prejudices against boarding school and are trying home schooling. For some, it is successful and for others, it isn't. For us there was no other option."

The answer to this complex problem which Bob's parents found was not even mentioned and was never an option for Bob and Belva. Certainly health conditions have changed drastically in the intervening years and so has the availability of books and courses for home schooling but even if these changes had not occurred, it's doubtful that Bob would have made the same sacrifice a second time around.

The family remembers these years at Cavango as the "golden years". The children roamed freely over the vast, verdant acres. There was plenty of opportunity to hunt and discover all manner of wildlife, even a rare elephant passed through now and again. Any event, like a birthday, was an excuse to have a picnic down by the river or a cookout under the expansive African sky. The children loved to gather fruits and vegetables from the large garden Bob put in. Shelley's favorite memory is riding around the station with Bob on a Saturday afternoon, looking over the gardens, checking the geese and chickens and other livestock. As she and Stirling grew older, they were given a lot of responsibility in the care of the garden.

Meat was a great delicacy and there was seldom enough available from hunting to feed everyone on the station. One noon, however, the workmen spotted three hippos in the river and sent word to Bob. By that time two other missionary families had come to Cavango so the three men grabbed their guns, followed by all five MK's on the station. Bob was still dressed in his hospital white shorts and shirt.

At the point where the hippos were spotted, the bank was quite steep. Bob took aim, but he was still at the wrong angle, so one of the missionaries crouched on the ground and Bob stood on his back. One careful shot to the head and the huge animal thrashed in circles and disappeared; but he emerged, still alive on the other side of the river - too far for another shot. Several workers crossed the river by way of the dam that was being erected, and shouted and threw rocks until the wounded animal swam back to the shore where Bob took one more shot at him. This time he disappeared.

Bob assured the worried children, "A hippo sinks when he dies, but then he'll bob up feet and belly on top, raised by the gasses in his stomach." Sure enough, in about an hour, the animal surfaced. By this time school children, leprosy patients and villagers crowded on the shore to see the sight. Most had never seen a hippo before. Using a truck which had just delivered bricks to the hospital site and a steel cable, they pulled the two-ton beast onto the shore.

For the next five hours, well into the evening, Bob and Darrell Hockersmith hacked their way into the animal. They had to be very careful not to knick the stomachs which would release the foul gasses. By the time they'd worked their way to the backbone, Bob almost disappeared from the waist up into the carcass, his hospital whites drenched in blood. The people waited patiently for the "miles" of intestines Bob pulled out. About three hundred people enjoyed this delicacy the next day. The carcass yielded hundreds of pounds of meat which, when cut up and dried, fed the leprosy patients for the next six months.

About once a month, the family drove the four-hour trip into Nova Lisboa (now Huambo) then a thriving city with paved roads and shops full of imported goods. The last few days before the trip, Bob and Belva spent every spare moment catching up on correspondence to be mailed in town and making lists for a month's shopping. Little did they dream that that four-hour drive would become a dangerous obstacle course of mines and ambushes, and that people would risk the journey only in convoy with military protection.

But in these early days at Cavango, the terrorist war was far away; something they heard about on the BBC news broadcast each morning before breakfast. In 1971, there was no fear; just the sense of new freedom and opportunity. Bob and Belva happily invited their three children back in North America to come for summer vacation. A family friend had paid for the girls' airfare. For Bob, it must have been a special delight to have Stephen helping in surgery. Now a third year med student, surgery was already his love and mission work his goal. Stephen says Bob never tried to pressure him into medicine; in fact, he warned him about how tough the competition would be to get into med school. Sheila and Sharon happily scrubbed up every day to help Bob in whatever way they could.

Bob's parents also visited them that July, for it was still possible to come to Angola through South Africa. It was a special cameo in time, as they sat together in front of the fireplace on those winter evenings getting to know each other all over again. As they returned to their lifelong habit of memorizing Scripture, the children listened with deepening respect to Grandpa Foster open up new thoughts like exposing the sparkling luminescence of a crystal inside a rock. Having immersed himself in translation for over fifty years, he could pull biblical truth together on almost every subject.

Bob also asked his father to speak to the patients and African staff. Stephen was impressed by the impact his grandfather made on the people there.

"He preached a series on tithing and practical Christian living. Man! The church elders came in at the end of the sermons and said, 'If that's what God says, then we want to get serious about this' and the offerings immediately increased five or six times over in one week. At the end of one month, they'd given more than they'd given in all the years before."

It was this kind of response to truth that Bob had been observing as he met with his staff every morning and for the Sunday evening fellowship time in their home. It was as though these men had seen the cover of the book but for the first time in their lives, they were reading the inside and realized it was talking straight to them. Within a few months, Bob felt confident that the men understood the full meaning of giving Christ a pivotal place in their lives; that faith and commitment to Him, and Him alone, would ensure life with Him in eternity; and that the Bible was trustworthy - the source of all truth and information a Christian needed to live a life pleasing to God.

He had already been taking them out to the surrounding villages on Sunday afternoons. When Bob first arrived, he had been unaware that this was a totally unreached area. Unlike the Catota area or around Mukinge and Luampa back in Zambia, there were no churches or pastors. The government had forced the Ovimbundu and Luchazi from miles around to move into new villages along the road where they would be less vulnerable to attack by terrorists. They had come from parts of Angola never evangelized. Mud brick and thatch houses lined the roads for mile after mile. Children, chickens and goats ran around in the dusty paths between the houses and the little plots of ground where the people planted their gardens.

Bob began taking his core group of African friends, Srs. Israel, Reinaldo, Augustinho and Festo, and later other men from the church, out to the villages on Sunday afternoons. At first, they concentrated on the four nearest villages. They started by paying their respects to the most influential people, the chief and leading men in the village, and asking permission to hold a meeting.

"We'd invite all the people. Out of a village of four hundred maybe fifty would come. We started with the men because we knew that if we got the men interested, the women and children would come. But if we started with women and children, we would never get the men. If you make certain mistakes in African culture, you can't ever make the transition," Bob explained.

For four to six Sundays, the team would concentrate on one village. Bob taught in Luchazi; then one of the African staff would repeat the lesson again in his own words, or in Ngangela. At the end of the time, they asked the people if they wanted to learn more. Usually, ten or fifteen indicated they did. At that point, the rest of the team would move on to another village, leaving one behind at the first village to continue teaching, evangelizing, and planting a church.

Bob found these Sunday ministries deeply rewarding though they would have exhausted most any one else. A prayer letter in November, 1971 written at the end of a typical Sunday, summarized his day: "Following a quick round in the hospital after breakfast, we have an evangelistic service with patients and their relatives. Today, four trusted the Lord. Since August, there have been about two hundred and twenty-five who have come to the Lord for salvation at these meetings.

"At the church, I teach the men's Bible class. Today, I had more than seventy men. After lunch, a team of us go out to the villages for evangelistic outreach. We have been concentrating on four large villages during these first few months and now there is a small group of believers in each. Chivango, where we were today, is a village of about a thousand people and we have a group of twenty-five believers already.

"Returning home, there is just time for a quick check at the hospital and bite to eat before our living room is full to capacity for our Sunday evening Bible study in Portuguese."

And he did not take Monday morning off! The hospital was not being neglected by any means and frequently the medical work opened new evangelistic opportunities.

After visiting every village on a road south, Bob and the team were able to begin visiting a whole new area. As they entered the village of Vicungo, Bob recalled that a man from this place had been brought to the hospital with a painful, dislocated shoulder. As Bob chatted with the chief, he asked about the man who had been injured.

"Oh," smiled the chief, "I'm that man." He called all the people together to hear what the doctor had to say.

For Bob, the rebuilding of the Cavango hospital was a special delight. By this time, he had developed a strong base of supporters back home who were fully committed to his program and impressed with his ability and drive. They saw results from their contributions; they received frequent letters from Bob. When he and Belva were in North America, they contacted as many individual donors as they could, personally and by phone.

Even though he couldn't reside at Catota, Bob felt responsible for the run-down "14th century" hospital there. He transferred funds that had been given for Catota to the station and, in a few months, the repairs and painting greatly improved the facilities and lifted the morale of the staff. Bob began visiting Catota about once a month to do surgery and treat seriously-ill patients. Turning Cavango from a run-down leprosy clinic, to a modern hospital would be an expensive, long-term project. But funds continued to come in in response to Bob's letters and he believed that God would provide everything that was needed for the project.

By April 1973, the re-building was almost complete, bringing the forty-bed clinic to a modern hundred-bed hospital with a new outpatient clinic, operating room and administration block. Some months earlier, the Hockersmiths, Zigrangs and Jane Williams had joined the team at Cavango. With two well-trained nurses, Bob was able to treat many more patients and, in spite of primitive conditions, he often performed two or three major surgeries a day.

The need for adequate electrical power continued to challenge Bob's ingenuity. He knew the fast-flowing Cavango River could supply cheap power all year round. All they needed was equipment, a plan, money and a work force. Once they had power, they could install an X-ray machine - unheard of in this part of the African bush - but so critical to good patient care.

Whenever Bob went into Nova Lisboa, he made friends with Portuguese businessmen and through them, he had run into an engineer who had experience installing hydroelectric power. Bob asked him to come out to Cavango to analyze the possibilities there.

By the time the hospital renovations were complete in 1973, work on the water wheel had begun. Once again Bob stepped out in faith. The initial estimates ran about $10,000 for the whole project. At the same time, he began praying about ordering an X-ray machine since it would take many months to get it through the bureaucratic red tape and have it shipped to Angola. Initial estimates for the X-ray machine came to $12,000 and he had funds for neither.

Getting the permits, licenses, signatures and all the papers in order to import such equipment was far harder than getting the money to pay for it but, in the meantime, the water wheel project began to take shape. First a dam was built to make a fall of ten or twelve feet. Then the Africans cut a channel to divert the river to the water wheel. This proved more difficult than expected and Bob had to hire a man from Nova Lisboa to use a jackhammer and to dynamite the passage. Bob ordered the thirteen-foot-high water wheel in town. Cups attached all around the rim would turn the wheel which, in turn, would turn the axle on the generator, thus producing twenty-five kilowatts of power and providing electricity to the whole station twenty-four hours a day.

When Steve brought his bride, Peggy, to Africa on their honeymoon in June that year, the project was well under way. Peggy recalls "how nice it was" in this part of Angola - the beautiful, well run station, the shops full of goods in town. There was a spirit of progress and no sign of the terrorist war which continued to simmer in other parts of the country.

Stephen recalls, "Things were booming in Angola in '73. You could eat in fancy restaurants and get the finest food. You could get the best Swiss watches, American imports, South African imports, Japanese stuff. There were dealers for every kind of car. The place was just a hubbub of activity."

Bob and Belva felt it was safe enough to drive through Angola to South Africa where Bob was to speak at a retreat for Christian doctors, giving the young couple an opportunity to see more of Africa. While Bob and Belva were in Luanda to pick up Steve and Peggy that June, he ordered the X-ray equipment - a $16,000 step of faith, trusting that money would be in hand by the time he took delivery months ahead. He never dreamed what a long lead time he would actually have!

By the time Sharon and her husband Rob, whom she'd met while attending Gordon Conwell Seminary in Massachusetts, came for a three-month visit at the beginning of 1974, the water wheel was turning and the station had electricity.

Belva wrote, "The X-ray equipment is still bogged down in red tape." Though the central part of Angola was relatively sheltered from the terrorist war, rumors were rife in the villages. The African grapevine works notoriously well, and reports of atrocities, pitched battles, and ambushes spread through the villages and leprosy colony. Only later would true figures come out that more than 100,000 Angolans died during the war of liberation, and many more were forced into exile. The displaced villagers around Cavango were blatant testimony of this.

Suddenly, the war of liberation was over. In a surprise coup in Lisbon in May, 1974, Marcelano Caetano, successor to Antonio Salazar, dictator for fifty years, was overthrown by General Spinoza who immediately began negotiations to give the colonies of Angola and Mozambique their independence. Even at Cavango there was a distinct attitude change, as formerly arrogant or uncooperative Portuguese officials hastened to mend bridges with their future "masters".

For Protestants, it meant the end of being "second class citizens" as a new religious liberty law went into effect. To Bob, the future never looked brighter. God had allowed him to come into Angola when the door had barely been open a crack. The hospital had already established an impressive Christian presence before the African community and it seemed certain that the new African government, whatever it was, would be kindly disposed to having more Protestant missionaries in the country.

As Bob conveyed this hope through his prayer letters, he also had a specific request for a replacement for himself. He and Belva were completing their five-year term and planned to go on furlough in mid-'75. The government had assured him that it would allow a replacement for six months without the usual language acquisition and complicated documentation. He did not dare leave the hospital without a doctor. Patient load had increased so much that he often had a huge back-log of major surgeries.

Although the Africans were euphoric over the coming independence to take place in November 1975, the Portuguese settlers were jittery. Ultimately over three hundred thousand fled the country, many leaving their homes, savings and possessions behind. A local Portuguese farmer had a prize herd of cattle he was eager to sell to Bob at very low cost. Excited at the prospect of more meat and milk for people living on the station, he brought them over to graze on Cavango's expansive acreage.

By the end of the year, there was still no word about a replacement for Bob but there was good news from Sheila. She had completed her nurse's degree and a year of nurse-practitioner training in pediatrics. Now she'd been allowed to take her required six-month internship in Angola under her Dad's supervision. Sheila arrived just before Christmas, hardly able to take in the changes in less than four years. Bob put her to work immediately.

"I was seeing a hundred patients a day in the out-patient department and I had forty patients in the hospital. Dad was the overseer and if I needed help I'd call him in. I could take a child from my department to Dad if he was in another room. He'd look at the child and say, 'I think he's got this,' and he would usually be right," Sheila recalls.

That Christmas, it rained a lot at Cavango, but sitting around the fireplace in the evening, the family felt cozy and sheltered from the storm raging outside and from the political storms churning all over the countryside. One night, as the family was sipping their cocoa before going to bed, the lights suddenly dipped up and down. Bob grabbed his flashlight and ran out into the pouring rain. He had a terrible premonition of what he was going to find.

Chapter 16

In a World of Disaster

"The general level of commitment, especially for life, is not the same in our generation of Christians. Among our contemporaries, very few are willing to go as missionaries. I was working as a nurse practitioner in Massachusetts among Portuguese-speaking people. [Their response] was 'You're absolutely crazy [to go to Angola]. There are great needs here; we need you here.'"

--- Sheila (Foster) Fabiano, B. Sc. R. N.

"You've been praying with us regarding our furlough. Many letters have been written and inquiries made to find someone who could relieve us for at least six months. The problem is finding people who are willing to go anywhere. So many have pre-set conditions. Only under certain circumstances and a

congenial atmosphere will they go and, since it is al-
most impossible to find the perfect situation, they do
not go and if they did, they would not stick to it."

--- Dr. Robert Foster

****

Bob ran through the pouring rain to the dam. His fears were
confirmed; the water was rising dangerously and would soon
overflow the waterwheel. He called some of the Africans to come
and help and they dug feverishly for several hours to divert the
water from the generator house.

About a week later, Sheila and Shelley were walking along the
river looking for wildflowers which grew in abundance in the rich
damp soil. As they neared the dam, Shelley recalls, "Suddenly,
we noticed that the water wasn't going down under the water
wheel, it was just shooting over the top."

Realizing that wasn't normal, they raced over to the generator
house and saw it was flooded. Water covered the generator. The
girls knew this could spell disaster for the electrical system and
raced back to alert Bob. Through the rest of the afternoon and
into the night, every ablebodied man and woman who could handle a shovel worked feverishly to dig a deeper channel to divert
the water around the generator. But the river had already done its
damage - the water wheel had literally shifted off its base and the
generator was mired in sandy water. Bob surveyed the damage in
dismay. The whole system had to be redone. He arranged for
help from town to dig deeper into the rock. Fortunately, the generator was reparable but it took several thousand dollars to get the
system running and the station operated without electricity for a
few months.

While the power was off, Bob received the good news that the
X-ray equipment ordered a year ago, had arrived in Lobito. He
began working on documentation for its release. Hopefully, he
would be able to bring it out to the hospital before their furlough
in July.

Bob had been writing letters for over two years to recruit a replacement for himself during furlough. Every night as they

prayed together, he and Belva reminded God of this need. Besides the usual red tape, the Portuguese government required language study and courses in tropical medicine, so whoever came would have to have a good lead time. But months passed and no one volunteered.

Then early in 1975, Bob received a letter from Steve which filled his heart with joy and pride. Steve and Peggy had been praying for a replacement for Bob. Steve wrote, "It was awfully easy to pray, 'Lord you know Dad needs a replacement. I can't be that replacement because I don't speak Portuguese, I haven't finished my residency and I don't have the tropical medicine certificate that the Portuguese want.'"

Steve contacted as many doctors as he could who might be able to go but, all along, he felt the Lord's prodding, "What about you?" So now Steve had written to find out if there was some way he could fill the gap even if he didn't have the requirements. As it happened, the interim government came out with new regulations late in 1974 which cancelled the language and special studies requirements because of the desperate need for doctors. Meanwhile, Steve approached his professor of surgery to ask for a six-month leave of absence, fully expecting that he would be refused because he still had two and a half years to go in the program. Instead the professor responded, "You know, Dr. Foster, that's the most interesting idea that any resident has come and talked to me about in a long time. If you'd like to go to work in Angola for six months, I think that's great. I'll do everything I can to see that you can go, and I'll guarantee your job when you get back here in January. We'll even give you credit for what you've done out there."

Even before Steve had the opportunity to tell anyone about the decision, one of his friends at the church came up to him after the service and, putting his hand on Steve's shoulder, said, "Steve, the Lord's told me that you're going to Angola. Here is some money to help get you there." He handed Steve a check for $50 - confirmation from God just like in his dad's day!

Bob felt confident that Steve and Peggy could safely serve the six months from July through December, even though independence was scheduled for November 11, 1975. He recalled the peaceful transition in Zambia and believed that the various factions in Angola would be able to work out an equitable solution.

In fact, Bob and Belva were overjoyed when they learned that Peggy was pregnant.

Bob saw no problem in Steve delivering their first grandchild here at Cavango in December so confident was he in Steve's ability, the hospital facilities, and God's leading. Yet as the weeks passed, unsettling news began coming across the African grapevine and over the radio. Heavy fighting had broken out in Luanda between the three parties vying for power and victory in the forthcoming elections. The Africans in the bush knew the names of the parties but they were confused about what Marxism or socialism was. They plied Bob and the other missionaries with questions, "Who are these people? Where did they come from?" Most of the Africans in the area tended to side with UNITA - not for political reasons but primarily for tribal loyalties. Unbeknown to Bob or the Africans at that time, the governor general appointed by Lisbon was a Marxist who saw to it that support and supplies reached the MPLA which had its strongest base in the cities and in the north.

By May of 1975, a full scale terrorist war had broken out between the three parties. Though there was no fighting around Cavango since it was so far off the beaten path to anywhere, they began seeing groups of armed men who barricaded the road, stopping all cars, asking for identification, where they were going and what they were doing.

Sheila recalls the intimidation of seeing fourteen- and fifteen-year-old youths with huge rifles which they waved dangerously. It was impossible to tell which party they were with because everyone wore the same ragged clothes and it was only by examining the origin of the weapons (which one would not choose to do) that their loyalties were revealed. By this time, rumors were rampant that the Russians were supplying the MPLA and the Cubans who were their mercenaries, and South Africa and the United States kept UNITA forces armed. The Portuguese left the country without a government in place or a trained and equipped army and the super powers seemed to have managed to destroy any possibility of a quick settlement of differences.

But it was hard to be pessimistic in the glow of God's work at Cavango. The hospital had served almost a hundred thousand outpatients in 1974. About three hundred and fifty new converts had been added to the family of God; twenty churches had been established in the surrounding villages since Bob and his co-workers started going out on Sunday afternoons. Most of the leprosy patients in the village had accepted Christ; many were well enough to return to their homes, but others replaced them so that there were still about two hundred and fifty lepers and their families on the station.

Belva worked on craft projects with the women and marvelled at the ingenuity of some who were terribly disfigured. One woman who became a dear friend, had only a thumb and stump of one finger on each hand, yet she knit beautiful sweaters and baby clothes.

Besides her work in the pediatrics ward, Sheila set up clinics for children under five, to give injections, weigh them, check on diet and teach the mothers simple health care. The infant mortality rate was very high and these clinics were aimed at preventing some of the common causes of death among infants. Sheila trained a team who went out with her each week. Eliseu, and his future wife, Sara were both trained nurses whom Sheila came to look upon as close friends. Eliseu also used the opportunity at the clinics to recruit local people for UNITA and later he was killed in an ambush.

When it was time for Steve to arrive, Bob and Belva drove to Lobito to pick him and Peggy up and, hopefully, to clear the long-awaited X-ray equipment. Bob filled out ten sets of documents but dock strikes, work slowdowns, red tape and lack of true authority frustrated his efforts once again. They returned to Cavango without the new equipment.

For three weeks, father and son worked in surgery together, each one learning from the other. Since Bob and Belva were going to be away only six months, they left everything unpacked and available for Steve and Peggy's use in their spacious home, "The nicest we've ever had in Africa," according to Bob. The Hockersmiths, their teenage son and nurse Jane Williams remained at Cavango. Peggy appreciated the companionship since she didn't know Portuguese or any African language.

When Bob finally received clearance on the X-ray machine, he made one more trip to Lobito before leaving for furlough to arrange to have it shipped to Cavango. This time, he found several crates, but in going through all the documentation, he discovered that one major piece of equipment was still missing. He told the customs officials that he did not want to take delivery until the order was complete and left it in storage until his return.

Bob and Belva had one difficult task to perform on their way home. The missionaries at Mukinge had made it clear that Dad and Mother Foster at 83 and 82, were no longer capable of staying in their own home alone. They felt that they should return to the United States where they could be with their daughter, Rhoda, and be near good medical care. Understandably, the busy medical staff did not feel it could assume the responsibility for two seniors. What if they developed a serious illness? Or fell and broke a hip? Who could stay with them in their home to keep an eye on them? They lived down the hill quite a distance from other missionary homes and from the hospital.

Never for a moment had Bob's parents expected him to give up his work to care for them. It was impossible to bring them into the insecurity of the Angolan situation even if they were to be granted residency, which was unlikely. Bob's family thinks he was disappointed in the missionaries' decision; that arrangements could have been made for them to stay on in their beloved Zambia. But he gives no indication of that when he speaks about taking his parents home. He just remembers the traumatic move after fifty- eight years in Africa - to leave the people they loved, the language they spoke as well as, if not better than English, the station they started - and to go back to a country whose culture and affluence was foreign to them.

In fact, at first they refused to leave. But Bob's mother, especially, had complete confidence in anything he said. After he explained why he had to pack up their things and take them home, she finally agreed. Bob recalls sadly, "It was almost more than she could take."

The whole family helped the folks pack up their belongings and escorted them to Rhoda's home in Illinois. As a final blessing on their years of ministry, God allowed the Fosters to see the first Kaonde Bible come off the press as they passed through London.

Little did Bob and Belva realize how close they came to being stranded in Angola. They left on one of the last regularly scheduled flights out of the country. Just before they boarded the plane Bob hugged Steve and reiterated, "Remember, if things get rough and you've got to leave, you send me an SOS. I'll come back and take over." But Steve and Peg drove home late that night enjoying the peace and rugged spaciousness of the African countryside, confident they had made the right decision. That would be one of the last times any of the missionaries travelled to town without some military personnel escorting them. Steve remembers young boys armed to the teeth demanding their papers at checkpoint after checkpoint.

"Your heart was in your mouth every time, not knowing if these kids had any inkling of what they were up to; whether they even know which side of the gun worked."

Far from the peaceful transition experienced in Zambia, Angola turned into a bloodbath. Portuguese who had lived in the country for generations fled, turned their homes over to their servants or drove the car to the airport, leaving the key in the ignition. The country lost its industrialists, businessmen, technicians - those who had developed the infrastructure of a sound economy - in a few short weeks.

While a few Portuguese were killed - one family near Cavango was hacked to death - most of the tens of thousands casualties were Africans, as opposing parties fought for control. Innocent villagers accused of complicity with the opposing side were shot or beaten to death. Villages were burned. Thousands of refugees fled out of the battle zones.

At the hospital Steve experienced an eerie calm. Most of the beds were empty; few people hazarded the roads to come to the outpatient clinic. He was usually finished at the hospital by noon and he and Peggy enjoyed lazy afternoons together that they hadn't experienced since their marriage, or Steve went hunting for meat for the leprosy patients and their families. More and more frequently, however, war casualties came into the hospital. Steve never asked which side they represented; he treated each one as best he could.

The hospital was well equipped with drugs. Darrell Hockersmith had been able to get an ample supply of fuel. They felt they could manage until independence and hopefully a settlement of the war.

One afternoon a man drove into the mission covered with blood and near death. As Steve examined him he found the man's abdomen had been shot away, exposing his intestines. Incredibly, the patient had had the foresight to wrap himself in a blanket to hold his organs in place, and had driven for six hours to the hospital. Steve and Barbara worked over the patient for three hours, cleaning up the horrible wound and two days later operated again to remove gangrenous tissues.

When the patient regained consciousness they learned that he had inflicted the damage on himself, carelessly handling his rifle as he bent over to pick up a rabbit he'd killed on the road. Years later a truck driver pulled up to the curb in the middle of Huambo and called out to Barbara Hockersmith, "Remember me?"

He pulled up his shirt to show the scars from his massive wounds, still grateful for the life-saving heroics she and Steve had undertaken for him. As the tentacles of the civil war began to engulf even such a remote place as Cavango, the staff and church leaders drew together even more tightly in a bond of love and fellowship. The Sunday evening Bible studies in their home continued after Bob and Belva left. The warmth captured Steve's heart.

"I had never been in a Bible study like that in my life, where you had eighteen Africans and two or three Europeans. This was totally reversed from the old traditional staff meeting with forty white faces and one African.

"Even though I understood little Portuguese, just the sense of electricity of interest, seeing people starting to apply this to their lives right away, was new to me. I was used to the jaded university environment where you discussed the Scripture but you didn't necessarily put it into practice. I think I'll always remember that excitement at Cavango."

Steve was especially impressed with Sr. Israel who had welcomed Bob and now welcomed him so openly, without any sense of competition or being displaced by a white man, after running the hospital for eight years himself. The magic of bonding with African brothers and sisters in this dangerous and lonely outpost sealed the call to Angola in Steve and Peggy's hearts. And then one morning in September, they received a message on the intercom from the missionaries at Catota, "We feel it's time to leave."

Fighting had increased near Catota which was on a main road with heavy military traffic. Rumors of Cubans moving into the interior were rampant. Steve argued that the Lord hadn't told him to leave, that life was relatively tranquil at Cavango. Though unable to convince him to go, most of the other missionaries in the country left. Steve had no peace about leaving himself, but it was becoming obvious that the war was escalating and that he might be caught without an escape route. He felt Peggy must go. Talking it over with Sr. Canjila and other church leaders, they agreed that her pregnancy posed too great a risk.

As the weeks passed, it would become more dangerous for her and the baby if they had to get away in an emergency, perhaps even hiking out through the bush. At first Peggy could not accept the thought of leaving Steve and returning to Canada, but being the level-headed young woman she was, she realized it was the only sensible decision. The U.S. State Department had made a whole series of refugee flights available out of Nova Lisboa (to be called Huambo after independence).

Arriving there for Peggy's flight, they found the airport jammed with people loaded with trunks and bags, everything they could possibly take on the plane with them. Some had been waiting for a flight for more than two weeks. Peggy was devastated. The panic at the airport left her shaken, as she read fear in the eyes of the thousands of Portuguese fleeing for their lives. She couldn't help wondering if she would ever see Steve again. She remembers going into the washroom and weeping uncontrollably. But once that was behind her she pulled herself together and calmly boarded the plane with 13-year-old Paul Hockersmith whom she was escorting out of the country. Fortunately she didn't know about Steve's near escape just hours after she flew out of Huambo. Steve, Darrell and Barb decided to stay in town rather than risk the dangerous drive out to Cavango at night.

They slept in a missionary apartment behind the Christian bookstore in town. About 2 A.M., a gang of FNLA terrorists (the smallest of the three parties vying for power) broke in; brandishing pistols they began to search the apartment from top to bottom. They demanded the keys to the car, and tried to take Darrell to the police station for questioning.

Darrell stood his ground, holding onto the doorposts and refused to move, even when one terrorist pointed a pistol at his head. After seemingly endless harassment, the men were convinced that Steve and Darrell were who they said they were, and finally left.

The next morning, the FNLA commander apologized profusely, saying it was a case of mistaken identity. He did not want the medical personnel to leave, and assured them over and over of his gratitude for their service. In spite of the accelerating civil war, Steve was determined to stay the promised six months to give his dad as much time as possible for a furlough and rest.

Originally, he and Peggy had planned to stay through December, since the baby was due on the 5th. But now she was having the baby in Canada and he wanted to be there with her. There was no way to phone to find out how she was and no way to get mail back and forth.

In November, Darrell slipped out of the country on a military courier plane to Zambia where he was able to call back to the United States to let everyone know they were safe and how the situation had deteriorated. Steve sent a message to his dad that, if possible, he should come back before the end of November, but he would have to find a way on military transport since all civilian flights had been cancelled.

On December first, Steve, Darrell and Barbara were having Sunday morning breakfast together. They all stopped their conversation as they heard a rare sound on this isolated outpost, a car drove up and stopped. Even before they could jump up to see who it was, there was a knock at the door and Dr. Burgess, a missionary doctor from a United Church of Canada hospital about a hundred miles away, burst through the door.

Chapter 17

Escape!

"It was amazing to me how the Lord undertook to provide us food, hospitality, transport. In every situation, we were very conscious that the Lord was with us. It was a miraculous thing to see how God had this person here, something there - just as though we were walking in a dream. Every time we needed some help, the Lord would have somebody there. If I had tried to plan it, it would have taken six months' preparation to organize it, but I could not have done it as wonderfully as the Lord worked it out.

"It's a wonderful thing to put your hands in the hands of God and to believe that He'll do what He says. It's great to look back and see what God has done, not only through His Word, but in your own experience. As

*you're reminded, it gives you tremendous courage to
ask God, believing Him."*

--- Dr. Robert Foster

****

The mission leaders were not at all sure Bob should return to Angola. Even the Red Cross was hesitant about sending medical teams in because of the heavy fighting and lack of communications. But once Bob received permission from the mission, he wasted no time in getting together a $5,000 supply of urgently needed drugs which he knew would not be available in Angola.

The parting with Belva and the children was difficult, but both she and Bob knew they had to stay behind until the situation settled down. There was no question in her mind that he was doing the right thing in relieving Steve. With commercial flights cancelled, Bob worked through military channels. On his final clandestine flight into Huambo, he was the only passenger and he sat on top of boxes of ammunition.

As soon as the plane touched down he was ordered to jump out. A soldier tossed his boxes of drugs down on the tarmac beside him and the plane was off, leaving Bob standing on the end of the runway in the late afternoon. Airport guards raced up, demanding to know who he was and how he'd arrived since no flight had been scheduled.

When they learned he was the doctor from Cavango, they agreed to take him to his friends in town, where he was able to make arrangements to get to Cavango, a hundred miles away.

The clock was ticking away for Peggy and the delivery of her baby, so Steve wasted little time bringing Bob up to date on patients in the hospital. His hope was to catch a military plane that would get him onto an overseas flight in the next day or two. Even with the urgency of getting away, Steve left with a heavy heart. He recalls his farewell with Silva, one of the student nurses.

"He just embraced me and said that he wanted me to remember that he and the others were going to be praying that God would never let us forget the people there, that there would always be a place for us to work in Angola. It's that kind of memories that have burned holes in my heart. Every time I think of going some place else more comfortable to work, I think, "What am I going to say to Silva when I see him in heaven? How am I going to reply when he asks me what I did about what I knew?"

"I felt I'd be dishonest if I said I'd sent my money, or prayed, or found a replacement, but that I didn't go myself."

Once Steve was gone, Bob settled into the busy routine of the hospital. Many nights he'd be wakened by emergencies as soldiers with gunshot wounds, or civilians injured by a mine explosion or beaten by guerrillas were brought in. When heavy fighting was reported in Huambo, Bob did ten major surgeries in 24 hours. He just moved from one patient to another, washing up and changing sterile gowns as the next patient was brought into the operating room.

Bob risked one trip to Lobito to get extra supplies and to check to see if the missing piece of the X-ray machine had arrived. Not only could he not find the missing item, he couldn't find the equipment at all! After hours of frustrating investigation, port officials told him it was now sitting in the port of Mocamedes, three hundred miles down the coast. Once again Bob came home with a fist full of documentation and no X-ray equipment.

These were precious days with the church leaders as they met together for prayer and Bible study, acutely aware that the communists were getting closer each day. The African grapevine was very busy, and each morning the Africans told Bob who had run away from town and where fighting had taken place. Bob knew that it was essential to have contingency plans in place. He was able to get the church leaders to reorganize the station so that every position, formerly held by a missionary, was now assigned to an African.

The people pled with Bob not to leave them. Understanding their fears, he assured them he would stay until they told him to go because the situation had become too dangerous for him to stay.

Then one morning in February, word came from the highest authority that the Cubans had reached Huambo and would be marching on Cavango within a day or two. If the western missionaries were going to get out, they had to go immediately. The church leaders came to Bob to tell him to leave.

Darrell and Barbara decided to go to Catota to pick up a vehicle that had been left behind when the missionaries had fled some months earlier. Bob drove his Chevrolet Carryall loaded with jerry cans of gas to get him to the border. They planned to meet in Menongue, three hundred miles to the southeast.

There was little room in the Carryall for personal belongings so it didn't matter that Bob had no time to think about what to take. He threw together a change of clothes, a few books and important documents in an overnight case. News of the missionaries' leaving had spread through the area, and people streamed into the church for a farewell service. Once more Bob stood in front of the people he had grown to love; people who had taught him so much about fellowship; people he'd seen grow spiritually with a zeal to evangelize their own people in the surrounding villages.

Many had lost family and friends in the civil war; some had sons who'd disappeared into the military camps; others had fled their villages ahead of the terrorists and resettled near Cavango. What would happen to them now? Once again they would be without a doctor just as they had been for many years before he'd come. As far as he knew there were only two doctors in the whole east and central part of Angola.

How would the communists treat them? Most were ignorant village people to whom political philosophies meant nothing. Their loyalties were formed by tribe and place of birth, and they were at the mercy of whatever power took control. Stories of Cuban atrocities were rampant. How would they treat the seriously ill patients in the hospital and the leprosy patients cruelly deformed by their disease, unable to care for themselves? Communists were known to destroy the sick and helpless, considering them an unnecessary burden.

Would they rob the villagers of the produce in their gardens, and destroy their very means of sustenance? What would happen to the churches in the villages surrounding the hospital? Would the church leaders be able to continue holding services here at Cavango and out in the villages, or would the communists forbid such meetings?

Bob stood before his weeping people, longing to stay and defend them, knowing he could not. He looked at Sr. Israel, now the director of the mission, in whose capable hands the mission had rested for so many years. What price would he have to pay for his leadership? Oh, that God would stay the enemy, halt their progress, put a hedge around this oasis of light and healing. How could God allow this ministry He had raised up to fall into the hands of atheistic communists who hated Him and His people?

Bob began to speak words of comfort to the packed congregation. He reminded them of how Habakkuk had heard God's terrible judgment upon Jerusalem - that the evil, merciless Babylonians would destroy His holy city. Habakkuk didn't understand either. He questioned God, *"Why do you tolerate the treacherous? Why are you silent while the wicked swallow up those more righteous than themselves?"* (Hab. 1:13).

But Habakkuk was sustained by his confidence in the sovereignty of God. Bob comforted the people, "Here's a man who tells us when everything goes wrong, when there's absolutely nothing to eat, 'Yet I will rejoice in God who is my salvation.'" He could only assure them that God who is their strength would enable them to be faithful in the midst of every difficulty. Even though they could not understand what seemed to be God's judgment coming upon them, God would sustain them and enable them to triumph.

The prayers of the people brought heaven to earth that night. But then it was time for Bob and the Hockersmiths to say their personal goodbyes. One after another, as men and women filed out of the church, they hugged Bob, many crying unashamedly. Bob tried to assure them, "I'll be back as soon as I can get permission from the new government, I'll come back."

But in his heart, he feared he would never see many of them again.

Early in the morning, Bob took his last look around his home and the magnificent hospital that he had brought into being. He and Sr. Israel embraced one another. In the five years they had worked together, the two men had become friends and partners in the ministry. Words could not express the depth of their feeling as they looked into each other's faces, then embraced one another again.

Bob handed his keys over to Israel, "Take care of everything till I get back."

Bob pushed the Carryall south towards Menongue as hard as he could. The easiest exit from the country would have been west through Lubango, but the city and all roads west and north were in the hands of the communists, so he headed towards the southern border, praying that he could outdistance the invading Cubans.

It poured all day, the van slipping and sliding in the muddy roads. Time after time, soldiers stopped him, demanding his identification papers and bombarding him with questions - "Where are you going? Why are you travelling alone?"

Finally, Bob picked up a few soldiers to answer the questions for him and save time at each barricade. He arrived in Menongue late at night to find the city full of harried looking refugees, seeking a place to stay or gas for their cars and trucks packed to the roof with their belongings. Rumors were rampant that the Cubans were just hours outside the city. Every available hotel room was full. Bob went to the hospital where the only empty bed was the examining table in the Outpatient Department. When the governor of the province, whom Bob knew, learned he was there, he sent for Bob to come to his home for a meal. He, too, confirmed that the Cubans were within a day of the city and warned Bob to get out. A doctor would be a prized prisoner!

It was a great relief to learn that Darrell and Barb were at the AEF Church in town. They had turned their vehicle over to Christians there. From here on, they would travel together. Everyone they talked to said the roads leading to the border were heavily mined, and even armed convoys were being attacked. Bob learned there was an army camp south of the city, so he went to ask them what their chances were of getting through to the border of South West Africa. The commander invited them to stay at the camp overnight and in the morning, he would provide an escort. The camp was an eery sight in the pouring rain, as grim-faced soldiers sloshed through mud churned up by army vehicles. The weary missionaries welcomed the shower and hot food provided and marvelled at God's provision of an escort over the dangerous miles ahead.

Early the next morning, a convoy of two hundred heavily-armed soldiers in armored vehicles headed south with Bob's

Carryall in the middle. He couldn't help comparing himself to Paul when the centurion provided an escort of two hundred to take him from Jerusalem to Caesarea.

The roads were a muddy mess, churned up by the massive tires up to eighteen inches thick. Several times, they ran into an ambush but when the soldiers saw the heavily-armed convoy, they disappeared. At one point, the convoy crossed a marsh. The troopcarriers maneuvered easily through the two feet deep water, but within a few yards Bob's Carryall konked out. One of the vehicles returned, attached a line from a winch, and pulled the van the rest of the way.

As the miles went by, Bob and Darrell became more concerned about whether the van would hold up. Every spring had broken; the shock absorbers were gone. Going through one rough patch, the battery box became completely detached. Three times, they had to signal the convoy to stop for a flat tire.

"It was a miracle that the car held together until I got to the military base at the border," Bob marvels.

But late that night, the exhausted travelers arrived at Rundu in South West Africa. Bob learned that one of the Portuguese Christians who had been associated with AEF at Catota was camped with his family on the Angolan side of the border. By asking around, he found Sr. Rodrigues who was waiting for papers to cross the border. When Bob left, he gave him the keys to the Carryall.

"It's in terrible shape but perhaps you can fix it up, or sell it for parts," he told Rodrigues.

Seven years later when Bob returned to Namibia, an AEF missionary told him one of the Hereros, an African tribe, was still driving the van!

Two days later, Bob called Belva from Johannesburg - the first direct contact he'd had with her in three months - to say he was on his way home. Her only information had been a tersely-worded telegram from mission headquarters, "Cavango evacuated. Missionaries safely out."

A weary and emotionally drained Bob arrived back in New Jersey to find the family still comfortably ensconced in the big old house they had been loaned eight months earlier. That had been another one of God's miracles. Rentals for a large family are not easy to find at the best of times; extremely difficult for a short period of time. But a friend in one of their supporting churches had told Bob they could use the house "until I sell it."

Bob had laughingly warned her, "If you let us have it, you won't sell it as long as I need it."

Sure enough, month after month, no buyer appeared. But now that Bob was back, the owner confided that she really needed to sell it before the year was up because of tax complications. So Bob assured her they would look for something else. Within a week, the house was sold and Bob and Belva had been offered another large home, rent-free, until their furlough was up.

The question now was, what to do after their furlough ended in July? As word got around that Bob had escaped from Angola, several organizations invited him to go to mission hospitals in other countries in places like Pakistan, Bangladesh, Nigeria.

To all he said the same thing, "I don't want to go anywhere until I know I can't go back to Angola."

In June, 1976, Bob received a letter from Dr. Brechet who had been able to remain at the Kalukembe Hospital because the Cubans had not come into that area. Brechet had been to the capitol and had spoken to the Marxist authorities in control there.

He wrote, "The authorities are willing to have you come back."

Bob immediately wrote to the Minister of Health in Luanda explaining, "I left on furlough with my family in July 1975. I have a return visa which is good until July, 1976 and I'm ready to come back with my family to work in Angola."

Within a few days Bob received a cable from Luanda inviting him to come back to Angola. The official explained that the situation at Cavango was still unstable and suggested that Dr. Foster work temporarily at Kalukembe with Dr. Brechet.

Bob wrote his prayer supporters, "We're happy to do this and believe that God will ultimately open the door for us to return to minister among the Nganguela people again. We have been assured that there will be continued freedom for the ministry of the Word of God. How long this will last is a big question. However, we believe that we should take the opportunity now available and trust God for the future."

Mission leaders and friends were strongly opposed to Bob's return. Bob agreed to wait for word from Don Lutes who had remained in Southern Angola, but time was short for the visa and return tickets would expire the third week of July. Why would Bob risk his life and put his family in jeopardy to return to the same battle-scarred country he'd left? Nothing had been resolved, and the civil war would continue until 1989 when peacetalks would be held.

Steve, who just a few years later made the same decision to take his family back to war-torn Angola, faced the same question.

"It wasn't easy to come up with answers! What kind of God allows us to get out scot-free and the rest to pay the price? Can we walk off the scene and let them stay? What are we saying about the Lord Jesus? What are we saying about the implications of the cross?"

The bonding at Cavango had become an identification, not only in ministry and service, but in suffering. If Bob and Belva could return, even if it meant working under the Marxist regime, they were convinced that God had called them and they could trust Him to care for them and their family just as easily in Angola as in New Jersey.

When word came from Don Lutes that the new government was a flexible type of Marxism and was willing to have missionaries return, the AEF leaders capitulated. Once again, Bob and Belva packed up their belongings, storing and sorting a year's accumulation of things. They shopped for supplies and personal needs, knowing that store shelves in Angola were pretty bare. God had beautifully allowed them to have a family reunion with everyone together, right after Bob returned from Angola.

Sharon and Rob were back in Jamaica, Steve, Peggy and baby Rebekah were still in Canada where he was completing his specialty in surgery. Sheila was working as a nurse-practitioner, directing a Portuguese children's clinic in Boston, and Stacey and his wife Ruth were in New Jersey.

The three youngest, Stuart, Stirling and Shelley, were excited to go back to Angola and continue their home schooling. With the major cities and much of the northern and western parts of the country in the hands of the new Marxist government, commercial flights had resumed and the Foster family arrived as scheduled.

What a joy to see the man who had originally invited them to Angola, Dr. Brechet, at the airport. But their joy quickly turned to sorrow as Dr. Brechet described what had happened at Cavango.

"It's very bad. Cavango is under the control of the Cubans. You can't go back there."

They listened, horror-struck, as he recounted that the Cubans had ransacked everything. They'd stolen drugs and equipment; even the beds had disappeared from the hospital. They had broken into the missionaries' houses and taken everything. Leprosy patients and their families had fled into the bush; staff had disappeared. Then in a voice broken with anguish, he reported the unbelievable. The Cuban soldiers had forced about thirty of the weakest and most deformed patients - the ones who couldn't escape - into one of the grass huts and set it on fire. No one had escaped.

Chapter 18

The War's Toll

"There are two ways a man can live: he can do his own thing and go his own way, or he can humble himself and take God at His Word. We put our lives into the Lord's hands long ago, and we are not about to take them away."

--- Dr. Robert Foster

****

The questions tumbled out over each other as Bob and Belva tried to comprehend the tragedy at Cavango. Where was the staff now? Where did the rest of the patients go? What about Sr. Israel and the other church leaders?

But there were few answers to their questions. Some Africans who had escaped to Kalukembe brought the terrible news, but few details. It seemed the hospital was functioning with a skeleton staff. Communications were completely cut and no one could safely travel into the region. Only as the news began to sink in, did Bob and Belva realize the full impact on them. Everything they owned at Cavango was gone - their furniture, dishes, books, wedding gifts, pictures. All they had were the few things in their suitcases and a few boxes they had brought by air freight.

They'd seen the impact the war had on the economy even in the months since they'd left. The shops were virtually empty. They could not replace most of what they'd lost here in Angola. But Dr. Brechet had already anticipated their problem and assured them, "Just come. We've got a house available, with everything you need in it."

So the Foster family once again moved to a new area. Bob had frequently visited the station which was operated by the Swiss Evangelical Mission. In fact, he had re-designed the hospital at Dr. Brechet's request, and the familiar U-shaped configuration of wards and administration block made him feel right at home. The hospital had a hundred and fifty beds, plus a TB unit for a hundred patients and another hundred leprosy patients - far too much for Dr. Brechet to handle alone.

When the African staff saw that Kahaya had come back, they pressed around him, greeting him warmly. Many knew him from past visits; some had been patients at Cavango.

"Now we know that you really love us," they assured him.

"What do you mean, NOW you know?" Bob retorted. "I've lived here, I've worked here. I've done everything possible to show you that I really love you."

"Oh, no!" they replied. "For you to be willing to leave your home and come back and suffer with us shows us that you really do love us."

Bob immediately threw himself into the medical work. A few weeks after their arrival, Dr. Brechet became ill and had to return to Switzerland for surgery, leaving Bob alone. During the first month, he did a hundred major surgeries.

He described these in a letter to one of his medical friends, "A typical day's surgery includes work in five or six different surgical specialties - ophthalmology (cataract extraction), gynecology (Ceasarean section), orthopedics (open reduction of a fractured femur), plastic surgery (skin grafts), urology (prostatectomy), and general surgery (hernia repairs)."

A particularly challenging case was a patient who was brought in with a bullet wound through his leg. As Bob cleaned up the wound, he saw that the bullet had also grazed the main artery. The patient seemed to be doing well until three days later when Bob received a urgent call to come to the ward. The man was bleeding to death. Bob himself admits he'd never seen as much blood as the artery was pumping through the wound. In a flash, he recognized that the effects of the bullet had killed surrounding tissue, weakening the artery so that it had broken down.

He gave orders for a tourniquet and an IV solution. They rushed the patient back into the operating room where Bob performed the first vascular surgery in his life. He clamped off the artery, and while the blood was temporarily circulating through smaller surrounding vessels, he had twenty minutes to stitch up the torn artery. With no medications available to prevent clotting and thrombosis, the patient remained in great danger even though Bob managed to close the artery in time.

He recalls, "Once again the Lord was good to us and the man recovered completely."

War casualties flooded the hospital as the war escalated. The Marxist government announced its policies of "strict scientific socialism" which no one really understood and which did nothing to improve the serious shortages of many basic necessities. The list of unobtainable items seemed to grow by the day - tea, yeast, laundry detergent, hand soap, baking powder. Yet, just when Belva reached the end of her meat, some friend would stop by with a piece of beef or pork. Air mail packages from home would bring a delectable piece of cheese which they hadn't tasted in months, or a precious hoard of chocolates.

The suffering of the African people was far more serious. Thousands became refugees as they were driven from their homes and gardens by terrorists. In one month, four male nurses at Kalukembe disappeared. News of the death of several Cavango friends, including Belva's cook, saddened them.

In spite of all this, Bob praised God that they had liberty to preach under a Marxist government and he began his normal pattern of preaching on Sundays and holding Bible studies with the staff. Shortly after they arrived at Kalukembe, an African from the Chokwe area, south of Cavango, came to the mission to ask Bob to speak at a church conference. This meeting was to be held in an area of relative peace, so Bob and Belva both attended. Two years earlier, Bob and several Cavango evangelists had started the ministry. At that time there were twenty believers. Now four hundred gathered, rejoicing and praising the Lord. When they saw Bob they could only call it "a miracle". About forty people made decisions to accept Christ during the conference. Little did they realize that God was preparing this Chokwe fellowship for trials ahead. A few months later, the military attacked their villages and forced them into refugee camps.

In the fall of 1977, Bob was able to travel to Donde Leprosarium to examine new patients and reevaluate others. How wonderful to meet some of the Africans from the Cavango district. The news they brought was devastating. As Bob listened incredulously, the Africans explained that the Cubans had begun moving into the Cavango area again. Savimbi feared they would use the hospital as a military base as they had done in other areas. Rather than giving them the comfort and protection of the sturdy buildings, Savimbi ordered a thousand local Africans to converge on the mission and systematically tear down the buildings brick by brick - the administration block, the wards, the operating room, the missionaries' homes, the church - everything, until all that was left standing was the enervated waterwheel.

Dr. Jim Foulkes of Mukinge recalls Bob's reaction, "The destruction of the hospital would be a problem to some people but it wasn't to Bob. Bricks and mortar don't count as much as people, and healing in the name of Jesus. I talked to him soon after that happened. What a beautiful testimony of a guy who has his priorities right! To see his beautiful waterwheel and hydro-electric system destroyed, after all the time he took to raise the money, was nothing. He believed it had been right at the time and that it had done all that it was supposed to do."

Bob and Belva still feel that Cavango was the highlight of their missionary career and that the growth in the church, the matured Christian leaders, the twenty new churches and evangelism in the surrounding villages was worth all the pain and loss.

There's no doubt Bob felt keenly the loss of the hospital into which he'd poured his creative energies, and to which God's people had given thousands of dollars but he wasted no time in looking back. The war had created a spiritual hunger in the hearts of the people and Bob was determined to take advantage of the openness.

"Opportunities abound on every hand," he wrote his prayer partners. "Every weekend since the beginning of the year, I have had the privilege of ministering God's Word in a different area: in two cities, in the country, on the frontier of the terrorist-held territory, in a refugee camp and at the hospital and neighboring towns. Everywhere I found hungry, troubled hearts."

While travelling was dangerous, staying on the station was no guarantee of safety. An elderly Swiss nurse on another station was abducted in the middle of the night. There was no word of her whereabouts for several months until the news came that she had escaped and walked more than a thousand miles to safety.

Bob risked several trips to Luanda for supplies and to inquire about the still missing X-ray equipment en route to Lobito. In November 1977, two years after the equipment was ordered, Bob finally found the crates which had mysteriously reappeared on the Lobito docks. He, personally, had to go through warehouses piled high with boxes, looking for ones with his name on them. He found four cases but the X-ray table was still missing. After lengthy correspondence the company agreed to replace it. In spite of the frustrations, Bob couldn't help praising the Lord for the delays which kept the valuable equipment from being delivered to Cavango where it would have been hacked to pieces.

The X-ray saga continued. The company had promised to send a technician out to install the equipment but because of the war's dangerous interruption, it would be another four years before someone was willing to go out to Kalukembe to assemble it. It was a miracle that a Portuguese technician remained in the country at all.

Even after Dr. Brechet returned from Switzerland, the case load remained extraordinary. At any one time, Bob had up to a hundred and fifty surgical cases on the waiting list. When government officials from Luanda came on an inspection tour of the hospital, they were impressed with the quality of medical care but they were concerned about the lack of medical staff and offered to send some Cuban doctors to help out.

Bob thanked them for their offer, but refused. He had seen too much of Cuban medical work. If an African came in with a leg smashed up from a mine, the Cubans would prefer to amputate rather than try to save the leg. They reasoned, "If we cut it off he'll be up and about in ten days and out of the hospital; if we repair it, it may take months before he's healed."

With Angolan visas more freely obtainable, Bob once again pled for more missionary doctors but the situation had changed little since his days in Zambia. Few doctors were willing to leave their good salary, their good equipment, their fine facilities to care for people in a bush hospital, to serve the Lord with limited facilities and resources.

It grieved him to admit that African doctors were even less likely to serve in a bush hospital after they completed their training. He recalled how the mission helped educate a number of Zambian doctors overseas, but few returned to Zambia. Those that did could not bring themselves to work in mission hospitals. Though some missiologists believed the era of planting and maintaining mission hospitals was over, Bob strongly disagreed.

"Having been involved in medical mission work and seeing the tremendous value both from the medical viewpoint and the spiritual, I believe there is a greater need today than there was in 1950 for medical missions. Governments that we hoped would be able to cope and take over mission hospitals are further from being able to do that today than they were twenty years ago."

Relief was on its way from another source. The two doctors' sons were coming back to Angola. Jean-Pierre Brechet and Stephen Foster had been friends at boarding school in Zambia years ago. Each had gone on to study medicine in his home country and each was now ready to return as a missionary doctor.

By early 1978, both young families were established at Kalukembe. Many days Bob and Steve operated in the same theatre, their patients separated by a screen. They shared skills as Steve explained the modern techniques and new procedures from his training and Bob made suggestions from his years of experience and ability to improvise.

Now there was one less Foster child to keep in touch with by correspondence. The family was scattered but there was a constant interchange of news and a great deal of evidence of deep caring for each other. Sharon and Rob still lived in Jamaica, and Bob and Belva could read between the lines that life was tough in that poverty-stricken island, too. Stuart, who had returned to America for college the year before, shared the exciting news that he had been accepted at Harvard for his sophomore year with all expenses paid. Though majoring in communications, Stacey was the one who seldom wrote, withdrawing not only from his parents but his siblings.

Sheila loved her work as pediatric nurse-practitioner and had become fluent in the language as she worked in the Portuguese community. Now she wrote that she had applied to the AEF to come to Angola as a missionary and she hoped to be at Kalukembe before the end of the year. In fact, her acceptance, support and visa all arrived in time for her to return to Angola with Bob and Belva after their mini-furlough at the end of 1978.

Steve drove to Luanda to pick them up and they had a joyous trip back to Kalukembe together. Two days later on the very road they'd travelled, twelve people were killed in a mine explosion.

Bob insisted that Sheila spend her first months learning an African language. He was fluent in Luchazi (a form of Nganguela he'd learned in Zambia), but the majority of the people spoke Mbundu which Sheila chose to learn.

After three months of lessons on another station, Sheila moved out to a village to live with an Mbundu family to put her head knowledge into practice. She became astoundingly fluent in the languange which was a great asset as she worked with village women and children in the clinics she was to establish.

When she returned from the village, Sheila began working in the outpatient clinic. It troubled her to see so many preventable diseases, especially among the children. Polio vaccine was readily available, yet she saw many cases of polio.

She made friends with the government medical officer who gave out the vaccines and learned that vaccines often sat around in airports for days in the heat, destroying their effectiveness. Worse, the live virus in the Russian vaccines was often too strong so that many children contracted polio from the inoculation. Through the medical officer, Sheila made sure she used only UNICEF vaccines.

Even more widespread, measles left devastating results in thousands of children. Malnourished children have immune systems which don't function well so they come down with pneumonia or other life-threatening diseases. Only recently have researchers discovered that the blindness connected to measles can be averted with heavy doses of vitamin A. Without it, a child's cornea can be permanently damaged within twelve hours of the onset of the disease and nothing can be done to alleviate the condition. Sheila was able to save the sight of many children through this simple procedure.

When she was ready to start her primary health care clinics out in the villages, word of mouth had already prepared the people to come. Once again, Sheila gathered a small team together - two nurses, and one elderly woman who had credibility and was respected by the village women. They travelled as far as thirty-five miles out from Kalukembe twice a week. Sometimes, it took them an hour to drive ten miles as they negotiated rough roads ever on the watch for mines or an ambush.

Alfonso, who was later appointed by the church as a missionary to another tribe, was also on the health team. He and Sheila became good friends as they worked together. Several years later, Alfonso was at Kalukembe for the Christmas holidays. He had promised his wife he would be back in the village where he was working for New Year's Day. Two young Brazilian missionaries who were visiting Kalukembe needed to get back to Luanda for their return flight to Brazil. Alfonso agreed to give the two women a ride, crowding them into the van with others from the station. A few miles out of the mission, guerrillas attacked the overcrowded church van. Everyone dashed for cover but a bullet struck Alfonso in the leg and he lay writhing on the road. Seeing that he was still alive, the Brazilian girls ran over to help drag him out of sight but, in that moment, the attackers surrounded them. They grabbed and bound the girls, one of whom had been wounded in the initial cross fire, and force marched them into the bush. Before they left, one of the guerrillas turned and fired point blank at Alfonso's head, leaving him dead on the road. Months later, news reached Kalukembe that the two women had been marched over a thousand miles across Angola before they were released.

In the late 70's, it was still relatively quiet around Kalukembe and Sheila and her team increased the number of health clinics to eight. Sheila and her Dad had many long discussions about the benefits of primary health care. Bob felt very strongly that primary health care had been overrated. An international World Health Organization Congress had declared that the answer to the world's medical needs could be met by the year 2,000 if the concepts of primary health care were promulgated. All that would be needed was clean water, contraception, basic education for child care and simple medical training for local health workers. Bob was quick to point out to Sheila that after ten years, the WHO had very little progress to show for the plan. In fact, population growth in Africa continued at more than three per cent. Africans had often told Bob that family planning was just a ploy of the whites so they could keep control of the country and in Angola, where one- third to half of children die before the age of five years, Africans feel they must continue to produce children or "We won't have any family to take care of us in our old age." In reality, Bob and Sheila did not differ on basic philosophy. They both agreed that it was not an "either - or" situation, and that both preventive and curative medicine were desperately needed here in Angola and across Africa.

Sheila enjoyed working with her father in the hospital. He was always available for advice if she had a particularly difficult case to treat. She recalls one set of tiny twins who had come down with pneumonia, an infant killer. In an American hospital, she would have had respirators, vaporizers, and instruments to clear the mucus out of the tiny lungs but, in this case, they had to improvise. Bob showed her how to tap the little chest with a cupped hand to loosen the mucus and then suction it out manually. He suggested putting the infants into the sterilizing room which was always hot and humid. Once again God intervened, and the little ones survived.

Not all of Sheila's little patients responded. One baby boy came in with the ever-common diarrhea and dehydration. She prescribed the usual treatment but, after a few days, her assistant Maria expressed concern that the child was not improving. All tests were normal - there was no fever, no infection and the child was drinking fluids. Sheila planned to be away for the weekend so she instructed Maria to keep a very close eye on him. In spite of every possible treatment, however, on Saturday morning the child died. When Sheila spoke with the mother, she broke down and confessed there had been great conflict between her and her husband about bringing the child to the hospital. Her non-Christian husband told her, "If you go to Kalukembe for treatment, I will put a spell on him and he will die."

Sheila believes that if the mother had told someone at the hospital about this before the child died, they could have prayed against the curse and saved his life but the mother was afraid that her husband would kill her as well, so she said nothing.

Bob was very cautious about attributing illness to a curse or evil spirit. He tended to look for the medical cause first. One of his patients went into a coma soon after coming into the hospital. When Bob first examined her, she told him she was going to die. He found no reason for her coma; still, she just faded away as he stood helplessly by. Later, he learned that a witchdoctor had put a curse on her. One or two of the pastors at Kalukembe had the gift of exorcism and regularly exorcised evil spirits. Bob admits that they might have gotten out of hand "to the point of finding evil spirits in anybody and everybody." But the Africans have seen so many uncanny and inexplicable things happen that they are very aware of the activities of the spirit world. Throughout his medical career in Africa, Bob had to convince his patients that surgery and medicines which cure are not manifestations of the spirits.

Late in 1979, Bob visited Cavango. He and Steve had been there only once before since the hospital had been destroyed. They walked around the ruins; only one wall of the church remained. Everything else had been leveled to the ground. At the river, the waterwheel rusted in its moorings like a giant relic of a past civilization. Some of the leprosy patients had returned to live near the mission. Bob heard how Sr. Israel had been forced by the Cubans to give up the keys to the missionaries' houses, and then he had fled into the bush with his family. No one had heard from him since.

Protected by a military convoy, Bob returned this time without Steve, not wanting to risk both of them to attack at the same time. He went with the express purpose of treating the leprosy patients. One of the tragedies of disrupting treatment is that the leprosy again becomes active and infectious, turning the clock back years in the eradication of the disease. Sixty patients and their families welcomed him.

His heart was deeply moved as he heard how Christians continued to meet together. At Catota, which had also been burned to the ground, the pastor had been imprisoned for more than three-and-a-half years. Everything had been destroyed so that Christians had no Bibles - not even a scrap of paper to write on. In the Cavango area, a group of Christians living in the bush had met together for worship out in the open. One night a gang of soldiers found them sitting around a fire, singing and praying. The communist soldiers told them they were meeting illegally and ordered them to throw their Bibles and hymn books into the fire. To refuse meant death so, reluctantly they tossed their precious books into the blaze. Within moments a thunder storm blew up, not uncommon here on the high plateau. A bolt of lightening split the sky. It struck the captain of the troop, killing him instantly. As the Africans told Bob the story, they shook their heads in wonder at God's retribution.

Wherever Bob went those days, the cry was the same, "Teach us, tell us about the Word of God, train us!" The more the people suffered hardship and privation from the war that tore the very heart out of the country, the hungrier the people were for spiritual sustenance.

Nor did the medical work let up. Between January and August of 1979, Bob and Steve performed more than fourteen hundred operations and three babies a day were born at the hospital. Bob was grateful for the fine African nurses and support staff that kept the huge operation rolling smoothly under these difficult circumstances.

Early in 1980, a new assistant administrator, Ezekiel Fabiano, joined the hospital staff. He seemed to be doing a good job but Bob hardly had time to notice him for he faced another major decision. The chairman of the international board of AEF had written asking him if he would be willing to let his name stand for election for International Director. The mission had made the same request in 1977 when Bob and Belva had felt very strongly that their place was in Angola. Now, the request came again and Bob found no easy answer this time, either.

However, while he struggled with this major decision, Sheila began to make friends with Ezekiel. He lived in a small room behind the Brechet's house and whenever she walked from her house up to Steve and Peggy's or to see her folks, she walked past his place. Often Ezekiel sat out on the steps enjoying the cool evening and Sheila stopped to chat. Ezekiel spoke no English but that was no problem to Sheila who was fluent in Portuguese as well as his native Mbundu. They began to take long walks in the evening, not intentionally hiding their growing friendship, but perhaps subconsciously realizing tongues would wag, especially in an ingrown community like a mission station.

Sheila admired Ezekiel's practical commitment to Jesus Christ. She had become very discouraged with the shallowness of the men she'd dated in America and met no one there who was willing to serve in Africa as she was. Here was an African Christian man who loved God's Word and wanted to serve Christ at any cost. Then one night, he told her that he loved her and wanted to marry her. It would be just as much a shock to his traditional Mbundu family as it would be to hers, but he was willing to try to convince both of them of the wisdom of their choice.

His proposal came as a surprise to Sheila, too. She wrote a letter to Sharon, asking her advice. She gave the letter to Belva to mail. Sometimes if Belva was also writing to Sharon, she mailed the letters together to save postage. On this day as Belva sat down to write Sharon, she skimmed Sheila's letter to avoid duplicating news. She was shocked by what she read. She'd had no idea of the growing relationship between Ezekiel and Sheila.

When she told Bob, he became very angry. Who did this fellow think he was? He'd seen so many Africans looking for ways to get to the United States that he suspected Ezekiel's motives. After a lengthy discussion and praying together, Bob and Belva decided they would not tell Sheila they knew about the relationship. Bob would ask the Pastor of the church to talk to Ezekiel and tell him in no uncertain terms to "lay off the doctor's daughter".

When the pastor spoke with him, Ezekiel intimated they were "just friends" and, indeed, Sheila and Ezekiel were having second thoughts - would such a cross-cultural marriage work? Would their parents ever accept the union? Sharon had responded that she and Rob saw no serious problems but encouraged Sheila to give the relationship plenty of time, not to make any decisions until after her furlough in 1981.

Meanwhile, as Bob and Belva continued to pray about the mission's invitation, Belva felt a deep peace that Bob should allow his name to stand for International Director. Bob struggled in prayer many hours, having no peace to refuse and not wanting to accept.

One of the major problems was that with Dr. Brechet retired, there was no senior missionary to serve as hospital superintendent. Most of the missionaries and church leaders felt that would be a disaster especially in the unsettled conditions in the country.

One morning as Bob was having his devotions, it seemed as though God clearly spoke to him. "Bob, do you know why you're not willing to do this?" Bob admitted that he didn't know. The Lord seemed to speak again, "Bob, you think more of medicine than you do of Me."

Bob realized that this was the same struggle he had faced before accepting the job in the American office years ago - except this time if he left medicine, it would probably be for good. Yet his response was immediate, "No Lord, that's not right. You're first."

"And when I said that," he recalls, "I knew I had to say, 'Yes'. From that moment on, I never had any doubt in my mind that's what God wanted me to do. I had the assurance that I should let my name stand and that if God was in it, it would work out."

Chapter 19

Go Forward

"We leave a rewarding ministry we love, and where we are loved, for a difficult position no one wants and whose job description no one can humanly fulfill. The verse of Scripture God gave me at the time says, 'Cast your burden on the Lord, and He will sustain you. He shall never permit the righteous to be moved' (Psalm 55:22). The word in Hebrew that's translated burden could be translated 'what He has given you' - 'Cast what He has given you on the Lord.' In other places, the word has been translated as a gift. As I thought about what a responsibility the Lord has given, it is a tremendous privilege to receive this as a gift from the Lord.

"When the Lord gives us a burden, He never promises to remove it. But He promises to sustain us in it. Ever

*since the Lord gave me these verses, I've had a light
heart about accepting the responsibility."*

--- Dr. Robert Foster

****

When Bob accepted the position of International Director, he
knew the mission was in danger of flying apart. The Africa Evan-
gelical Mission had been founded in 1889 in Capetown as the
Cape General Mission under the inspirational leadership of
Andrew Murray. The mission's motto became, "God First - Go
Forward" as it reached north into the Rhodesias (now Zambia and
Zimbabwe), Angola, Swaziland, Portuguese East Africa (Mozam-
bique), Nyasaland (now Malawi) and later into Botswana, South
West Africa (now Namibia), Gabon, Mauritius and Reunion.

At the same time, councils developed in the United States,
Canada, Great Britain and Australia to recruit and send out
workers to these fields. Missionaries not only learned how to
adapt to the culture of the people whom they served, but had to
adapt cross-culturally to their colleagues. On the whole, the nearly three hundred AEF missionaries worked together well in spite
of differences in support scale, methods, church government, and
a variety of denominational positions within the basic evangelical
framework.   But over the years, the councils became more
polarized in some of their positions and Bob realized that some
council members feared the power of the American influence
which was often perceived as arrogant and self-confident.

Admittedly, the Americans sometimes resented the fact that,
though they provided by far the most money and missionaries on
the fields, in the International Council their vote carried no more
weight than that of the smallest council. One answer to this
dilemma had been to place the international headquarters in Great
Britain, geographically more central to Africa and the other councils. It was also felt to be politically somewhat more neutral than
the United States, especially when dealing with Marxist countries
like Angola.

Bob spent a whirlwind ten days in and out of Britain in
August, 1980, visiting all the councils, looking at houses near the
AEF office in Reading and buying supplies unavailable in Angola

for the staff at Kalukembe. The Warburtons met Bob at the plane. Mike was serving as Acting International Director.

Frances remembers, "In ten days, he bought a house, a bed, an electric blanket and shopped for the whole family in Angola. He flew to the States, to Canada, to Australia, to Switzerland. When we went to pick up the ticket, the agent said he had never issued a ticket for anybody going to Australia and back almost in the turn of the plane."

Bob made this grueling flight to establish rapport with each council and to deflate the notion that he was going to "come in and turn the mission upside down," as Mike described their fears. Bob had been in this position several times before! Eight years later, Bob would testify, "I think that if God has done anything through me, it's been to draw our councils together and give a sense of direction to AEF so that there's a more unified goal and approach to our work."

But on that first morning in Britain in January, 1981, when the family gathered for devotions around the breakfast table, there was still that sense of uncertainty as to how God would use them in this new capacity. What a comfort to read, "Not one of all the good promises of the Lord failed; all came to pass" (Joshua 21:45 and 23:14). Their hearts were still tender after leaving friends and family in Angola and the thousands of Christians still suffering in the "furnace of affliction". Bob was particularly concerned that there was no one to take his place in the leadership of the church; it would be two years before another missionary couple replaced them.

Belva was still hobbling around recuperating from a broken ankle. Bob threw himself into helping her settle into the little house in Tilehurst, purchasing furniture and equipment. What a culture shock to see the stores piled high with goods after the empty shelves in Angola. Bob complained, "The dollar seems to buy about half what it does in the States."

Before the month was out, Bob would begin a routine that continued relentlessly through his eight years in office. He flew to Portugal to confer with AEF missionaries studying the language, and to meet with Steve and Peggy on their way back to Angola. Then barely back from there, he left for a conference in Zambia, going on to visit Botswana, Zimbabwe and South Africa. In the remaining months of 1981, Bob was in the USA three times for speaking engagements, meeting with councils and dealing with family matters. Mother Foster broke her hip and the senior Fosters had to be moved into a retirement home. Stuart graduated from Harvard and was married two days later.

In August, Bob flew back to Africa for his first crucial International Council meetings, then on to Brazil to develop contacts with Brazilian missionaries who could serve with AEF. While Bob rejoiced in what he saw on the fields, he was concerned that such a large percentage of the missionaries were involved in institutionalized, status quo ministries; that on some fields, South Africa in particular, the number of churches had remained virtually static; that Bible schools faced chronic shortages of staff and finances while the churches everywhere suffered from lack of trained leadership. As he reviewed the history of the mission, he realized that most of the expansion into new fields and unreached people had taken place before the forties! While pioneer visionaries had moved into new areas such as Mauritius and Southwest Africa, such expansion had not received the major focus and thrust of the mission. The majority of the missionaries were involved in what might be called service ministries. Half of AEF's motto - "Go Forward" - was stuck in quicksand.

Never to be discouraged, Bob probed church leaders and missionaries about the possibilities of new areas of service and pockets of unreached people. In his report to the field directors he wrote, "Look at what I've found!" He sensed a stirring for greater outreach as those he talked to shared their vision and needs for personnel; in Zambia for the Balozi and the Ba Bemba people, in South Africa for the Muslims in Durban, in Botswana for the Bushman and the Ba Kalanga, in Namibia for the Mbukushu.

Expanding current ministries wasn't enough for Bob. He'd done a lot of thinking about the direction he'd like the mission to go in order to "Go Forward" and, to him, that meant new countries and unreached people.

One day, Bob learned that a young Mozambican had attended London Bible College and was now back home. Bob wrote to ask him if it would be possible to visit the Christians in Mozambique. The young man wrote back saying that the government's position was changing and that Bob should apply for a visa. Mozambique's history paralleled Angola's - both countries had been Portuguese colonies, both had been given independence in 1975, both had Marxist governments and both were suffering from bloody, debilitating civil war.

In the 1950's, AEF missionary, Gordon Legg, had seen a growing church develop at Mihecani in northern Mozambique (then called Portuguese East Africa) in spite of the harassment of the Roman Catholic authorities. Then in 1959, while the Leggs were on furlough, a terrible incident gave the hostile colonialists an excuse to close the mission down. No one can really explain the circumstances but one of the church leaders claimed God had given him supernatural powers to raise people from the dead. Carried away in a frenzy, he threw a child into the fire to prove his claim. When the authorities investigated the child's death, they closed the station, boarding up the windows and doors of the church to keep people from meeting. The AEF missionaries were expelled.

In the early 70's, Gordon Legg was able to return once to visit the believers in Mozambique. They told him that the government had not allowed more than five people to meet together at a time. They had met in homes until the colonial government once again permitted them to build a church. They proudly showed him their new building, rebuilt with bricks from the demolished church; the motorbikes they'd purchased for their pastors; the benches and other furnishings they'd made with their own hands; the power plant they'd acquired.

When the Marxists took over in 1975, they were far more ruthless than the Angolan government. They closed churches and schools, banned missionaries and imprisoned pastors. Everything the Mihecani believers had was confiscated. Once again, the church was forced underground and contact with other Christians was totally cut off. Now, Bob's correspondent told him, the government's attitude had softened. There was a greater desire for acceptance in the international community and a desperate need for relief and assistance for the shattered economy. Caught in a guerrilla war and suffering the effects of drought and famine, Mozambique had become almost uninhabitable. The Population Crisis Committee says Mozambicans endure the world's highest level of human suffering.

The government needed help and it knew Christians would be more likely to give it than anyone else. One provincial governor would say later, "If it weren't for the church, the country wouldn't exist today."

Visa in hand, Bob traveled to Mozambique to contact the Christians and to find out if the time had come for AEF to reenter the country. Signs were encouraging; he learned that "parent organizations" could send a representative once a year "for the purpose of encouragement, instruction and edification of local churches."

He came back to Britain with a shopping list for the Mozambican Christians: 10,000 hymn books which would be sold and the funds used to rebuild churches; yearly pastoral visits to train church leaders; a qualified Bible translator; financial assistance for formal training for church leaders either within or outside of Mozambique; doctors and other professionals to go as tentmakers. It was a simple step of faith for Bob to promise the 10,000 hymn books and a joyous step of fulfillment for Gordon Legg to agree to go back for six weeks of Bible teaching.

Bob had barely returned from Mozambique when he left for Brazil. While there, he received a call that Sharon's husband, Rob, was seriously ill. Bob was able to stop in Jamaica on his way home just when they learned the fearful diagnosis of inoperable cancer.

"It meant so much to Rob that Dad would come to see us," Sharon recalls. "Rob saw that tender side of Dad that he'd not seen before. I think he always thought of Dad as being very disciplined, able to cope in almost any situation."

In the next few months, the family rallied to Sharon and Rob's side. Belva spent some time with Sharon, taking turns at Rob's bedside during long days at the hospital. In February, Bob was again in North America and spent a few days with Sharon and Rob who was home from the hospital but extremely weak and in a great deal of pain. Knowing that Sheila was in Nairobi at a medical conference where she could be reached by phone, he put a call through to her suggesting that Sharon needed her and that if she wanted to see Rob again, she should come immediately.

After Rob died, Sharon and the two children moved to England to live with Bob and Belva for several years. Sharon still marvels at their warmhearted love.

"Mom and Dad had had kids at home for thirty-three years. Shelley and Stirling had just left for college. I suppose they could have felt, 'Free at last!' It wasn't easy to adjust to little children again but they did it with so much acceptance."

Bob and Belva planned to return to Angola in July when they were in Africa for the first conference of leaders from all the AEF churches but somewhere in some government office their papers were lost and they never received their visa. Bob reapplied successfully and January, 1983 found them back in Angola feeling "as though we'd never left". The guerrilla warfare had intensified and travel was more dangerous than ever. So much food disappeared into the black market that an egg cost $5 and a scrawny chicken the equivalent of $100 yet the people seemed to take the hardships in stride; there was great eagerness to listen to the Word of God and many requests for more missionaries.

One morning while Bob was speaking to several hundred patients and staff at the Kalukembe hospital, gunfire broke out just outside. Everyone flew for cover while two groups of local militia fought it out. Once calm was restored, the audience returned and Bob continued to preach on his text, "My peace I give unto you."

It was a special time of fellowship for Steve and Peggy and the grandchildren, and for Sheila to have Bob and Belva there. Because of the dangers on the roads, they would not leave the station for months and few visitors risked coming to them. Food shortages meant a monotonous diet and Belva knew just what special treats to bring with her.

Though Bob seldom made reference to Sheila's relationship with Ezekiel, he made a point of asking Steve how it stood. Since the beginning of the year, Ezekiel had studied in Switzerland. Unbeknown to the family, he and Sheila had decided to give themselves a two-year separation to see if their love would withstand the test of time. They wrote to each other regularly, and became more and more sure of their love and the rightness of their marriage, if only their parents would agree; neither wanted to marry without parental blessing.

Ezekiel had already spoken with members of his extended family. His parents were evangelists in a remote area of Angola and he had not seen them for more than ten years because of the war. When Ezekiel asked his uncle, the traditional authority figure in the family, he told him to forget her, "We have another lady for you. You must see her." His brother also feared that Ezekiel would lose his culture by marrying a western woman; still, he did not adamantly oppose the marriage.

Ezekiel himself had times when he felt the alliance wasn't possible. "One reason was the culture," he recalls. "The second one was, she was from overseas. I had never visited her in the United States or Canada. I know Portuguese, Swiss and French but not enough English to know her culture."

Their friends and members in the church encouraged them. "It's not a matter of color or culture," said one. "If the Lord wants you to get married, then do it."

Sheila almost hated to bring up the touchy subject during the happy holiday visit but she knew the time had come to settle the matter with her parents. Steve and Peggy both knew that she and Ezekiel were writing regularly and, though they had their doubts about the wisdom of the relationship, Peggy especially, had been a great listener and comfort.

Her father's reaction couldn't have been worse. He bluntly told Sheila that he believed the isolation and her age were getting to her; if she transferred to someplace else, she would get over it. For the first time in her life Sheila became really angry with her father.

"What did you expect?" she asked. "You raised us in Central Africa. We've grown up here and these are our roots - these are the people we've come to love; for whom we've worked all our lives.   It would be natural to consider joining forces, wouldn't it?"

Steve understood where Sheila was coming from; that she was more comfortable with Ezekiel in terms of common goals than someone in North America who wanted to be successful and make money. He could also appreciate Bob's perspective.

"It was a sense of fatherly concern that his daughter might wake up and find out that confronting the realities of the stresses and strains of a black-white, Angolan-North American marriage was a more bitter pill than she thought. He was also concerned about who was going to carry the burden financially."

While Bob seemed not to listen, Sheila felt she had gained an ally in her mother.

"Mom was more ready to listen," Sheila remembers, "but to Dad it was a closed book."

Four months later, Sheila found herself in Britain. A tenacious bout of hepatitis weakened her to the point that Stephen sent her away for rest and recuperation and the necessary diet unavailable in Angola.

While Bob was away for meetings in the United States that June, he stopped to see his parents. They had weakened visibly and it was evident to him that his mother's heart would give out soon. Only a year earlier, the two intrepid warriors had made one last trip to Zambia alone. At 88 and 89, they must have known this was to be their final farewell. Now, grateful that God had so dictated his schedule that he could be with her, Bob watched his mother slip quietly into the Heavenly Port.

Though the family sensed their loss, Mother Foster's homegoing just heightened their anticipation of a family reunion that July - as maintaining family ties became even more important. For the first time in seven years, all seven children and their families would be together, spending a few days at a missionary guest house in Wales. Stephen and family were on their way to Canada for a much needed furlough; Sharon and Sheila were already in England and Stirling and Shelley had come home for the summer holidays. Stacey, who was separated from his wife, planned to take time off from his job. Stuart and Sindia would be joining Bob on his next trip to Mozambique where they were considering serving as missionaries.

When Sheila first asked Bob if she could invite Ezekiel over from Switzerland for the reunion, he adamantly refused.

"I spent a lot of time crying and praying," Sheila recalls. "By this time, I was sure we should be married. Ezekiel had been in Switzerland for almost two years and our relationship had maintained itself."

The day before Sheila left for a two-week visit in Switzerland, Bob wrote a letter to Ezekiel inviting him to the family reunion.

"Mom persuaded him. That's one time Mom changed his mind," Sheila concludes. Belva encouraged Bob to give Ezekiel a chance and get to know him personally.

The family reunion was a warm and exciting time for everyone except Sheila and Ezekiel. Sharing kitchen duties and memories, debating issues, telling jokes; the week went all too fast. Shelley remembers her brothers as being very self-confident and that they often debated an issue while Bob sat listening. The family included Ezekiel, trying to make him feel comfortable and seemed genuinely to like him. Since all except Sharon spoke Portuguese, there was no language barrier and they all began to recognize his abilities and spiritual insights.

Until the marriage issue was settled, however, neither Ezekiel or Sheila could enjoy the week. Ezekiel decided to confront Bob early in the week, asking him once more for permission to marry Sheila. As Ezekiel presented his case, Sheila could see Bob wasn't listening. Once again, he refused to give his permission, reminding them again of the cultural and educational gap, the dangers of settling in Angola, and questioning whether Ezekiel could provide for her.

Each evening, the family gathered in the huge living room to share their dreams and problems with each other and one of the boys would lead in devotions before they all prayed. On the last evening, Bob led the devotions, reading from I Samuel where God gives Solomon the opportunity to ask for anything he wants. Solomon did not ask for riches or power, but for wisdom. Bob looked around at his family. He told them that as he'd been reading this passage in his devotions that day, God used it to speak to him about each one in the family.

As Solomon had done, the most important thing was that each of them should ask for wisdom to do the ministry to which he'd been called and not to worry about financial security, physical security or protection from danger.

"I looked at Ezekiel," Sheila remembers. "Those were the exact arguments Dad had used as to why I shouldn't marry Ezekiel!"

Then Bob looked directly at her and Ezekiel as he shared how God had spoken from this passage to show him that he should give his blessing on their marriage. There wasn't a dry eye in the room as each one hugged Sheila and Ezekiel, assuring them of their prayers and love, welcoming Ezekiel into the family as a son and brother. As Bob hugged Sheila she wept with joy, not only for the blessing on the future, but that the barrier between them was broken. They had always been so close and Sheila knew it was not pride or prejudice but his love for her which had made the decision so difficult.

A year later, Bob and Belva attended Sheila's wedding at Kalukembe, a wedding put on by the groom's family in the traditional manner, as well as a beautiful western-style ceremony in the Kalukembe chapel. More than a thousand Africans attended the wedding feast - entirely provided by Ezekiel's extended family.

"We didn't go so far as to make Sheila get up and cook breakfast for all the guests on the day of the wedding as is customary among the Mbundu," Ezekiel says with a twinkle in his eye. "Nor did she have to go out and prove her worth working in the field the next day!"

When Bob and Belva saw the love lavished upon their daughter and the total acceptance the family gave her, the last vestige of concern disappeared. Sheila was in good hands and they knew they would care for her as their own.

Acceptance and bonding between missionaries and nationals became a major issue in the mission's policies. No doubt his experiences in Angola, and perhaps what he'd learned watching Sheila adapt, helped Bob to articulate this need to new candidates. He challenged aspiring missionaries at the candidate school:

"I believe the first priority is to earn or gain acceptance with the people you've come to serve. No missionary is automatically accepted, no matter how highly trained or experienced he may be. This is often hard to take for a new missionary who has been on the pedestal for months at home and suddenly drops to the bottom of the totem pole. Gaining acceptance comes from meeting, mixing with and getting to know the people, thus sharing yourself and life's experiences with them."

As a result of Bob's encouragement, the mission recommended that all fields implement a program of "bonding" by placing a new missionary into an African home for a period of time immediately upon their arrival on the field.

Bob also saw the need for working closely with the church. He challenged candidates:

"There is no place in the work today for running your own 'show'. God has given His church, in each country, spiritual men who, though not necessarily highly educated, are faithful, godly men whom God has raised up. It is to be deemed a privilege to work with such men and learn from them. They will welcome new ideas when you have gained their confidence and you will enjoy rich and fruitful ministry as you work together."

It was proof of this very concept that Bob saw when he returned to Mozambique in 1983 to teach church leaders. Here was a beleaguered and persecuted church, without training of any kind for over twenty years, yet the Spirit of God had used the godly wisdom and earnest prayers of its leaders to cause the church to mushroom. Over four hundred and fifty congregations now met together. The three thousand believers at Mihecani had grown to over a hundred thousand! What a deep joy to fellowship with these believers! Bob hardly noticed that many were dressed in woven plastic sacks and bark rope - no cloth had been available for years.

Their plea was not for cloth, however, but for New Testaments and hymn books. They told him how they shared their few Bibles around the growing congregations. They tore one New Testament up into books and left one with each group in the hands of someone who could read. When they'd finished reading that book, they passed it on, until each church had the opportunity to read the whole New Testament. Bob could hardly hold back the tears as he listened to this story.

"The eagerness and hunger for the Word surpassed anything I'd ever seen," he commented. When he asked them how the AEF could help them, they told him they would like at least five missionary couples. One pastor said to him, "We don't need missionaries to evangelize. That is a job we can do. We need help in training elders, pastors, and evangelists."

When Bob recruited for Mozambique, he always made it clear that the Mozambican church was looking for "church workers" not missionaries. Within five years, AEF had nine missionaries in Mozambique.

They started a seminary and planned an agricultural and medical program to alleviate some of the suffering. Tons of relief supplies have been sent to the church. The missionaries have suffered along with the people.

One night, a band of armed men surrounded Stuart and Sindia's home, trying to break the door down so they could get to the container of supplies that Stuart had received that day. Most of the goods were for the church but some were essential food items for the family which were absolutely unobtainable in the country. Nightwatchmen at a warehouse down the street heard the commotion and shot their rifles into the air, frightening the bandits away. When someone asked Bob how he honestly felt seeing his own child in a situation like that, his unhesitating response was, "I'm grateful." He has every confidence that a child of God can be in no safer place than where he is obediently serving God.

Wherever Bob travelled, he kept his ear open for opportunities in new fields. While in Reunion speaking at a Bible school, several Malagasy students came up to him, urging him to visit their island nation. Madagascar, the fourth largest island in the world with thirteen million people had been a French colony but since independence, the government had maintained a very isolationist posture. Though forty per cent of the island's inhabitants claim to be Christians, most combine the traditional worship of the dead with a ritualistic, untaught form of Christianity. Bob learned that one of their horrible practices is to exhume the bodies of their dead relatives, re-wrap them in colorful fine silk and parade them joyfully through the streets. Before the parade the body is brought into the church for prayer and blessing.

The young men who contacted Bob were from the G.B.T. (Workers Christian Union), an evangelical body which has groups all over the island. The two were the only Bible-trained people in the organization and they urged Bob to send teachers to help them. Bob promised that he would carefully consider visiting the island to see the situation for himself.

A short time later, Bob received a letter from a French-speaking pastor in Gabon saying that AEF had been recommended as a mission that might help their church. Would someone please come and visit them in order to discuss their situation? Bob had never had any contacts in Gabon but an inner urging told him this might be another opportunity to reach out. It seemed God was answering his cry to help AEF "Go Forward".

The hot climate and healthy economy of this oil-producing nation were a stark contrast to Angola and Mozambique. The leaders of the tiny evangelical church had two requests. One was for missionaries to train their leaders and the second was for help to begin a work among two unreached people groups in Gabon; the Ikota and the Seke. Pastor Sima travelled with Bob to see the Ikotas who had never heard the Gospel.

On the journey, Bob asked the pastor how he happened to get in touch with AEF. The pastor said he didn't know of any mission agencies so he went to the British Embassy and asked if they knew of any organization that might be interested in helping their church. The Ambassador said that he didn't know, he wasn't much of a churchman except for Easter and Christmas, but that he would write the Foreign Office in London. A few weeks later, Pastor Sima received a short list of British missionary societies and he wrote to the first two names which appeared on the alphabetical list. The other organization wrote to say they didn't send missionaries but would pray that God would provide the help they needed. Bob had replied that AEF was very interested in missionary outreach!

It seemed like a God-given match and Bob was eager to present this new opportunity to the councils. Bob knew that some of the missionaries in the older fields were feeling neglected that he was recruiting for new fields while they struggled understaffed. Some council members believed he was stretching the organization too thin. The number of career missionaries had remained relatively stable over the years, yet Bob was convinced that the mission mandate to "Go Forward" had stagnated too long. In his heart, he longed to see AEF "in every country south of the equator in Africa."

In 1984, Bob and Personnel Director Keith Donald initiated a recruiting campaign of "100 more in '84." There was real concern that the number of retiring missionaries would outnumber new recruits. Though short-termers gave valuable service, Bob believed that only career missionaries could produce long-term results.

As Bob spoke tirelessly to churches of the opportunities in Mozambique, Gabon, Madagascar and other AEF fields, he challenged them, "I don't think for a moment that God gave us this task and won't enable us to do it."

Dr. David Krentel of the Wheaton Bible Church described Bob as "forthright," "pulling no punches" as he presented the challenge of missions to them. Bob told of one North American church that raised $5 million on one Sunday for a covered parking lot. A month later, the total offering for a special missions Sunday was $200,000 - only a fraction of what they had given for a parking lot!

His voice almost breaking, Bob testified, "I don't think any enterprise in the world pays more eternal dividends than what you invest in missions. The Lord says, 'Be generous today; you may not have the opportunity to be generous tomorrow.' We're never, ever impoverished by liberality. Accumulation eliminates faith. We don't need God if we've got a big bank account! We're complacent if we don't have to depend on Him for our daily bread."

His zeal for the expanding work of God, and his faith that God would provide all that is needed according to His promises, was infectious. But the lack of sufficient candidates to keep up with the exciting opportunities, continued to weigh heavily on Bob's heart. That did not keep him from looking for new fields and unreached tribes, stretching the mission's vision into new areas all across southern Africa.

In November, 1985, Bob and Belva spoke in meetings in Vancouver, British Columbia. The demands of deputation; staying in people's homes, talking with strangers and answering countless questions were lightened by having Belva with him and he encouraged her to travel with him in North America whenever possible. He had come to depend upon her as an oasis of peace and strength in the accelerating demands and pressures upon him. Fortunately the gifts of churches and supporting friends covered these expenses so that this was never a burden upon the mission.

When Belva was asked to give her testimony that Sunday morning, she spoke on how much she'd learned about being able to say, "Thy will be done."

"I hadn't found it nearly so difficult in the early years when we went out to the field in the first place," she testified. "But as life has gone on, it's become more and more difficult. When it comes to the lives of your children, to say, 'Thy will be done' and to mean it, is not easy at all."

Driving to the airport that afternoon, the snow-capped mountains emerged out of the clouds in breathtaking beauty. Belva found herself thinking about her testimony that morning and something seemed to say to her, "God is going to test you on what you said this morning."

Two weeks later back in England, Bob told her that he had found a lump below his ear while shaving and that he was going to have it checked out when he went to the States for a board meeting later in the month.

"What can it be?" Belva asked, knowing that his diagnostic skills would already have narrowed down the possibilities. Bob assured her that it could just be a cyst or possibly Hodgkin's Disease. Belva knew that there was a reasonable rate of recovery from Hodgkin's and took her cue from Bob that it was nothing serious. Indeed, tests gave no indication of malignancy and the doctors at the Indianapolis Hospital presumed they were going to operate on a benign tumor that Tuesday afternoon.

Bob remained groggy from the surgery all evening and without family members at his bedside, he remained pretty much alone except for nurses coming in to check on him. He thought it somewhat strange that none of the doctors came to see him but he drifted off to sleep, still wondering what they'd found.

About 6:30 in the morning, a Christian medical friend who worked at the hospital came by to see him.

"It was malignant Bob - a nodular lymphoma of the parotid gland."

How many times had he given such a diagnosis to a patient he'd operated on? How many times had he uttered comforting words of courage and faith. How often had he seen that stark, unbelieving look in his patient's eyes?

Only now, alone in his hospital room without family or friends around, did Bob know what it really felt like to be told he had cancer.

Chapter 20

Sharpened Urgency

"The Lord has encouraged me through the word of the Apostle Paul in Philippians 1:13. Sitting chained in that dark Roman prison, Paul could triumphantly say, 'My chains are in Christ.' As I pondered those words, the Lord helped me to see that my chains, all those limiting circumstances that would tie me down, come from the hand of my heavenly Father, who in love sends what is best for me, and not only for me, but also for my family and the whole mission.

"This reminder of the goodness and faithfulness of God and the positive joy with which Paul accepted his circumstances have been an encouragement to Belva and me at this time in our lives. We don't know what

lies ahead...but we do know that whatever happens will be wrapped in His love."

---Dr. Robert Foster

****

Two days after his surgery, Bob flew home to Britain to recuperate and to have further tests and treatment at a leading cancer clinic in London. He felt he was in the best of hands.

After several days of testing, the specialists revealed there were microscopic lymphoma cells in his bone marrow. But they were confident that his body's own immune system could handle them for some time to come, and recommended that he receive no chemotherapy for the present.

"Go home and live a normal life," they advised. "Do whatever you have strength for as long as you are able."

As Bob regained his strength and regular tests continued to reveal no cancer cells in the blood, he resumed his hectic schedule, fulfilling speaking commitments around the world as well as seeking out new areas of service.

But Steve noted, "I think that he has a sharpened sense of urgency; the sense that the sands of time are running through the timer. Dad seems to reflect a more prophetic voice, a greater interest in the Old Testament Scriptures with regard to prophecy and with regard to calling men into consideration of their God. I think that perspective comes out of the situation in southern Africa which has been sharpened by war, and also Dad's personal sense that he may be moving off the scene physically and wants to leave a voice that will ring on."

When Bob spoke at the Wheaton Bible Church missions conference, his challenge to them from the book of Zechariah had a prophetic ring as he urged the people to see God's perspective of the world.

He drew a parallel between the man with a measuring tape trying to measure around Jerusalem in Zechariah 2, with the limited vision most people have, trying to quantify the task. "God wants us to see that the task is much bigger than anything we can imagine. We're so limited to the money, materials and men available," he remonstrated. "God wants to do more through us than we believe He can."

He likened the "wall of fire encompassing his people" (v. 5) to God's ability to protect those who serve in obedience to Him. He told them of the many times God had protected the missionaries from terrorists in Angola. "The center of God's will is the safest place in the world."

Just like the thousands of Jews in Babylon who didn't want to move back to Jerusalem to get involved in the task of rebuilding the city, so are many Christians. Bob warned, "A lot of us are very comfortable, content, happy to be saved, to take life easy - not to be concerned about the part God wants us to have."

At one point in the conference, Bob challenged people who were willing to be involved in preparation for full-time service to come forward. Both the pastor and his wife joined many of the parishioners in the counseling room.

The zeal for new recruits was matched only by his desire to expand AEF's ministry to the unreached. Mike Warburton, his associate in the international office voiced his concern. "Bob has a tremendous drive right now. I believe that he's pushing himself harder that he should physically because he's got some goals which he wants to fulfill before the Lord takes him to his reward."

One day when Mike and Bob were riding together in a car, Bob began talking about his cancer, and the uncertainty of the future. "He was really concerned," Mike recalls, "that the Lord would give him the three years he had left to complete the current term (as International Director), and to be sure that Belva was established and looked after should the Lord take him."

And each time Bob returned for tests to the cancer clinic in London, he received the good news that though the cancer cells were still present in the bone marrow, his condition was stable. Belva says they all laughed when one report came back saying it was "static". "If there's a word that doesn't describe Bob, that's it."

Indeed, the difficult travel schedule to the fields seemed to increase rather than decrease. Opening new fields involved arrangements with government officials, meeting with local church leaders, introducing missionaries, working out problems of adjustments - and Bob would not spare himself, if he thought his presence would smooth the way or if he had opportunity to preach.

In 1985, the mission sent its first missionaries to Mozambique. The Hardys were soon to be followed by the Morgans and the Stuart Fosters, and later by Stirling Foster.

Work among the Mbukushu and the Damaras tribes in Namibia opened that same year. Missionaries began work among the Muslim Indians of Durban, South Africa, and the Bushman of Botswana.

The first AEF missionaries to the Bakota people arrived in Gabon in April 1986. In that same year, a missionary couple went to study language to reenter the long-resistant Huila tribe in Angola. A survey of needs and opportunities in Malagasy indicated AEF missionaries would be welcome there.

In 1987, the International Council of AEF approved Madagascar as a new field, and by the end of the year an associate worker arrived to run a farm to raise support for an orphanage and work among "garbage eaters." That same year, through Bob's repeated contacts, the first Brazilian missionaries associated with AEF arrived in Angola, with about ten other candidates preparing to serve in Portuguese-speaking areas.

Before the end of his second term in 1988, Bob had responded to invitations in Zaire to consider opening work among the Muslim, and in Guinea Bissau and Tanzania.

But he had not lost his love and concern for the work in Angola. Each time he revisited that war-torn country, he tried to find out more about the Christians in the Cavango area who had been so violently scattered in 1976.

He began hearing rumors from this one and that one that Sr. Israel had been seen in Namibia. Thousands of Angolan refugees had fled across the border, and the town of Runtu overflowed with Portuguese-speaking Africans.

On one of his trips to the border town where AEF was planning to open a Bible school for the refugees, one of the missionaries took him to the refugee area where someone had reported seeing Sr. Israel.

They drove up and down the dusty streets looking for the small store where Sr. Israel was said to be working. When Bob stepped into the shop, he stood looking for a moment at the man who'd been his close friend and colleague at Cavango, hardly recognizing him. An older Sr. Israel, with suffering etched in his eyes stood and stared for a moment, unbelief and joy flashing across his face as he recognized Bob.

The two men embraced, laughing and crying, both talking at once. It was more than five years since Bob had handed him the keys to the mission in the wake of the attacking Cubans. Neither had ever learned how the other had escaped.

Sr. Israel began telling his painful story. Once the Cuban soldiers had forced him to give them the keys to all the buildings, he knew he and his family were in danger. While the soldiers began their destructive break-ins, Israel furtively slipped back to his home and hastily gathered together what he and his family could carry into the bush.

Sadly, Sr. Israel recounted how he could do nothing for the deformed and seriously ill lepers who were left to the mercies of the Cubans. He and his wife and two children waited until he was sure the marauding soldiers were fully occupied before they escaped from the mission. For weeks, they walked through the bush. Sometimes they were able to find a place to stay for a few days with friendly villagers, but most of the time they kept off the beaten path, afraid they would be apprehended by soldiers of either side.

They lived out in the bush for several months until their ten-year-old son came down with a high fever. The family tried to get into a town where they could find medical care, but their son died before they could get help.

Half starving and weakened from exposure, they continued to head for the border and relative safety. Once in Runtu, the Namibian government offered refuge to thousands like him, but jobs were almost impossible to get so he was reduced to selling staples and beer.

Later, Bob was able to help them financially and encouraged him to start a little business cutting and selling wood. And when Runtu Bible School opened, the mission offered him a job as Business Administrator, once again using his years of experience to serve God.

But Sr. Israel could tell Bob little of the whereabouts of the rest of the Christians from Cavango. Bob had learned that the communist government had forcibly moved hundreds of Africans from their villages so they would not be able to offer food or shelter to the enemy. But no one knew where they had gone.

When Bob returned to Angola in 1987, he found the people reeling under the crushing tide of civil war as never before. Describing the suffering, he wrote, "The city streets of Luanda are littered with filth and garbage the like of which I have never seen before. Pigs, dogs and children scavenge in the streets, trying to find a morsel of food."

The worst cholera epidemic in Angola's history ravaged the capitol.

At the airport, people pushed and shoved and fought for space on the planes, the only means of transport left in the country. Bob was not able to go out to Kalukembe to see Peggy and the children because of heightened terrorist activity on the road. Peggy had not left the station for over two years because of the danger, and Steve was only able to get out for hospital business in a Red Cross military convoy. Just a year later on that same road, all of Sheila and Ezekiel's household goods and supplies were ambushed and stolen or burned.

While in Lubango, Bob heard rumors on the African grapevine that hundreds of Cavango people had been resettled just twenty miles outside the city. They had spoken to some of the Christians in town when they came in to buy supplies. At the first opportunity Bob and one of the missionaries drove out looking for the refugee camp.

They passed other villages along the way and Bob recognized they were in Huila area, the very tribe that AEF had been trying, for over 25 years, to evangelize with little success.

At last, they reached the settlement out on the dry barren-looking soil, so different from the "bread basket" around Cavango. Bob jumped out, and speaking in Nganguela, asked the first person he saw if there was anyone here from the Cavango area.

The man nodded and pointed down the street. The news began to spread like a brush fire in a wind storm as people came out of their homes. "Kahaya has come," the word travelled. Soon a crowd of laughing, smiling faces surrounded Bob. Hands reached out to grasp his, men embraced him, not ashamed of their tears.

Then the crowd parted to allow an elderly man through. Pastor Johan Gonzalves, one of the original team at the Cavango church, welcomed Bob with joy and led him to the crude church building. Sometime during the exuberant singing and confusion, Bob learned that about three hundred Cavango Christians had been moved to this camp. Many had lost family members in the attacks on the mission. Husbands and sons had disappeared into Savimbi's army, never to be heard from again. Several of the other Cavango pastors were dead.

When at last everyone had been gathered and Bob stood up to speak, his heart was overwhelmed as he remembered that morning more than eleven years ago when he last spoke to this congregation. He remembered how they had flourished under the teaching of the Word. Many of these glowing faces before him had come to know Christ through the early evangelistic outreach around Cavango. Some had travelled into the villages with the team to share with those who had never heard.

Many bore signs of pain and loss on their faces, yet he could sense an inner peace as they had matured through suffering. They listened expectantly as he began to speak, reminding them of the goodness of God in saving and preserving them.

He told them that for many years, AEF had tried to establish a work among the Huila people, but after all that time there were only a few Christians. He pointed out how God seemed to have used evil things to advance His work for He saved thousands around Cavango, and then He used a Marxist government to move hundreds of them to an area where the Gospel has never gone.

"All of these Huila people around you have never heard the Gospel," Bob challenged them. "God's brought you here for that purpose, and I expect that He's going to do something special through you."

Though he was speaking to poor, homeless refugees in a country ravaged by war and death, the message was the same he'd been preaching all around the world. Bob Foster knew from experience that God honors those who trust Him and are obedient to His Word.

Chapter Twenty-0ne

A Family Under Siege

"Blessed is he who is not offended because of me"
(Matt. 11:6, NKJ).

"My Bible reading this morning included Psalm 55. I was encouraged by verse 22 where David says, 'Cast your burden on the Lord and he shall sustain you.' The word translated 'burden' is a word which means 'what he has given.' He does not promise to remove the burden, but He does promise to sustain through it."

---Dr. Robert Foster

Prayer letter, Aug., 1989

****

Retirement was never in Bob's plans, but mission rules required that e step down as international director when he turned 65.

A few weeks before Bob and Belva left England to retire at the end f his second term, he received the World Vision Robert Pierce Award or 1988 for outstanding Christian service. Belva proudly watched Dr. 'om Houston, Minister-at-large of the Lausanne Movement, hang the ilver medallion around Bob's neck and present him with a special ertificate and check, while many of their old friends watched the eremony with her. It was a fitting climax to the eight years of leadership ob had given AEF.

Belva wrote in her Christmas letter at the end of 1988, "We are not etiring, and our diary is already fairly full. Hopefully there'll be more lective travel and fewer problems to face on returning home, the first ome of our own we've ever had."

In January of 1989, the Fosters settled in their own townhouse in Greensboro, North Carolina. An aura of peace and satisfaction seemed to permeate the whole family. Each of the children had finally moved into his or her place of service or career and 1989 seemed to promise a less hectic life. Though living and ministering in different places around the world, five of their seven children and their families were able to spend a holiday together in the mountains of North Carolina right after Christmas. What a joyful time of reunion and sharing ideas and plans!

Sharon had recovered from her grief after Rob's death some years earlier and remarried. She and Martin lived nearby and had opened their home to Sheila and Ezekiel and family who were preparing to return to minister in Angola shortly. Shelley, the youngest Foster, lived in Greensboro where she worked as an obstetrical nurse in preparation for training in midwifery.

Steve and family were on furlough in Canada from Angola where he was developing a postgraduate training program for Angolan doctors. Stacey still worked as vice president of Broadway Video. He and Ruth, a post-video tape editor, had remarried and with their son were also able to joining the mini-reunion.

The two remaining family members were in Africa. Stuart and Sindia and their two girls seemed to be happily settled in Mozambique where Stuart trained pastors in an extension program. Across the continent, Stirling was spending his first Christmas in Angola, where he had started an agricultural ministry among the Vangambwe people, an unreached tribe who are semi-nomadic cattle people. It was gratifying to Bob and Belva to see how God had led their children to serve Him, four of them right back in some of the most needy areas of Africa. None of them imagined the extent of the testing the next few years would bring to the family.

When Bob had his annual checkup to see if his lymphoma was still controlled, he received an "all-clear" report. He felt energetic and eager to continue serving both in the USA at mission conferences, and as special representative for the AEF, ministering to current missionaries and investigating potential new areas of work among unreached people groups.

AEF celebrated its 100th anniversary in 1989 so Bob was particularly busy representing the mission at various celebrations. June found him and Belva in South Africa for the annual conference of Africa Evangelical Churches where Bob was the main speaker. While there, he received a call from Steve in Canada to say that Sheila's husband, Ezekiel, had had a grand mal seizure in Luanda, the capital of Angola. He had gone there to do the paperwork and facilitate bringing in a plane for MAF, since he was one of the few church leaders fluent in both English and Portuguese.

At about five in the morning Ezekiel's roommate was awakened by sounds of thrashing and choking. Realizing something was seriously wrong, he called a missionary doctor who was also staying at the Brethren guest house. They took the unconscious Ezekiel to the nearest hospital. The authorities admitted Ezekiel but refused to allow the doctor or Ezekiel's friends to see him, and would answer no questions about his condition. When friends called Sheila in Lubango, they could tell her little except that as far as they knew, he was still in a coma. She listened incredulously—she'd spoken to Ezekiel just the night before and he'd been perfectly fine.

Did Sheila know at that moment that life would be forever changed? She arranged to leave the children with Ezekiel's family and she and her brother-in-law, Ambrosio, caught the first flight to Luanda. By the time she arrived Ezekiel had come out of his 12-hour coma and had been released from the hospital, without tests or diagnosis. Deeply concerned, Sheila called her brother, Steve, still on furlough in Canada, who in turn was able to trace Bob at the conference in South Africa. Both doctors concurred that a grand mal seizure at this stage in life could indicate a serious problem and that Sheila should take Ezekiel to the USA for tests as quickly as possible.

Sheila recalls the miracles of the next two days, as they located Ezekiel's passport in a government office, collected the children from another town, and booked a flight to the USA. They flew straight to Greensboro to stay in Bob and Belva's home while tests were carried out to determine the cause of the seizure.

Ezekiel seemed to be prepared for the devastating news. Shortly before he'd gone to Luanda he had one of his prophetic dreams. In the past he had occasionally dreamt about someone riding in a bus, or getting off a bus, which had proven to be a prophecy of death. Now he dreamt about someone forcing him onto a bus. He'd ignored the dream until he'd had the seizure, but now he wondered if his own death had been predicted.

A CT scan and needle biopsy revealed a highly malignant brain tumor. Growing in the left side of the brain, it had begun to spread its tentacles throughout the gray and white matter. It was inoperable! But doctors expressed cautious hope that radiation could eradicate the tumor since Ezekiel was only 33 years old. Ezekiel started on a series of 35 treatments, and he and Sheila both experienced a sense of confidence and peace as a great outpouring of prayer surrounded them.

A month later, Bob and Belva returned home after teaching in Mozambique and visiting with Sindia and Stuart. They helped Sheila and Ezekiel find a small house near Sharon where they could settle with their family for the months of treatment. Though Ezekiel was weak and uncomfortable from medications, he was up and about most of the time. He was able to be with Sheila when their third child and first son, Daniel, was born that September.

In the meantime Steve and family returned to Kalukembe Hospital in Angola while arrangements were being made to inaugurate the graduate level training program in Lubango. Terrorist activities around the hospital heated up and communications broke down, so Bob and Belva heard little from their oldest son for months on end. But having lived so long themselves in the heat of war and terrorism, they felt at peace leaving Steve and Peggy and the children in God's safe care.

Then they received an exciting announcement from Sharon and Martin that they had been accepted by a mission, Reciprocal Ministries, and were preparing to leave in January for Jamaica to manage and develop a conference center for the Missionary Church. Though Bob and Belva had felt uncertain about the marriage because of Martin's rebellious years, they conceded that he had grown spiritually and that his mechanical gifts were a good fit for this new assignment. Of course, Sharon and the children were delighted to be going back "home" where they had spent so many happy years.

That fall Ezekiel's condition lay heavy on the family's heart. He completed radiation treatments in December; a follow-up scan revealed that most of the tumor had receded. The doctors tried to be encouraging, saying that the remaining white spots could simply be dead cells, but there was no way of knowing--no other treatment. Chemotherapy in brain tumors isn't very effective.

Bob was fully aware that the prognosis was poor. Without a miracle the radiation treatments simply bought Ezekiel a little more time. With her medical background Sheila understood what lay ahead, but she and Ezekiel were hopeful that God had truly healed him. There was never any question that they would return to Angola as soon as the treatments were over. Belva recalls, "Even though we knew that without a miracle Ezekiel was going home to die, it was important that he go back to his family. As for Sheila--it was home for her."

They decided to return to Angola in January with their three children. Sheila recalls, "We felt that whatever time God gave us, we would like to be in Angola and not sitting in the USA waiting to see what would happen."

In anticipation of their likely return, they had been accumulating clothing, staples and other supplies to take back to Angola with them since there was little they could purchase in the war-devastated country. There was a sense of anticipation that the worst was behind them and that 1990 was going to be a good year. Three weeks before their departure, Sheila and Ezekiel and the children moved over to Bob and Belva's so they could finalize their packing and close down the rented house. It was the first night since they'd moved into the house six months earlier that they did not sleep there. At five the next morning the phone rang, and a hysterical voice shouted, "Your house is on fire!"

An Afro-American friend of theirs had been jogging past their house that morning. He was shocked to see flames pouring out of the living room window. He raced to the next house and pounded on the neighbor's door. At first she refused to open, fearful of the black stranger on her doorstep, but when he shouted, "Fire" pointing to the house, she flew to the phone.

Bob, Ezekiel and Sheila threw on their clothes and rushed over to the house, hoping they might be able to salvage their things, but by the time they arrived flames had engulfed the house. Everything was gone! Had they remained in the house, the smoke from the fire, later discovered to have started with an electrical short in the basement, would have killed them all.

Bob recalls the devastation in Sheila's eyes as she blurted out, "What have I done wrong? Doesn't the Lord love us?" Later Sheila said, "I've never been so fearful in my life. It was just like preparation for something worse. They only worse thing I could think of was that Ezekiel was going to die."

Memories flooded her heart. In Angola less than a year earlier, their household goods had been destroyed while moving their things in a truck convoy to the city of Lubango. The convoy was attacked by terrorists and everything was either stolen or burned. Now once again they had lost all their possessions, yet God provided in ways beyond their imagination. Friends in supporting churches in Greensboro and High Point asked Sheila for a list of the things they had lost. They more than replaced everything that had been destroyed, packed it and paid for the shipping costs. The Fabianos were delayed only one week, and left for Angola late in January, 1990.

As they left Bob encouraged Sheila and Ezekiel with the Scripture, *"Blessed is who is not offended because of Me."* He reminded them that Jesus had said these words to John's disciples when they came to find out why Jesus hadn't done anything about John's imprisonment. "No matter what happens," he told them, "you can see the way God has provided for you all right now, and you can be sure He'll take care of you in the future."

With their missionary children all back on the field, Bob headed for Guinea as part of a delegation of the World Medical Mission. Some years back a 20 million dollar medical facility had been built, but never used because of lack of medical staff. The WMM agreed to open and staff the facility on the condition they would have freedom to evangelize and teach the Word of God. Though the country is 85% Muslim, the officials assured the delegation there would be no problem. Bob returned elated, though a few months later he learned that the project had fallen as the government reneged on its promises.

Sheila and Ezekiel arrived safely in Lubango and settled in their third-floor apartment. Water and electricity were on only a few hours a day. Under these circumstances it took all of Sheila's time and energy to care for three small children and watch over her husband. Ezekiel had been asked to serve as the medical work administrator under the African church, but within weeks after their return he began suffering weakness on his right side. His ability to think clearly and concentrate diminished and he was not able to carry on his responsibilities, Sheila knew the tumor was on its final, relentless onslaught, but Ezekiel refused to accept the fact. Harder still, he would not discuss future plans and arrangements with Sheila in the event of his death.

Just about this time, God in His providential mercy sent Belva and Sharon to Angola. Peggy had to fly home for her mother's funeral, so Belva offered to take care of the children while she was away. Since the two families lived only a few blocks apart, they were able to provide care and support for Sheila as well. It was no easy task. Belva wrote her prayer supporters, "The next five weeks were some of the most strenuous I've ever spent. The meals for 8-10 people even with some household help, and supervising four children's schooling, in a house with no running water, but everything running hectically took everything I had."

As Ezekiel grew weaker, his older brother, Gabriel who held to Mbundu traditions, came to visit. Mbundu tribal custom dictates that when a man dies, everything that belongs to the husband reverts to his family. Sheila and Ezekiel had made arrangement at their marriage stating what would happen to the material possessions of the spouse, should the other one die. Sheila recalls, "It was clearly stated at that time that whoever died first, all of our belongings would belong to the one who stayed behind and to the kids, and that the other family would have no part in anything."

Gabriel came for a weekend visit which stretched into a whole month. Again following tribal male culture, he did not lift a finger to help her even in her care of Ezekiel. When he finally left, he went through their cupboards and helped himself to soap, razors, towels, sheets, anything he pleased, to take home with him. When Sheila queried Ezekiel he simply replied, "He's my oldest brother, I can't say anything." As the time came for Belva to leave, she could see that Ezekiel was steadily growing weaker. He spent more and more time in bed and spoke little. Often what he said made no sense. He seemed to be in little pain and had none of the excruciating headaches common with a brain tumor.

The morning she left, Belva kissed Ezekiel goodbye as he lay silently in his bed, but she clung to her daughter, wishing she could relieve the suffering she was going through. It was obvious Sheila was exhausted, caring for her husband and children--the baby, Danny, was just nine months old. Yet she sensed an inner confidence that God would be her strength and her Husband in the days ahead. Shortly after Belva left, Ezekiel's brother, Ambrosio, pastor of the local church, offered to care for him in his home to relieve Sheila of the 24-hour caregiving. One morning three weeks later, Sheila left Ezekiel's side to check on the children at home, and when she returned she found he'd made his final journey.

Bob learned of Ezekiel's death on his way to a meeting of the board of Samaritan's Purse. When he received the news he called the president, Franklin Graham, to tell him what happened, and Franklin generously offered to pay for his ticket so that he could go to Angola. Though he could not reach Angola in time for the funeral, since burial takes place within 24 hours of death, Bob was anxious to be there to protect Sheila and the children. Some of the non-Christian members of Ezekiel's family wanted to take her vehicle and other things, leaving Sheila almost penniless. However, Ambrosio and other Christian family members honored the promises made at the time of the wedding and held to them despite pressure from others. Bob was able to work out an agreement that the Foster family would be responsible for the care and upbringing of Ezekiel's children. What comfort to have her dad there, to handle the business affairs and deal with the family. How it soothed her broken heart to see him romping with the children and hear their peels of delight. He brought a sense of normalcy and strength into her shattered life.

She had to consider another major decision--should she stay in Africa or go back to the USA? She wondered if the African church would want her to stay as a single mother, especially in light of the unsettled conditions in the country. "I wasn't sure what the mission policy would be, or how useful I would be as a single parent, trying to keep the family together, as well as doing something that would justify my being in Angola." Bob and Sheila spent a lot of time talking and praying about her future in the days he stayed to help her. His advice was, "If you can find somebody to help in looking after the kids, you can think seriously about staying, but if you don't have help, you don't have much option."

Mercifully, just a few weeks after Ezekiel's death, God sent Teresa, a young woman from the Mungambwe tribe, an unreached people group in Angola, to work for Sheila. She later became the first Christian in her tribe. She had already spent nine years working in the household of a Portuguese farmer and knew how to cook and do everything in the house. By Christmas Teresa was living with Sheila and the children.

"She is really good with the children and keeps the household going," Sheila explained. "When Ezekiel died the children were so small--Helena was four, Sarah two and Daniel nine months old, but she was a very good disciplinarian. I could go away for the day and know that what I had done was not going to be undone by the end of the day in terms of the rules of the house and how the kids behaved."

So Sheila was able to fulfill the request of the church to teach in the seminary in Lubango, and later served as acting principal. She also worked at the Rio de Huila clinic several days a week. Her training as a pediatric nurse-practitioner and in Bible at Regent Serminary in Vancouver plus her knowledge of Portuguese, Mbundu and English were all invaluable gifts to the church; while her willingness to continue to serve alone after her painful losses were a model of faithfulness and obedience to believers in Africa and to all who know and love her.

Bob returned to the USA to fill his many summer speaking engagements and visit supporters. Now it was Belva's turn to face a test. During this time she suffered increased difficulty walking. Her condition was diagnosed as "intermittent claudication" affecting the circulation in both legs. In September she had vascular surgery which unfortunately was not completely successful.

As Belva was preparing for her surgery, news of a horrible accident in Angola reached them. On their way to Canada for a six-week leave, Steve's family spent a few days in the capital city of Luanda. One day Steve dropped the three youngest children off at a children's playground in the care of a new Brazilian missionary, while he went on to attend to business in town. Peggy had remained at the guest house. The small park adjoined a zoo, divided by a stone wall. Ten-year-old Rachel, a natural tomboy, loved to climb and the wall offered an enticing challenge. As she balanced precariously along the top of the wall, the young missionary called for her to come down. She could see Rachel was getting close to the gorilla cage just on the other side of the wall.

In a flash, the gorilla reached through the bars with his powerful arms and grabbed Rachel's leg, pulling her down against the cage. Bystanders watched in horror as he twisted her leg so he could get her bare foot in his mouth. Two soldiers rushed to help, shouting and screaming at the monster, but the animal would not let go. One of the men thrust the end of his rifle through the bars into the gorilla's eye. Furious, he opened his mouth to cry out, and Rachel fell free, breaking her leg.

A circle of stunned bystanders crowded around the weeping child now covered in blood. Someone had presence of mind to wrap something around her leg, but what to do with the girl? No one knew how to reach Steve, and since the young missionary had only been in the city a few hours, she could not give them directions back to the guest house. However, learning it was a missionary home, the two soldiers knew where it was and took Rachel there. Crying hysterically, Heather and Robbie stayed behind to wait for Steve as he wouldn't know where they had gone.

At the guest house, Peggy took one look at Rachel's foot and knew she had to be hospitalized immediately. She was in shock and the danger of infection from an animal bite could be fatal. When Steve finally arrived at the hospital, demanding to see his daughter, he was denied entrance. It didn't matter that he was a surgeon. Communist hospitals had tight security and not even family members were allowed to see patients.

When Rachel was later released, her leg heavily wrapped in bandages and plaster of Paris, they were told that the wound had been cleansed and sewed up, but no drain had been inserted--an absolute necessity to prevent infection. The doctors told Steve that the gorilla had bitten off Rachel's small toe, had torn four tendons and broken bones in her leg. Angry at the poor care given his daughter, Steve could only keep Rachel as comfortable as possible until they reached Toronto at the end of the week. Gangrene had already set in when surgeons operated, but they were able to save her leg.

Rachel spent the next six weeks at Sick Children's Hospital in Toronto enduring surgery, skin grafting and physiotherapy after her broken leg healed. Part of her foot had to be reconstructed to give it a better shape, but fortunately she was able to walk fairly normally within a few months. Rachel suffered severe shock and really remembers little of the frightening incident, but Heather and Robbie had nightmares for months, recalling their sister in the clutches of the massive animal.

In December 1990, Bob and Belva returned to Angola where Bob replaced Dr. Steve Duncan, missionary doctor at a new medical work at Jamba Iron Mines, while he went home for a much needed rest. Life at Jamba (150 miles east of Lubango) brought back memories of the early days of Luampa Hospital. Though they lived in a house rather than a Quonset hut, there were many other similarities.

When they first moved into the house they found cockroaches, bees, snakes and rats in residence. After the first ten days they seldom had electricity or running water, so they were back to rain water, candles and kerosene lamps. Belva wrote, "Our bathtub was a plastic dishpan and we either scrubbed out our laundry by hand or sent it out to be drubbed on the rocks in the river by a local lady who ironed it all with a charcoal iron." Belva reminded her friends it sounded worse than it was for they had done it all before.

Meanwhile Bob reveled in being back in medical work again--his first opportunity since he'd moved to England in 1981. The Brazilian doctor he was working with had little surgical experience, so Bob was happy not only to practice but to be teaching a younger doctor. With fighting getting closer and closer, the two doctors treated many casualties under primitive conditions. In one month Bob operated on three ectopic pregnancies at night "with only a 15-watt bulb." He found skillful hands could still work quickly and perform intricate procedures, but he found his legs, especially his right one, throbbing as he stood and worked for long periods of time though he passed it off as inconsequential.

Often they could hear bombs and gunfire as they worked. One night they literally jumped out of bed when a bomb exploded blowing up a bridge just eleven miles away. They wondered how long they could safely stay. Except for the "African grapevine" they were completely out of touch with the outside world. The MAF place was supposed to come in once a month to bring supplies and welcome news.

In February the MAF plane did not arrive on schedule. After several days Bob went to police headquarters to put a call through on the radio, only to find that all three radios were out of service. They were totally cut off from the outside world. Then on February 28, the plane arrived late in the afternoon with the shocking news that they had come to evacuate Bob and Belva and the Bragas immediately. The area was almost totally cut off by UNITA forces and it was unsafe for the plane to fly into the region any longer. It had taken the pilot all day to get permission to come for them.

Bob convinced the pilot to give them a few days to prepare the African staff at the hospital and to give final treatments to the wounded who filled the hospital. Once again Bob found himself speaking words of comfort to African believers in the surrounding villages--believers to whom he'd been preaching every Sunday--knowing that many of them would die as the terrorists moved close. They had been through so much, even a devastating famine the year before that had left many dead. Now they would be left without any doctors.

The plane returned on March 5, bringing the news that Belva's mother, who had been in failing health for several years, had died. Under the disastrous and confused circumstances in Angola, Belva was thankful to arrive home ten days later for the funeral in Brantford, Ontario. She was deeply comforted by the memories and eulogies of the great gifts and rich input her mother had made into so many lives.

Sadness soon gave way to joyous anticipation as the family prepared for Stirling's wedding that May. Under extremely primitive conditions, Stirling had made great progress with the farm in Angola which was to provide training and jobs for the Africans in the region and begin to open doors for the Gospel into a very resistant tribe. He was obviously his father's son--an entrepreneur, willing to try big projects under the most trying conditions. He had recently installed a water system and purchased 100 head of cattle. A sawmill was on its way, donated by a manufacturer. His fiancée, Donna, had just completed her veterinary training, and he was anxious for her partnership in this new venture.

The wedding date was set for May 25, and most of the family arranged to be there. A few days before the wedding, however, Donna decided she could not get married at that point. There were unresolved issues she needed to deal with, and no amount of discussion was able to change her mind. She just couldn't go through with it. Marriage held fears for her that she could not face. However, in the ensuing months Stirling stood by her as she worked with a Christian counselor, and God healed her. They were later married in a quiet ceremony in September.

During that summer Bob and Belva served at the Muskoka Baptist Conference on Mary Lake near Huntsville, Ontario. Many years earlier Bob had served as conference director one summer before going to Africa, and now the board asked him to do so again., What a joy to listen to some of the greatest teachers expound the Word of God, and to meet old friends and make new ones. It was a hectic, but delightful people-filled life.

Some weeks before going to Muskoka, Bob twisted his right ankle and suffered excruciating pain in his right leg. However, as the ankle healed the sever pain subsided, and he was able to carry on his busy schedule, trying to ignore the nagging pain which continued. He attributed the continuing discomfort to the steep terrain he had to negotiate every day. Even while directing the camp, Bob was making preparations to visit Madagascar in mid-September to assist in plans for new medical work started by AEF. His fall schedule was filled with conference and Bible teaching ministries.

However, when Steve, who had come on a business trip to Canada, visited the conference ground, Bob mentioned the pain in his leg. He did not admit even to himself, that it might be caused by more than muscle strain. Steve felt an abnormality even through a cursory examination and advised his dad to have it X-rayed. The diagnosis was devastating. A biopsy revealed that the lymphoma he had battled in 1985 had returned. Doctors found an infiltrating tumor in one of the bones in his right leg and on September 12th they removed five inches of the fibula. The doctors knew they couldn't remove all the tumor in his muscles without amputation, and neither they nor Bob were ready for that. As they did tests to prepare for radiation, they discovered further tumors in other bones in both his legs. Radiation was now out of the question.

When Sheila heard the news she was upset and angry with the Lord. She remembers, "I didn't think it was fair to me to allow Ezekiel to die and then to take Dad away too."

Bob understood clearly every step of the treatment. When the doctors prescribed a severe regimen of chemotherapy, Bob questioned the protocol which had never been used on anyone over 65 before, but the doctors told Bob he could probably handle it because he had the physique of a 55-year-old and the heart of a 45-year-old. However, there were days when Bob thought he couldn't handle it all--days when he felt near death's door. The treatment cycle was to last six months, but it seemed like an eternity. Bob thought since he would be home and resting, he would be able to read and study, but he became so weak it was impossible to concentrate on anything.

Belva wrote in one prayer letter, "Although he has had some nausea he hasn't lost weight or his appetite. However most of his hair is gone. His energy sinks to a low point in the middle of the second week when his white blood cell count falls drastically. Fortunately it gradually picks up during the third week of each cycle so that he feels relatively good, just in time to be hit again by the chemotherapy." Personally she admitted, "It was terrible to see him turn into an old man with transparent skin and no hair. After three days of chemotherapy he was so weak he could barely walk up the stairs to the front door, and in his weakest moments he could not even hold up a book."

At Christmastime Sheila and Peggy flew to Namibia to do some shopping and phoned Bob from there. When Sheila heard his weak voice her heart stopped. He sounded as though he were going to die any minute. For all of Bob's extraordinary strengths, she remembered his voice as one of the strongest. Bob himself wondered if he would ever be able to minister again. He felt he had let people down by having to cancel all his speaking engagements, but he found the love and support of God's people overwhelming in an outpouring of prayer and comfort.

In February, 1992, Bob completed his sixth cycle of chemotherapy. He would take another six to eight weeks to regain his full strength. In a month, more scans and biopsies would take place to determine if he needed radiation therapy as well, but the adrenaline was already flowing and in his February prayer letter Bob wrote, "We're planning to be available for meetings and fall and winter conferences. We have been invited to go to Angola in August for special ministry at a pastors' retreat." In his heart he was ready to go--he only needed final clearance from the doctors.

Chapter Twenty-two

A Vision Without End

"I the Lord have called you in righteousness; I will take hold of your hand. I will keep you and will make you to be a covenant for the people and a light for the Gentiles, to open-eyes that are blind, to free captives from prison, and to release from the dungeon those who sit in darkness" (Isaiah 42:6,7).

"How we finish is most important. Jesus spoke of a man who laid a foundation and didn't count the cost, and was not able to finish his building. We must count the cost of being a disciple so that we can finish well. It is a disgrace not to finish well. Paul wrote, 'I have fought a good fight. I have finished the race. I have kept the faith.' I pray this will be true of me."

--Dr. Robert Foster

****

During the months of chemotherapy and recuperation Bob wondered many times if his ministry were over--if God had marked the finish line. But as his strength began to return, an inner compulsion drove him to think more and more of the people of Africa, especially the hidden, primitive tribes where the Gospel had never penetrated. He knew that Africa was generally considered nearly evangelized, with reports of new Christians coming to Christ at a rate of 16,000 a day, but he also knew from his years of living deep in the bush that there were yet many who remained in spiritual darkness, caught in their webs of tradition and demonism. When the team of radiologists met to evaluate his case in March 1992, Bob and Belva waited for their report, ready to accept their prognosis, hardly daring to admit even to themselves, the possibility that the cancer had not been whipped.

Instead Bob reported jubilantly in his handwritten note t friends and supporters, "There is no evidence of any tumc remaining in the tissues in the area operated on last September. There were still empty spaces in the bones where th chemotherapy had killed the cancer. But no more chem treatments; no more debilitating radiation. Doctors warned it coul take six to eight weeks to regain his strength. When he complaine of weakness, Belva teased, "Now you know what normal peopl feel like." She wrote in her prayer letter, "His hair has begun t grow, progressing from a halo to a convict cut so far."

A sense of urgency seemed to envelop Bob--a need to redeer the time. There was no way of knowing if or when the lymphom cells would break out again. So by April Bob and Belva were o their way to England to visit the international headquarters of AE to discuss his next assignment. The Spirit of God had prepared th leadership of AEF and there was a beautiful sense of harmony an focused vision as he spoke with Ron Genheimer, his replacemen about the need to help the church reach unreached tribes. By th time he left England, Bob's assignment had been crystallized-t get information about twelve unreached tribes in southern Afric and to help the churches accept the responsibility to reach them.

Though Bob had accepted an invitation to be the speaker a one church conference that spring, he really needed more time t recuperate, so he and Belva planned to spend several weeks i Jamaica with Sharon and Martin. It was encouraging to see ther happily working with the Missionary Church. Sharon did a lot c the preparation and purchasing for the teams that came from th USA to do construction work. Martin seemed to flouris supervising the teams as they worked in remote and often primitiv situations. In spite of their busyness, there was time for relaxatio and fellowship that bonded them even closer with the your couple and Bob's earlier misgivings diminished.

Once they were back home in Greensboro, life returned to i hectic pace. In between speaking engagements Bob was preparir twenty Bible studies to be given at the pastors' conference in Angola. This conference would bring together leaders from all over Angola and hopefully mobilize them to evangelize and disciple the remaining unreached tribes in the nation.

Civil war had been raging in the former Portuguese colonies of Angola and Mozambique ever since the Portuguese pulled out in 1975. Most of the eastern part of Angola had been in the hands of UNITA guerillas, while the Marxist government controlled the cities and the southwest. A peace treaty had been signed in 1991, and a tenuous cease-fire was in effect. Elections were scheduled for September, 1992. In this window of opportunity pastors from both sides of the "grass curtain" came together for the first time in sixteen years.

Bob realized they would come with suspicions of each other, hostility because of diverse loyalties, and tribal animosities which are a part of the African scene throughout the continent. Yet, these men had been serving faithfully in the Union of Evangelical Churches of Angola (UIEA) and Bob believed the opportunity to worship and study the Word together would overrule the divisions. He was thankful to discover that the men who had been isolated in the bush behind guerilla lines had remained faithful to the Word of God, and demonstrated a deep sense of gratitude for God's faithfulness in adversity. However, he spent many hours listening to accusations and complaints, and helping the men to understand that both sides had been caught in a political noose about which they could do nothing.

How precious it was to see pastors coming into the church in Menongue in tattered clothes, some barefoot, having walked almost two weeks to get there. Trucks or MAF planes brought others from distant places through the generosity of Samaritan's Purse which had underwritten much of the costs of the conference. Tears flowed unashamedly as they lifted their voices in praise.

Colleagues who had not seen each other in years embraced; some had been thought dead since news between the two political entities was scarce. When the leader of the UIEA saw the desperate poverty of some of the men, he challenged the delegates to help them. "If you have two shirts, or two pairs of trousers, share one of them with a brother who has nothing," he urged. Many, out of their poverty, brought what little they had to share with those who had spent years in the bush.

The most gratifying experience of the conference was to see the enthusiasm and willingness to accept the challenge of reaching the remaining unreached tribes. Bob wrote later, "God wonderfully answered prayer in reuniting the brethren and giving them a spirit of love and unity to press forward in the work of evangelization. Ten unreached tribes in the southern half of Angola were targeted by the church as their objective for missionary outreach during the next ten years in cooperation with the AEF."

A month later peaceful but flawed elections took place in Angola, only to have UNITA leaders denounce the outcome, so fighting broke out once again. In Lubango soldiers broke down doors, dragging people who had shown sympathy for the opposition out of their homes and shooting them in cold blood. Steve was away on business so Peggy and the children were evacuated. Further to the north Kalukembe Hospital became the target of attack. In the months ahead bombs fell on the hospital destroying many of the buildings and by September, 1993 all missionary personnel there had been removed.

It was disappointing to see the promises of peace destroyed, especially since the church had planned to move into areas once again closed to them, but Bob was not discouraged. His annual medical tests early in 1993 revealed no sign of cancer. "With that green light," Belva wrote, "Bob hasn't stopped since and shows no sign of doing so."

He began his first survey trip in January, traveling to Tanzania and Madagascar with Ron Genheimer to minister to missionaries there. In Tanzania they learned more about three large tribal groups, nominally Muslim, which also stretched across the border into Mozambique. So it was to Mozambique that Bob and Belva traveled that June, accompanied by pioneer missionary Gordon Legg, who had served in Mozambique many years before. Now in his eighties, Gordon had seen the church at Mihecani flourish, only to be closed and boarded up by Portuguese government officials after a tragic death for which a pastor was responsible.

Bob and Gordon had been asked to teach the Bible at several conferences for church leaders. In recent years, more than 700 churches have been planted among the primarily Lomue-speaking people in the northern provinces, in spite of continuing civil war and abject poverty. After years of anarchy with most schools closed, less than 33% of the people are literate. Mozambique is considered the poorest country in the world with an annual per capita income of about $ 80.

Nevertheless, more than 1,000 people singing and dancing at the airport exuded joy and gratitude as they welcomed Bob and Belva and Gordon Legg to Nampula, the second largest city in the country. As they were taken in a motorcade to the main evangelical church in the city, more than 10,000 people lined the streets, waving and cheering. It was an overwhelming homecoming for Gordon Legg.

Among the welcoming throng at the airport were a couple of men wearing skull caps like yarmulkes. They appeared again at the church, sitting on the front row. Bob's curiosity was finally satisfied when he learned that they were Muslim Imams, leaders of the mosque in Pastor Vicente's area. When the pastor passed out used clothes to all the needy people in his neighborhood, he included the Muslims. The Imam was curious why the pastor offered help to his people. He began meeting regularly with Pastor

Vicente to discuss Christianity, and now asked if he could attend the Bible teaching sessions Bob and Gordon had both in Nampula and Alto Molocue.

After teaching in Nampula for a week, they drove to the city of Alto Molocue for a second Bible conference. Once again crowds of joyful singing people gathered around their truck as they arrived. Bob was struck that among those waiting to welcome them were several more men wearing skull caps like yarmulkes.

These Imams (Muslim priests) smiled and reached out to greet them with the same eagerness as the others. Not only did they come each day to listen intently, but they invited Bob and Gordon to come to their mosque to teach their people. At the end of their time there, Bob asked the Imam what he thought about the teaching. He confessed that he was very interested, and he was thinking about what he'd heard.

Bob learned later that the Imam had asked Pastor Vicente if all his people could join his church. The pastor explained as gently as he could that it was not a matter of simply joining the church; the people would have to believe the teachings about Christ, and accept Him as their Savior. That would take some more thinking the Imam concluded.

While the visit with the leaders of the Lomue-speaking churches filled Bob with joy and thanksgiving for the work of God among these people, his visit to the northeast province of Cabo Delgado filled him with sadness. As he and some of the church leaders visited villages of the Makonde- and Makua-speaking people, they sensed a deep presence of evil "like no place on earth." These nominal Muslims have long been resistant to the Gospel and the people received them with obvious suspicion. Bob felt that at any moment they might turn on them. Though no census has been taken for many years, it is estimated there may be a million to a million and a half people living there--with no evangelical witness. While some can speak and read Portuguese, a portion of the book of Mark is the only Scripture translated into their language, but Bob learned that Wycliffe has allocated several couples to do translation work there.

Upon their return to Nampula the men sat down to evaluate what they had seen and what could be done. Now that the civil war had ended, the government welcomed missions and churches to work among these neglected people, and the Christians were ready to commit prayer and workers into the area. Would AEF send 10-15 missionaries to work with the church among these unreached people? Bob assured them he would do all he could to challenge young people to come, but in his heart he wondered how many would be willing to spend their lives in this lowliest spot on earth serving among a resistant and even hostile people.

As Bob spoke at conferences and churches back in the USA in the months ahead, did his hearers note a special poignancy to his message? Did some of the burden he carried transfer to them? Did the urgency of his vision move them to fervent prayer, or a willingness to lay down their life on the altar of sacrifice so that the Makonde and Makua could move from darkness to light? Did they care?

There was encouraging response. In a few years sixteen AEF missionaries were on the job in Mozambique, plus others in AIM and Wycliffe. Bob and Belva continued to care--Africa had a tug on their hearts that nothing could dissuade.

When Sheila considered whether or not to go back with her three little ones to Angola after her furlough, her biggest concern was the education of her children. The church had asked her to teach at the seminary. If finding a teacher for Sheila's children was the only thing holding her from returning to Africa, Belva felt she should go and teach the children until a replacement could be found. It was decided that Bob would follow in a few months, after he'd completed his fall conference schedule, to help out in the medical work at Rio de Huila. They looked forward to a nine

month stint with Bob expanding the clinic and getting bac[
into surgery again.

In the 1920's a pioneer AEF couple, Jack and Minnie Procto[
began working among the Olumhuila people, under an agreemen[
between mission agencies that assigned the southern third of th[
country to the mission then known as the South Africa Genera[
Mission. Then as now, the people were extremely resistant t[
Christian teaching, and after a few years with no results, th[
Proctors transferred to Mozambique.

It would be almost forty years before another AEF couple, th[
Willie Brandles, started a medical clinic for the Huila people wh[
were not only resistant to the Gospel, but refused to adapt t[
modern culture. The women wore only beads around their neck[
wrists and ankles and oiled their skin with rancid butter, clay an[
cow dung once a year. The clinic waiting room had a distinct odo[
as the women came with their naked children for the only medic[
care available to them.

The rugged waterless terrain where the Huilas lived had neve[
been of interest to the government--not even to provide schools fo[
the children--so it had been relatively untouched by the civil wa[
With Marxism dead, the government was more than willing t[
allow missions to provide for help for the people. After more tha[
fifty years of spasmodic attempts to win the Huilas (now[
numbering more that 250,000), the missionaries were beginning t[
see some response.

The clinic was overcrowded and inadequate, and there ha[
been no one with the vision or know-how to improve it. In th[
months that Bob was there he found himself back in hi[
Mukinge/Luampa/Cavango mode-drawing up plans, orderin[
supplies from as far away as Namibia, and overseein[
construction. Before he left an operating room and outpatients[
clinic were well underway. Eventually a 30-bed hospital extensio[

would be planned. He even had time to do surgery one or two mornings a week at the hospital in Lubango.

During the time he was there, Bob met with the leaders of the church in Lubango to plan a survey trip into the remote mountainous regions where they knew there were other unreached tribal groups. Pastor Chimuko had lived in the region some years before and was able to speak some of the local dialects. They packed a four-wheel drive pickup with their supplies, pup tents, even water, and headed out following narrow paths and well-worn tracks.

From his prior research Bob knew there were Bushmen-like people living in the forest, and they could see evidence of their presence. In fact at night as they pitched their small camp to settle for the night, they could hear voices and laughter in the distance. But where were the people?

One morning several old women, their naked bodies covered with red ochre, peered out at them from behind the trees. They had been sent to spy on the strangers. When they were satisfied they were not government soldiers, they motioned for their men to come out. Pastor Chimuko was able to ask them where they lived. They said they were nomadic cattle people. Were there any churches in the area? They shook their heads. Christians? They didn't understand what he was talking about. Bob later found out that there were few people outside the tribe who could speak their language and it had never been reduced to writing.

Another day the men came upon a government food distribution center, where several hundred people gathered. A drought in the region had caused severe food shortages. Here pastor Chimuko was able to talk with more people to find out more about where the people lived.

One group, the Vahakavona, were cattle people. Tall and strong, they resembled the Masaai of Kenya for they had lots of protein in their diet, drinking sour milk and eating meat. Of all the

people the research group met, these seemed to be the mos
interested in what Bob and Pastor Chimuko had to say. In fac
they asked them to send someone to their people to teach ther
more about this God they'd been talking about and Pastc
Chimuko promised to return.

In all, Bob and the team discovered the existence of at leas
seven or eight unreached tribes living in southern Angola. Thoug
no census had been taken for many years, the estimated number c
people was at least 500,000. While the mission would help throug
its medical work at Rio de Huila clinic and the model farm Stirlin
was developing, the bulk of the responsibility would lie squarel
on the shoulders of the African church. In the remaining weeks i
Angola Bob challenged the Christians with the desperate nee
right on their doorstep, with the same zeal he would exercise bac
in North America.

On June 10th, a few weeks before they were scheduled t
return to the USA, Bob received a message on the MAF radi
which had been transmitted from Stuart in Mozambique. Over th
crackling airwaves he heard the devastating news, "Yo
granddaughter, Belva, died of malaria yesterday." Was their no en
to the tragedies the families would have to endure? Questions fille
their minds as Bob and Belva and Sheila tried to decide what to d
next. Bob and Belva felt they should cut their stay in Angola shor
and get to Mozambique to be with Stuart and Sindia as quickly a
possible. That night a young missionary couple came to Sheila an
offered to stay with the children if she would like to go t
Mozambique as well.

Through a seemingly miraculous turn of events, they wer
able to book flights, changing planes four times across th
continent. None of them had visas for Mozambique, but authoritie
showed great sympathy for the grieving family and provided th
necessary permission. In three days Bob, Belva and Sheila arrive
in Alto Molocue. The funeral had taken place several days earlie
but Stuart and Sindia fell into the arms of their family, desperatel

needing comfort and to talk through their grief. Both nine-year-old Cara and the baby Luke, had high fevers, and Sindia was afraid she was going to lose her other two children as well. Bob arrived with a well-stocked bag of medications, and soon put her fears to rest.

Gradually the events of the last two weeks came out. Belva Joy had developed a low-grade fever which got worse toward evening but in the mornings she seemed to perk up. Sindia suspected flu. Stuart had a trip scheduled to another mission station that weekend and he debated whether he should stay, but they both decided that if Belva seemed better Saturday morning he would go. He had an appointment with a linguistic expert as well as meeting with the couple who would take over his duties when Stuart and Sindia left for furlough in a few weeks.

Saturday morning found Belva relatively chipper, so Stuart left confident that whatever had caused the fever had run its course. He took their last few doses of chloroquin with him since he was going into a highly infected area. However, over the weekend, Belva's fever returned and by Monday morning Sindia was concerned enough to radio from the town administrator's office for malaria medicine. Since her request did not sound urgent, the doctor gave Stuart a less potent drug to take home which did little to bring her fever down.

Belva Joy celebrated her seventh birthday on Wednesday. She was strong enough to sit up and eat some birthday cake and go right back to bed. The chloroquin Stuart had given her upon his return wasn't helping either. Seeing their daughter weaken visibly before their eyes, Stuart and Sindia took her to a government clinic in town for a blood test. Though the clinic had no medical personnel or nurses, they did have a fairly well equipped lab. Blood tests revealed a high parasite count, indicating that her red blood cells were being destroyed. A transfusion may have saved her life, but the nearest hospital in Johannesburg was 1,000 miles away. Even before they could consider the possibility of taking her there, Belva fainted away in their arms and was gone.

Bob and Belva tried to relieve the guilt Stuart and Sindia felt for not recognizing the symptoms earlier, or taking stronger measures to find out what was wrong. As Bob explained later, "To lose a precious daughter and granddaughter is difficult to understand. We shared our grief and cried out to the Lord. God gave peace as we were reminded that she was safe in the arms of Jesus and we would see her one day again."

As Sindia packed to prepare for furlough, she found one of Belva's books in which she had declared her six-year-old love for Jesus, "Dear God, I love you. I trust you too. Thank you for your love and the Bible. Thank you that your love attaches us to you forever. Oh Lord, I love you. Signed, Belva Foster."

Bob and Belva returned to the United States for a busy summer of conference engagements. With renewed zeal Bob challenged his listeners to respond to God's call to the yet unreached people in southern Africa, while knowing in his heart that there could be a heavy price to pay in the remote, disease ridden and war-torn regions where they would have to serve. Never for a moment did he believe that the cost would ever be too great for those who followed the call of God in faith and obedience.

Perhaps God permitted so many testings in the Foster family so they could say with Job, "When he has tested me, I shall come forth like gold" (Job 23:10). The testings were still not over.

On August 9 the three Angolan siblings were together and decided to call Sharon on her birthday. Sharon had been in the United States for several weeks working on her permanent resident status. When she picked up the pone, she heard Sheila's cheerful, "Happy birthday."

"It's not a very happy birthday."

"What do you mean?" Sheila asked.

"Martin's disappeared." Sharon went on to explain that she was to have picked him up from Kingston at the airport the night before but he had not arrived, nor had his name appeared on the manifesto. Had he been killed? Had he been mugged? Fear gripped Sharon's heart. Further investigation, however, revealed that Martin had taken a different plane in the company of a woman he'd known before their marriage. He had given no sign of unhappiness or indication of unfaithfulness. Bob and Belva returned home to find Sharon deeply distraught and in total shock.

In the months ahead she had to work through feelings of rejection and loss. Both of her children left Jamaica to study elsewhere, but for the time being at least she continued on alone, preparing the way for service teams coming into Jamaica. Her father had taught her well the importance of faithfulness and commitment, and she was not a quitter.

During the fall and winter of 94/95 Bob continued to travel extensively in the United States, including a trip to Madagascar where he had the joy of opening a new medical facility, but once again his heart was turned toward Angola. He and Dr. Don Mullen, then president of World Medical Mission visited Angola in May to assess ways to help rebuild the country. While a peace accord had finally been signed the previous November, it was only six months later that the welcome UN "Blue Helmets" arrived to help enforce the peace.

Bob wrote in his prayer letter, "Don and I were able to visit almost all the major centers of central and southern Angola. Such destruction as I have never seen before greeted us in the central cities of Huambo and Kuito. Whole city blocks were leveled to the ground. The faces of many high rise apartment buildings were completely blown away. There were no electrical or water systems operating in most areas we visited. No hospital was really functioning. Equipment has been destroyed or ransacked.

Medicines were non-existent." This was the first time since 1976 that Bob was able to visit the hinterland, and it was indeed a devastating sight.

Yet, signs of spiritual strength and growth were everywhere. The church had taken its commitment to the unreached tribes seriously. When Bob and Dr. Mullen arrived in Lubango, they were greeted by three men from the Vahakavona tribe. They asked if they could come to see Bob because they had a gift for him.

Bob chuckles recalling the burly men (at least six foot four), dressed only in loin cloths, sitting on spindly chairs in Steve's living room. The glow on their faces outshone the oil on their skin, as through an interpreter, they thanked Bob profusely for sending the pastor back to their area. They came as the first converts of a new church-the first ever among the Vahakavona people.

Then they asked Bob to come outside where the biggest goat Bob had ever seen was grazing. One of the men picked the goat up as though it were a toy and presented it to Bob as a thank offering. Bob thanked them for this generous gift, knowing it represented the best they had. Unbeknown to them, that goat became the main course at the next church conference!

The Lubango church itself has caught the vision of reaching out to other parts of Angola and appointed one of the seminary graduates as director of evangelism. They started out with an eight day campaign in the largest theater in Lubango. By the time the campaign ended 1,000 people became Christians. The church committed itself to working alongside AEF in outreach to the tribes, and under skyrocketing inflation stretched themselves to support a full-time worker.

Money and workers are the only answer to reaching the missions of people in Angola and Mozambique who are living in spiritual darkness with no opportunity to hear that God loves them. When Bob returned to Mozambique at the time of his granddaughter's death, Pastor Vicente told him about a breakthrough among the Makua people they had visited two years earlier.

One night a Muslim man had a dream that he was to go to a pastor in Nampula to get a holy book. He traveled more than 60 miles and eventually found pastor Vicente. When he explained his dream, Pastor Vicente understood immediately that this book must be the New Testament and gladly gave him one. He explained that this was the Word of God and would show him the way of life. The Makua man urged the pastor to come to his village, and with that he left.

Some time later Pastor Vicente was able to visit the Makua's village. There he learned that upon his return, the man had called his villagers together and began reading to his people. As they listened, truth broke into their hearts and many accepted Christ. With the zeal of a Spirit-led revival, they spread out into surrounding villages sharing what they had learned. By the time of Pastor Vicente's visit he found seventeen groups of believers in 17 villages, many of them truly converted.

Bob cannot stop challenging Christians to respond to the call to Africa's unreached people. He's seen their hopelessness and spiritual darkness. He's seen the wasted minds as no one has cared to teach them, and the weakened bodies without medicine or doctors. His greatest burden is to see gifted and trained young people make the spiritual sacrifice of their lives on the altar of missions. More than that he longs that God in His sovereignty and mercy will break through, as he did in those Makua villages, with the Truth that will set them free. That will be his prayer and vision as long as God gives him breath.

The Foster Family Today

Dr. Bob and Belva Foster now live in Greensboro, NC. Since AEF merged with SIM in 1998, Bob has served as a special representative for that Mission, available for missionary conferences and other ministry opportunities the Lord gives. Once a year, he is a speaker for Prescription for Renewal at the Cove in Ashville, NC., a medically-focused weekend of spiritual refreshment and challenge sponsored by World Medical Mission, medical arm of Samaritan's Purse. Yearly check-ups have revealed no recurrence of lymphoma since '96 and treatment for prostate cancer has been successful.

Dr. Stephen and Peggy Foster have been back in Angola for five years, after 4 years in Canada while their children were in college. Stephen is now Medical Director of the Evangelical Medical Center of Lubango, a fine new hospital that opened its doors in October, 2006.

Sharon Mills has been working with USAID for several years after doing an MPH degree. She is currently in Nepal focusing on their program for HIV/AID's treatment and prevention.

Sheila Foster-Fabiano still teaches at the Evangelical Seminary in Lubango, Angola, and is working on a doctorate in teaching theology in Third World cultures.

Stacey and Ruth Foster live in Greensboro although much of his work as a Technical Consultant in TV takes him traveling.

Stuart and Sindia Foster still serve in Mozambique, focusing on translating the Bible into the Lomue language along with a great deal of Bible teaching. He earned his theology doctorate recently.

Stirling and Donna Foster are still developing the work at Tchincombe Ranch in southern Angola where they now have a nucleus of believers, and they continue church planting among the Ovongambue.

Sharon Foster married Peter Duplantis in '99 and they both joined the work in Angola in '06 where she trains midwives and does OB/GYN work. They visit outlying clinics regularly to give oversight.

This picture, taken in 1975, shows the elder Fosters, ages 82 and 83. Charles and June Foster went to Africa as newlyweds and remained to see their grandchildren take up the work they had begun as pioneers, hundreds of miles from civilization.

Charles S. Foster is seen here being decorated by the Governor of Zambia. This honor, Member of the British Empire, was bestowed upon him in 1963 for his many years of service to the people of the territory that had been known as Northern Rhodesia.

Their house at Musonweji was the site of tragedy and triumph as the Fosters lived in these primitive surroundings. June Foster was known for her energetic management and amazing ability to grow vegetables in her large garden. Dr. Bob Foster was born here and it was here that he returned with his bride, Belva.

Bob and Belva raised a large family and taught them to trust God in the face of insurmountable difficulties in Africa even during civil war and unrest. The faith of their parents and grandparents also reached them. ABOVE: A family picture in 1969 proved to be a rarity. The family was not together again until 1983 when the picture below was taken. Left to right: Shelley, Sheila, Sharon, Belva, Bob, Stephen, Stacey, Stuart and Stirling.

One of three hospitals Bob built in Angola and Zambia, the hospital at Cavango, was built in 1975 before the destruction of the civil war. In the operating room, Bob was at his best with an amazing ability to improvise under less-than-ideal conditions. Most of all, however, his confidence in the power of God to help and to heal gave him courage to tackle every problem.

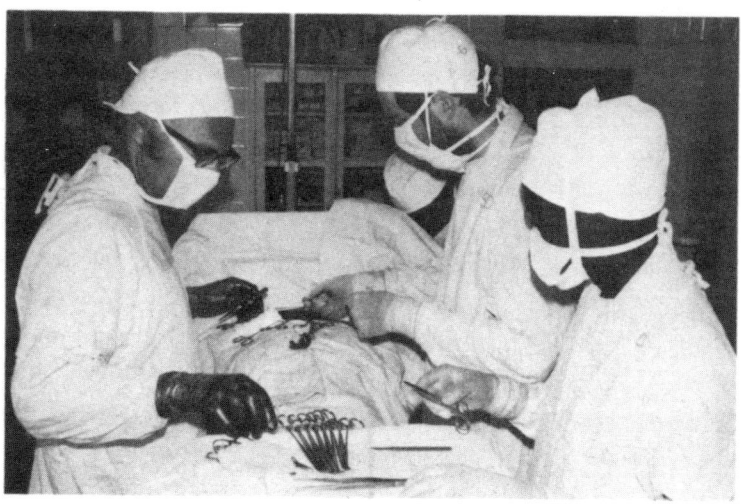

Other AEF Offices

Australia
P. O. Box 100, Kingsgrove, NSW 2208

Zimbabwe
P. O. Box 8164, Causeway, Harare

Canada
SIM – Canada
10 Huntingdale Blvd.
Scarborough, ON M1W 2S5

South Africa
Box 23913. Claremont 7735

U.S.A.
SIM-USA
P. O. Box 7900
Charlotte NC 28241

New Zealand
P. O. Box 1390, Invercargill

U.K.
6 Station Court, Station Approach
Borough Green, Sevenoaks, Kent, TN15 8AD